BUBBY'S HOMEMADE PIES

BUBBY'S
HOMEMADE
PIES

Ron Silver and Jen Bervin

Illustrations by Elizabeth Zechel

1807
WILEY
2007

JOHN WILEY & SONS, INC.

Published by John Wiley & Sons, Inc., Hoboken, New Jersey
Published simultaneously in Canada

Designed by Cassandra J. Pappas
Illustrations by Elizabeth Zechel
Wiley Bicentennial Logo: Richard J. Pacifico

For general information about our other products and services, please contact our Customer Care Department within the United States at (800) 762-2974, outside the United States at (317) 572-3993 or fax (317) 572-4002.

Wiley also publishes its books in a variety of electronic formats. Some content that appears in print may not be available in electronic books. For more information about Wiley products, visit our web site at www.wiley.com.

Library of Congress Cataloging-in-Publication Data:
Silver, Ron.
    Bubby's homemade pies / by Ron Silver and Jen Bervin.
        p. cm.
    Includes bibliographical references and index.
    ISBN: 978-0-7645-7634-8 (cloth)
1. Pies. 2. Pastry. I. Bervin, Jen. II. Title.
    TX773.S497 2007
    641.8'652—dc22

                                                                        2005032310

Printed in the United States of America

10 9 8 7 6 5 4 3 2 1

CONTENTS

CHAPTER 6 DEEP-DISH DESSERTS: CRUMBLES, CRISPS,
COBBLERS, BUCKLES, PANDOWDYS, AND BROWN BETTYS   193

ACKNOWLEDGMENTS

Without the unflagging commitment to excellence and the diligence to try, try again by Jen Bervin, this book would never have been written. I could never begin to thank her enough. That said, there are many people to be thanked for helping with this book: Elizabeth Zechel, for her steady hand, for making such lovely and helpful illustrations; my mother for her lovely food and cooking; my grandmothers for loving me so well, and for cooking food that inspired me to try to cook better food; all the staff and customers at Bubby's for their unflagging enthusiasm for this book, and equally steady support for the spirit of Bubby's. Stacey Glick, and the Jane Dystel Agency, who convinced me after years that this book ought to be written, thank you. And Pam Chirls, our editor at Wiley, whose experience and insight has been invaluable, and thoughtful, and wise. Her ability to hear and see what it is that we have tried to accomplish with this book has brought it to life. Immeasurable thanks to Jen Bervin's mother, grandmother, aunts, and great-aunts for their real love for pie. I would also not have near the passion for cooking were it not for James Beard and Alice Waters, my heroes and, unknown to them, my great mentors. This book would not have happened without a lot of help from a lot of loving generous folks who love pie, nor would it mean anything without Emmy, Abraham, Luc, and all the other sweet mouths that I can make pie for.

—RON SILVER

My sincerest thanks to Ron for our countless collaborations in pie and mind; to Elizabeth Zechel for her profoundly beautiful drawings; to our agent Stacey Glick; and to editor Pam Chirls for smart, supportive direction with this book. My mother, Dinah Kerksieck, deserves a lifetime of thanks. My earliest memories of her magnificent garden and homemade pies allowed me to develop an imagination for tastes I love. I deeply admire anyone who can grow and make such beautiful things now. Her enthusiasm for this book has been present throughout—reading, testing recipes, offering many of our family favorites. I'm grateful to my Grandma Adeline and aunts for our family gatherings thick with homemade pies, and to my Tanté Dorothy for food made in the best spirit possible: Please let me stand in my own kitchen at age 94 repeating "Isn't this fun!" like you did, sharing much of it with the neighbors. Special thanks to Catherine McRae and many dear friends and pie socialists who have generously shared recipes, and inspired, nurtured, and fed the spirit of this book.

—Jen Bervin

BUBBY'S PIES: AN INTRODUCTION

When I was a young boy in Salt Lake City, if I wasn't dropping hints to be invited to dinner at my neighbors, the Pedersons, the Kelgreens, the Frishnichts, or the Phillips, I was plotting my route to school, or to friends' houses based on what was growing in the fields. In springtime I knew where every stand of grass-thin asparagus was sprouting and I would sit in the field eating the raw stalks until my stomach ached; in June there were fences overgrown with English peas that led to stealthy walks through early cornfields, where I was at times chased off by salt rock blasts from .410 gauge shotguns fired by displeased farmers. I knew every strawberry patch, plum tree, apricot tree, peach tree, Concord grape vine, apple tree (and which sour or sweet apple would scratch the itch that day); when my stomach was full, I went off in search of crabapples to chuck at my younger siblings or at moving vehicles. All of it was absolute mischief for me. Even cooking began as mischief, since my mother forbade me to cook without her supervision. I made my first chocolate soufflé one fine Saturday afternoon while my mom took a long nap. I came bearing that first soufflé into her room with oven mitts covered in chocolate; her eyes popped out in amazement when she lifted her black silk eye cover and she seemed to find it hard to punish my disobedience.

However, I was not born into a life of pie making. I made my first pie when I was twenty-seven. Though I had been a chef for a few years, pie making was a mystery to me. I had never eaten a good pie. Pie was something that came from supermarket chains and tasted like cardboard crust filled with gelatinous canned fruit, and was wholly unappealing, or it was a fancy glazed fruit tart, the fruit carefully placed with pretentious symmetry, glistening with canned apricot glaze. But my imagination for good pie was strong, and curiosity and the notion (held in good faith) that pie must be inherently good, as well as some competitive notion that I might be able to win a pie-baking contest drove my desire to learn. I started baking pies with the goal of competing against seasoned home bakers in the New York State Fair. At the time, I was a breakfast cook at Restaurant Florent in the Meat Packing District of New York City. I had taken the job—which I was overqualified for—because I wanted to pursue a more artistic life; that is, I wanted to write and paint, and being an executive chef did not allow the time or energy required to learn what I needed to in order to be an artist. My job at Restaurant Florent entailed coming in at six in the morning to cook breakfast for the locals: transvestites, meat packers, and young up-and-comers who were either on their way to work, or had been up all night and were in need of a hearty breakfast. My job was to cook breakfast until eleven o'clock, then prepare for the next day until two o'clock in the afternoon. Being diligent about my work, I was always done cooking breakfast and prepping by eleven, so I would leave early and go to my Harlem apartment to write and paint. After some months, the chef at Florent sat me down to say it was unacceptable to leave work three hours early since she was paying for a full shift. By that time I was fully, if mistakenly, convinced I could place or win at the New York State Fair, and had been baking pies at home with mixed results, fueled by a good deal of enthusiasm. I suggested to the chef that I make all the desserts for the restaurant. She was happy with the idea, so I began baking pies for Florent. With diligence, I finished baking and prepping by eleven. One day I received two pieces of seemingly bad news: The chef said she had to let me go for leaving my shift early, and the New York State Fair sent notice that I was disqualified from competing because I had sold pies professionally. I took my cue and set out to start my own company, Bubby's Pie Co.; Restaurant Florent became my first wholesale customer.

When I opened Bubby's Pie Co. in 1990, I was twenty-eight. I told both of my grandmothers, Grammy and Nanny, I was naming the company after them. I scraped together $10,000, got permission to use a catering company's kitchen, and started selling pies wholesale all over New York City. On the day before Thanksgiving, the most popular pie day in America, Bubby's opened to the public on the corner of North Moore and Hudson Street with just four tables. We soon added twenty seats, becoming a cozy café where regulars crammed into mismatched chairs for satisfying piles of eggs, bacon, and pancakes. The space next door became available in 1996 and Bubby's grew to one hundred seats, adding a bar and more kitchen space. By this time, we were serving 2,500 people a week. (Now we serve twice that every week.)

Bubby's sits just ten blocks from Ground Zero, so September 11th had a very direct impact on us and our neighbors in lower Manhattan. While the area was still cordoned off, we reopened as a place for neighbors, cops, firemen, and a slew of volunteers to gather and have free coffee, pie, and pancakes. We got the restaurant up and running so we could serve meals to rescue workers, Red Cross workers, and displaced locals.

In October 2003, Bubby's Pie Co. opened a second restaurant in the Brooklyn neighborhood of Dumbo beneath the shadows of the Brooklyn and Manhattan bridges, and with a full and fantastic view of Manhattan across the East River.

Bubby's Pie Co. is often mentioned in the press as a favorite eatery for locals and out-of-towners. It's a place where, on any given day, you'll find neighborhood regulars sitting elbow to elbow with politicians, truck drivers, artists, bartenders, housewives, chefs, lawyers, and famous actors. From the beginning, our food has acted as a great equalizer. It is a language that everyone shares.

Bubby's is dedicated to family dining in its purest form; that is, all kinds of families eating good home-cooked food together. We have no secret recipes (except for one: our barbecue sauce), and I have always made it clear to our customers that I would rather they eat great food at home, and if they want our recipes I am happy to share them. After all, I've gleaned most of them from moms, grandmas, dads, and diners across America.

When planning menus at Bubby's, I try not to forget the pleasure I got from my childhood neighbors' dinners of fried pork chops and cream of mushroom soup gravy. My mother was more inclined to cook something fancy, like fondue or a curried leg of lamb and, though her macaroni and cheese is on the menu at Bubby's, it was rare that she would cook from the American lexicon of home cooking. Even after I became a professional chef, homey cooking always felt more convivial than fussy, fancy food— exemplified by the overly designed, squiggle-riddled giant plate with a teeny little precious morsel in the middle of it. At Bubby's, we make almost everything from scratch; even our mustard and pickles. Real home cooks, with traditions that they and their families have been proud of for generations, have given us many of our recipes. They have trusted Bubby's to uphold their reputation.

Pie goes back a long way in American history. While testing recipes and writing this book, I spent time at the New York Public Library researching old cookbooks. The oldest recipe for pie that turned up was in an English cookbook from 1326 for a suet and beef pie. All the recipes for pie that exist prior to Pilgrims landing at Plymouth Rock in 1620 were for meat pies. Before then, sweet pies were referred to as tarts. Somewhere between 1620 and the early 1800s, "pie" came to mean either sweet or savory.

If you look back to early American cookbooks, there's very little detail on how to make fruit pies. There are recipes for pie dough and meringue, and for old-time pies like sugar pie, shoofly pie, chess pie, and vinegar pie, to soothe a sweet tooth when the fruit cellar is bare. Nothing's spelled out for you in an old recipe though; most are written in a terse, almost reluctant shorthand for cooks who already knew their way around the kitchen, like this recipe from *Skilful Housewife's Book* (1853):

Green Apple Pie

Stew and strain tart apples, grate the peel of a fresh lemon, or rose water and sugar to your taste. Bake in rich paste half an hour.

Pie was something you learned first by watching and tasting, then by helping and paying attention, and then through lots and lots of practice. Pies were made with whatever could be harvested from fields, orchards, gardens, and nearby woods—rhubarb, gooseberries, blackberries, apples—and were patterned by nature's cycle, not the supermarket. There weren't recipes so much as learned methods—the way your grandmother did it, or your mother, or sister, or good friend. The ladies' auxiliary cookbooks of earlier times are more likely to give advice on how to raise a polite child or keep a husband happy than they are to intimate why a "No-Fail Crust" might flop.

Whether you're a beginner or a seasoned baker, this book will help you think about pie and the infinite possibilities available to you. For beginners, the Primer chapter will help you understand the various elements of pastry making: how weather, humidity, and temperature affect your efforts, to understanding the finer points of rolling out dough, par-baking, blind-baking, and what it means when your crust is "set" in the oven. Beginners will want to read a recipe all the way through before shopping for ingredients. It is important to have all the tools and ingredients you will need on hand before beginning to bake. We have included detailed step-by-step illustrations to make it easier to visualize and understand some of the more complicated processes. You can follow the recipes as they are here and you will have a wide-ranging palette from which to bake all kinds of pies, and the things that go well with pie, like ice cream and crème fraîche. We have made use of sidebar instructions for bakers of all levels in an effort to highlight tricks and tips. A seasoned baker might simply look at the general idea of the recipe for reference, and scan the sidebars for pointers, tricks, and tips. The recipes can be changed to reflect your own creative powers, tastes and desires, and local produce.

Seasonality is a very important aspect of pie making. If you get acquainted with your local growing cycles, you will experience the thrill of anticipating each fruit of the season, and the abundance of your region. For example, at the end of a long winter, a pie baker relishes the idea that rhubarb is coming to market. Then the fun begins when the first strawberries show up—starting with a slow but exciting trickle, accelerating into piles and mounds of juicy red strawberries just begging to be turned into pie, jam, and shortcake. By then, it's the season for berries, peaches, plums, and gooseberries and the farmers' tables groan under the abundance of summer. There are traditional pies for holidays, which also tie into the season. After all, pumpkin pie became a Thanksgiving tradition because November is the heart of pumpkin season. After some years of baking, a pie maker has a recurring notion of what is coming to the market and when—to this end we offer a Perpetual Pie Calendar (see page 339) to show what a year of seasonal pies might look like for us here in New York.

There is nothing quite so thrilling as meandering through the farmer's markets pondering what kind of pie can be baked for the evening's table. It's always good to have an open mind, an eye for thrift, and a willingness to think on your feet when it comes to shopping at the market. One summer day there was an abundance of lovely berries at the market, and I had some graham cracker crumbs in the freezer, and some crème fraîche left over from a dinner I had made earlier that week. It occurred to me that a custard made from crème fraîche would be an interesting base for a fresh berry pie. By spreading a thin layer of crème fraîche custard in a graham cracker crust, and substituting the freshly purchased berries for the blueberries in the fresh blueberry pie recipe, I was able to make something similar in idea, yet different from the original recipe, and the pie was wonderful. That is perhaps the poetry and practicality of pie: the fluidity of ingredients combined with the eye of the pie baker.

The journey of becoming a chef, of finding a particular passion for pie, and seeing other people not only enjoy the pies but also become interested in learning how to make them, has been more surprising and spiritually rewarding than I ever could have imagined. I sincerely hope this book, the techniques, recipes, and ideas conveyed herein will allow you to share this enthusiasm. My hope is that this book will soon be punctuated with fruit stains, the pages slightly tattered—even a bit stuck together—and that you can hand it down in that shape to your nieces, nephews, great-grandchildren, or whoever is chosen to carry the pie torch on into the future. Good pie making to you and yours.

Ron Silver

BUBBY'S
HOMEMADE
PIES

CRUST BASICS:
AN ILLUSTRATED PRIMER

When you become a good cook, you become a good craftsman, first. You repeat and repeat and repeat until your hands know how to move without thinking about it.
—JACQUES PEPIN

Most pies begin with a crust; crusts are also the reason why most bakers hesitate to make pies at all. Crust making is definitely a craft; plenty of practice through many seasons and weather conditions is the best way to learn the ropes. Study this chapter and use it as a guide.

In this chapter, we'll address questions most often asked, show you helpful techniques, and give you some insights about the inner life of the crust. Temperature, humidity, and aridity can greatly affect the process and end results of crust making, and this chapter will also address how to factor in these variables. Like most serious pie bakers, we'll discuss and debate fats—butter versus shortening versus lard, and so on—and show you how your choices affect your pie's flavor and structure.

Flaky pastry crusts—composed of flour, fat, water, and a pinch of salt—are our most versatile favorites and the surest choice for any classic double-crust pie. The flavor of flaky pastry crust is influenced by the kind of fat you choose—most typically butter, lard, or shortening. Flaky crusts take practice to mix correctly, and benefit from good rolling technique and cool working temperatures or intermittent chilling. Fully baked, golden, flaky crusts offer a crisp, buttery contrast to fruit pie fillings, saucy savory pies, and cream pies alike and are an especially good choice for pies with juicy fillings that need to thicken up inside.

There are many options for finishing off pastry crust edges and topping pies: double-crust vent slits, lattices, crisp toppings, and crumble toppings are but a few. We even give you tasty ideas for using your crust scraps to keep children (or adults) busy while the pies are baking.

Slender open-faced tarts call for denser, more stable crust walls to support the filling when the freestanding tart is removed from the tart pan. Tart crusts are made with the same ingredients as flaky pastry, but with an egg added for structure (a classic French *pâte brisée*). If a little sugar is thrown into the dough to complement a sweet filling, the crust is considered a classic *pâte sucrée* (sweet). Tart crusts are easy to make in a food processor or electric mixer and are less sensitive to overmixing than flaky pastry crusts.

Crumb crusts, made from crushed cookie crumbs and melted butter, are often used for ice cream, custard, and pudding pies; their sugary cookie crumbs cling to the rich creamy filling and remain flavorful when refrigerated or frozen. They are the easiest crusts to make in hot weather because they are made with melted butter. There is a wealth of information included here on how to be inventive with nut crusts, crumb crusts, and cookie crusts. The base cookie recipes are also included, since we find that using homemade cookies vastly improves the flavor of a homemade crumb crust. It's Bubby's aesthetic to make simple foods from scratch using quality ingredients. In the case of the crumb crusts, the flavor payoff is exponential.

Understanding the Structure of Flaky Pastry Pie Dough

A flaky pastry pie crust is made of three parts flour, one part cold fat (lard and/or shortening), a pinch of salt, and just enough ice cold water added sparingly until the mixture coheres into a supple but firm ball of dough.

Mixing dough seems simple and straightforward at first glance—and it is—but a pie baker needs to have a good grasp of the variables that yield good results. Mixing and rolling techniques, temperature, and weather conditions all shift the balance of the dough. Keeping everything in equilibrium takes practice. The fat in the dough must remain very cold, solid, and distinct from the flour and water that surrounds it in order to correctly form a light, flaky crust.

Cold butter is essential to a flaky crust. When the fat is cut into the flour and salt, the largest pieces of fat should be about the size of shelling peas; the smallest pieces of fat should be no smaller than lentils. Don't overmix the butter into the flour. Here's why: When you roll out the pastry dough, those cold, solid, and distinct little pea-sized pieces of fat flatten into disks between the floury layers. When the pie goes into the oven, the fatty layers heat up and expand open with steam to form a pocket. These airy pockets set amid the floury layers make the finished crust light and flaky.

A warm room temperature can make the separation of fat and flour layers difficult to maintain on a hot summer day (or in a commercial kitchen). It might be a comfort to know that centuries of pie bakers have struggled with the same dilemma, especially before refrigerators came along. Old recipes call for mixing dough in a cold room or cellar. Factor in more time for dough making in the summer to allow for chilling and rechilling everything, and keep your hands, ingredients, and implements as cool as possible. If the butter softens or melts into the flour during the mixing process, the flour essentially becomes waterproofed and will repel the water when you add it, making your crust mealy and dense instead of flaky and light. (Make the dough the day before if you need to take some pressure off yourself in a hot kitchen.) Great pie dough can still be achieved on a hot day if you take time to chill things between each step or whenever you notice the fat softening up. Chilling relaxes the dough and slows down the gluten development; it also makes the butter lumps colder so they remain distinct when rolled out.

Acidity also inhibits gluten development, which is why some pie-crust recipes have lemon juice or vinegar in them. However, good technique can accomplish the same result.

Rolling out the dough takes practice, and requires a fast, light, even touch. Pie dough can only be rolled out once for best results, otherwise the gluten in the flour gets overdeveloped and forms little elastic strands—resulting in a tough, leathery crust. When gluten has been overstimulated through rigorous mixing or overly warm, overly wet dough conditions, the dough (more precisely, the gluten in it) is considered "overworked." Dough scraps can be cut into interesting shapes and used to decorate the top crust, or they can be used for making little snacks we call Cinnamon and Sugar Scrap Buddies (page 22), but they are not suited to reuse or reroll for a top or bottom crust.

Choosing Flour

For pie pastry, use all-purpose unbleached white flour. The gluten in all-purpose flour is an ideal proportion for pastry-making; it's like the thin muscle in the floury layers of a crust's structure. If there is little or no gluten in the flour, as in cake flour, rice flour, or nut flours, the crust will crumble when rolled and the flour layers won't have the tension and flexibility needed to stretch around the fats as they expand during the cooking process. Use flour with too much gluten, however, and your layers will have too much muscle. If you've ever used bread flour for a pie crust by mistake, you'll recall its unpleasant, unpalatable, bready, cracker-like texture and flavor. Pastry flour is acceptable for pie dough but, despite its name, it's a distant second choice to all-purpose flour due to its heavier, crumblier texture. This texture issue is also the case with whole wheat, spelt, oat, and other whole-grain flours. If you want to experiment with them, it's better to do so in a short crust or nut cookie crust where the gluten has a less significant role to play.

Handling and Choosing Fats

Fats hold the key to both the flavor and the texture of a crust. The better the fat flavor, the better the crust flavor. A flaky crust can be achieved with any fat, as long as proper consideration is shown to keeping the fat cool and well below its melting temperature. The reputations fats have among pie bakers (as easy or hard to work with, flakiest, etc.) have much to do with their different melting temperatures. This is the case for two reasons: It is necessary to keep fat in its solid state during mixing and rolling to achieve a desirable crust texture and structure; solid fat softens easily at room temperature. The way to address this dilemma is by factoring in the behavior of the kind fat you're using and taking adequate precautions—typically, chilling the dough intermittently.

There are many options for fat in pie dough, but the most common are butter, lard, and shortening. Whatever fat you choose, it should be very cold when it is mixed into the dough.

BUTTER: This fat, especially high fat–content "European-style" butter (more than 80% butterfat, and less than 20% water), is the best for pie crusts. Lower-quality butter can have a lower ratio of butterfat to water content and milk solids (as low as 60/40), which means you won't get optimum flavor from it. However, a crust made with low-quality butter is still pretty flavorful, much more so than a shortening crust. Butter softens quickly at room temperature and can be a little tricky to work with on a warm day, but it adds wonderful flavor and texture to a pie crust. Never use whipped butter or margarine for pastry.

Lard: This fat has a wonderful reputation among pie bakers for its flavor, texture, and stable structure, especially when it's organic or rendered from hogs raised on small farms with good husbandry practices. Lard is magnificent for pies because it is 100% pure fat (no water) with a wonderful flavor. Look for organic "leaf lard"—the best-quality lard from around the kidneys—at the local farmer's market, a family-owned butcher shop, or online. It is normal for rendered leaf lard to be sold with some fatback mixed in, but it should be primarily leaf lard. Organic lard has a better flavor than commercial lard, but there are other important reasons for choosing it. Commercially produced supermarket-variety lard is sometimes hydrogenated and may have an off taste due to chemical additives (BHT), excessive fatback added in (this gives it a bacon taste), poor husbandry practices, or all of the above. Moreover, animals store toxins (and whatever growth hormones and antibiotics they're fed) in their fat, so stick with the quality organic lard, and you'll be pleased with your pies.

Shortening: Shortening crusts are a bit lackluster in flavor, but yield a very flaky texture. Shortening keeps for long periods of time and is the cheapest option for pie crusts. It's easy to work with because it's less sensitive to warm temperatures; it's solid at room temperature and will not melt into the flour during the mixing process. It's our last choice for flavor, but it can be improved by mixing both shortening and butter in dough to capitalize on the positive characteristics of both fats—stability and flavor. Most shortening comes as hydrogenated fat (cottonseed or soybean oil with hydrogen added) and contains trans-fatty acids. A fully baked all-shortening crust served at room temperature can leave a waxy feeling in the mouth.

Flavorful rendered meat fats: Goose, duck, bacon, etc., have a strong flavor and can be used in pie dough sparingly by substituting 1 tablespoon of cold, solid fat for 1 tablespoon of fat called for in your favorite crust recipe. For instructions on rendering meat fats, follow the lard rendering instructions (see page 45). Stronger meat fat flavors are best used in crusts for savory pies or for autumn and winter fruit pies. There are some curious old pioneer cookbooks that even call for using bear cub fat or wild game fats for pie crust—certainly not for the sake of being exotic, but rather, to use what was available locally.

Crusts made with liquid oil are unpleasant in texture—mealy and heavy—and are generally not recommended. Our only exception to this is the Hot Water Pastry Crust used for Pork Pie Hats (page 45), because the dough is soft and pliable and holds its form well when baked. Its baked flavor and texture are reminiscent of fried empanadas—delicious and solid next to the spicy pulled pork; it is a great pastry for little meat pies.

Preparing Pastry Ingredients

Wash your hands in cold water. No matter how hands-on or -off you are in the kitchen, you'll need to have your bare hands on the dough to get a feel for it during the process. Maintaining cool hands, ingredients, and dough throughout the pastry-making process helps to prevent the fat in the dough from melting. If ingredients or tools feel warm, chill them in the refrigerator or freezer; if your hands warm up too much, cool them down under cold water and dry them well before returning to the dough.

Measure out the water for the crust (with a touch more extra water in the measure in case your dough needs it) and then add ice cubes. Chill it in the freezer.

Dip a dry measuring cup into the flour and level it off. Sifting is not appropriate for pie dough; sifting flour fluffs it up and may leave you shy of the amount needed. By the same token, don't pack flour down or you'll have too much. In a mixing bowl, mix flour and salt.

To use butter, measure out the amount you need, and then dip the cold, solid stick in the measured flour to coat it. Sprinkle a little of the flour for the recipe on the butter wrapper and place the flour-coated butter on top of it. Using a dough scraper or a long butcher knife, cut the butter length-wise in half, and then in quarters, coating each cut side with flour as you go. Then dice the butter into ¼-inch cubes (1-inch pieces for food processor method) and add them and any remaining flour on the wrapper back into the bowl of flour.

Mixing the Fat into the Flour

HAND METHOD: Using a pastry cutter, press the blades through the mix-ture, bearing down repeatedly like you would to mash potatoes. Repeat this gesture until the largest pieces of fat are the size of shelling peas and the smallest are the size of lentils (none smaller). Do not get overenthusiastic here: this size range makes for excellent flakiness. Rechill if the fat is no longer cool to the touch.

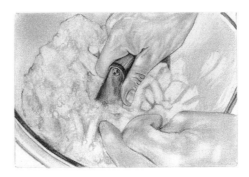

FOOD PROCESSOR METHOD: We use a food processor to cut the fat into the flour when we are making a batch of dough for three or more pie crusts. It's worthwhile and fast, but be careful not to overmix the fat. Always use the pulse button for this method, never use the ON (continuous) setting.

First pulse the flour and salt in the food processor. Chop the fat into 1-inch pieces with a knife and add it. You need to cut the fat into larger pieces when using a food processor because the machine cuts it down very quickly—much more quickly than a hand pastry cutter. Pulse a few times. To get the fat to cut in evenly, stop and give the entire food processor and its contents a jostle by tilting it from side to side every couple of pulses. Pulse the mixture until the largest fat pieces are the size of shelling peas. Do not overmix. Watch closely—it only takes about 10 quick pulses to get there. If you have a few bigger chunks of butter in a mixture that is otherwise perfect, pour the mixture into a large bowl and cut the bigger chunks down to size by hand so that the whole mixture remains consistent for flakiness.

Transfer the fat and flour mixture to a bowl and chill it. Do not use the food processor to add the water to a pastry crust. Always mix in the water by hand.

Mixing in the Water

Keep in mind that flour absorbs humidity from the air. If you're mixing pie dough in a hot, dry, and arid climate, you'll need a little more water than you will if you're making pie dough in a cool, moist, and humid climate. The ideal texture, a pastry that holds itself in a ball, supple and slightly tacky to the touch, is what you're ultimately looking for, rather than adding an exact amount of water; the recipes call for an approximate amount of water, but you need to use your hands to feel when it is right.

Begin this phase with a fully chilled flour and fat mixture. Be judicious, even stingy, with the ice-cold water. Do not add all the water at once; it must be dispersed into the mixture incrementally. Add water a couple of tablespoons (or later, drops) at a time, quickly tossing the mixture with your hands after each addition. Emphasize upward motion and lightness in your tossing and try to distribute the water evenly throughout the mixture. Work the dough as little as possible.

When there are no floury bits anymore—just little comet-like cobbles that don't quite cohere—slow down and sprinkle or flick water in at this point (don't pour or spoon it in now). The balance can shift quickly from crumbly to wet. Again, one drop can make the difference and bring it all together.

To test the dough for consistency, lightly pat together some dough the size of a tennis ball. If the ball crumbles apart or has lots of dry-looking cracks in it, the dough is still too dry; let it break apart. Add a drop or two of water to the outside of the ball and work it just a little. If it holds and feels firm and supple, mop up any remaining crumbs with the ball—if they pick up easily, the dough is probably wet enough. If they fall back into the bowl, you might need a touch more water to pull the dough together. The pastry should be just a little bit tacky when you touch it.

Wet dough may seem easier to work, but because the extra water overdevelops the gluten, it makes the crust tough. If your pie dough is stretchy (glutinous) and quickly retracts when you roll it out, chances are you have added more water than you need and your pastry is overworked. If your dough is quite sticky, soft, and wet, it is better to pitch it and start over. At this point, you can't just add flour to fix it.

Dough can feel like it's holding together because the butter is melting. If at any point the dough ceases to feel cool to the touch or the butter pieces feel melty, soft, and warm, put the whole mixture in the freezer until it's cooled down again—about 10 minutes. It's impossible to gauge the water ratio accurately if the fat is melting into the flour.

If you're making a single crust, shape the dough into one round ball with your hands. If you're making a double crust, divide the dough into slightly uneven halves and shape each half into a ball—the larger of which will be for the bottom crust, the smaller ball for the top. Cover each ball tightly with plastic wrap and refrigerate it for at least half an hour to relax the gluten and rechill the fat. In practical terms, this cold rest makes the dough easier to roll out. The dough will feel cold and firm when you take it out again.

Rolling and Shaping

Only take one ball of dough from the refrigerator at a time, beginning with the larger of two balls if you're making a double crust. Unwrap it and place it on a clean, smooth, lightly floured surface like a wooden chopping block or a countertop. Flour sprinkled on the surface of the dough and the work surface keeps the dough from sticking to the rolling pin; it allows the dough to move and expand freely without resistance. Keep a little mound of flour off to the side to pull from as needed. You don't have to be shy when applying flour, but just brush the excess off the dough with your hand before rolling it out. Too much extra flour can dry out the dough.

Gently press the ball down with the palm of your hand to flatten it into a round, flat disk, about two inches high. Sprinkle the flattened dough with flour.

The more circular the shape you start with, the easier it is to keep it that way, so pat the edges of the puck into a circle again if any cracks formed there. (If the cracks are many and resistant to mending, brush off any flour and add a drop or two of water at a large crack and give the dough a very brief knead to incorporate it.)

Start rolling in the center and keep rolling the dough from the center outward—using more pressure in the center and less as you near the edge. Take care not to roll beyond the outside edge or it will get too thin. If the edges start to crack and separate, gently squeeze them back together. Scatter flour across the rolling surface and flip the puck over.

Strive to make the thickness of the dough as even as possible—about ⅛ inch thick by the end.

Think of the dough like a clock—balancing a 12 o'clock stroke with a 6 o'clock stroke, a 2 o'clock stroke with an 8 o'clock stroke and so on, lifting and turning the dough incrementally so that all directions are addressed. Use each stroke to try to maintain the circle's integrity as it grows larger.

If you get subcontinents, pinch them back together before they have a chance to spread out too much.

You should be able to see the fat take on a marbled look in the dough as it spreads out under the pressure. Try not to handle it too much with your hands.

Be quick to note if the dough is sticking. Scatter flour across the dough and the rolling surface and flip the dough over. To flip it, you can loosely roll the dough around the rolling pin to support it and turn it over. If dough clings to the board, use the pastry scraper to help lift it off. If you are having trouble with dough sticking to the pin or the counter, you either need more flour on and under the surface of the dough or you need to chill the dough before moving on. If you start feeling soft butter, gently scrape the dough up with the pastry scraper, put the dough on a baking sheet, and chill it in the freezer for one

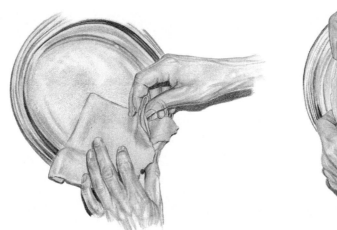

minute. (This won't happen as you learn to work more quickly. Practice makes for improvement.) If the dough is cold to the touch, you probably just need more flour to prevent sticking.

For the bottom crust, hold your pie tin over the dough circle to test the round for size. The edge of the crust should extend beyond the lip of the tin about two inches in all directions. Brush off the excess flour with your hand or a dry pastry brush. For pies, you don't have to grease or flour the pan. The fat in the dough is sufficient for an easy release.

If you are using the dough right away, loosely fold the circle in half, then in quarters. Center the tip of the wedge in the pie plate and unfold the pie dough very gently.

Lift the edges inward a bit to help the dough settle into the edges of the pan on its own accord without forcing it. Don't press or stretch the dough, or it'll pull back in baking. Let it take the shape itself. Refrigerate the crust-lined pan. If you're making a double crust, scrape the counter

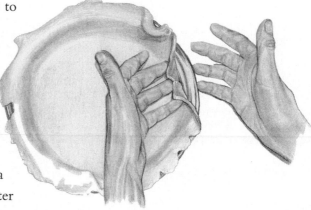

clean with a dough scraper. Reflour the counter, take out the next ball of dough, and repeat the process.

Trimming and Crimping a Single Crust

A single crust can be used alone, with filling exposed, or in conjunction with a crumb, a crisp, or a meringue topping. A single crust is often par-baked or blind-baked before the filling is added. It is good for custard pies, cream pies, or fruit pies with very juicy fruits that can afford to lose some extra moisture during baking.

After lining the pie pan and allowing the dough to settle into it completely, trim the excess dough—about ¾ inch beyond the edge of the pan—with the pastry cutter or the tip of a sharp knife. If you don't have quite enough crust on one section of the edge, you can use trimmed bits of excess dough to patch into scant ones by pinching the overlapping dough edges together.

Roll the trimmed dough edge and rest it on the lip of the tin. Work your way around the edge continuously, striving for a rolled edge pretty even in thickness—about ½ inch. Avoid creating super thick edges; they're likely to turn out undercooked and gummy inside.

The benefit of crimping an edge—in addition to tying up loose ends—is that it helps strengthen and stabilize the crust's edge on the lip of the pan. The easiest way to crimp the edge of a single-crust pie is by pressing the tines of a fork evenly around the edge. You might need to dip the tines in flour occasionally to keep the dough from sticking to them.

To make a fancier scalloped edge instead, use your outside hand as an armature and your inside hand as the primary mover, to push the rolled edge into a little V-shaped crimp. Repeat and turn until you've made it all of the way around.

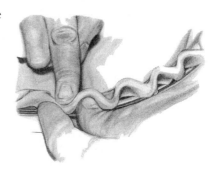

Chill the fully formed crust for at least 20 minutes before filling or baking it.

Blind- or Par-Baking a Single Crust

There are two reasons to bake a single crust alone without its filling: The first (blind-baking) is if the filling is not baked but the crust is, as with a pudding pie or a glazed fresh fruit pie. Sometimes, a crust is par-baked (partially baked) and then a custard filling is added to it and the two are baked in the oven together. What's the reason to do this somewhat cumbersome par-baking if it's going to be baked again? Have you ever eaten a gummy-tasting, doughy bottom crust from a pumpkin pie? A custard filling is wet and bakes for only a short time at a low temperature, preventing the crust from getting very far along in its baking process. In this case, the solution is to bake the crust alone until it is blond, blistered, and the pastry is "set" in the oven, then to finish baking the crust with the filling in it. (This is the case with pumpkin pie.) You can prepare a par-baked crust a few hours in advance to get a head start, before going on to make the filling.

To blind- or par-bake a fully formed, crimped, uncooked crust, refrigerate it for at least 20 minutes first. Before baking, dock the bottom of the entire crust with a fork. Line the inside of the crust with parchment or foil and fill it with dried beans or commercial pie weights (dried kidney beans work well and can be used over and over), spreading them evenly all the way up to the top edge. (See Equipment and Source Reference, page 321.)

(See Equipment and Source Reference, page 321.)

PAR-BAKING. Bake the crust at 450°F for 15 to 20 minutes, or until the edge looks blonde and lightly blistered. The bottom of the crust will look partially cooked and there may still be some translucency to the dough. Carefully lift out the liner and weights. Cool the crust completely on a rack or trivet. It is now ready to be filled and further baked.

BLIND-BAKING. To fully blind-bake a crust, turn the oven down to 375°F and bake it for 10 minutes more after removing the liner and weights, or until the crust edges and bottom are golden brown. Check on it from time to time during the first few minutes after returning it to the oven. If the crust starts to balloon up, you can lightly pat it down with your hand or a clean dish towel (yes it's hot, but just move quickly) and then prick the ballooning area with a fork before returning it to the oven. Cool the crust completely before filling it.

Caring for Your Rolling Pin

Only use water (don't use soap) to clean a wood rolling pin—you don't want to wash the oil off the wood. It should feel supple, like healthy skin. Instead, just wipe it down with a clean dry cloth until all the flour and bits of dough have been removed. There should be a sheen to it.

Trimming and Crimping a Double Crust

A double-crust pie has a top crust that works like a lid on a pot—it traps most of the steam from the fruit filling as it cooks. The perk is that the top crust responds beautifully to everything that happens above and below it and tastes marvelous.

Fill the pie, dot the filling with butter if directed in the recipe, and lay the second rolled-

 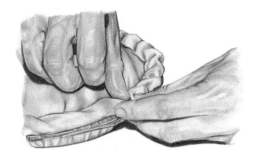

out pie crust over the top of the pie, aiming to center it correctly the first time, either using the quarter-fold method (see page 13) or by transferring the dough on the rolling pin.

Because you'll have two layers of crust at the edge, you can trim the edge of the bottom crust slightly shorter than you would a single-crust edge. Trim off the excess dough along the edge to ½ inch, roll the bottom and top edges together, and crimp as desired (see page 14). Refrigerate the filled pie for 10 minutes before making the pie vents.

Pie Vents, Markings, and Pie Birds for Double-Crust Pies

Vents are small holes or slits in the top crust of a double-crust pie to allow the excess steam to escape. At Bubby's, we think of pie vents as language or signage—each kind of pie has its own characteristic design. With so many different pies at the restaurant, we find it necessary to differentiate between whole uncut pies, especially ones that look similar, so we use distinctive vent patterns to indicate different types of pies.

To make vents, cut into the top crust of an unbaked pie with the tip of a sharp knife once the crust is already crimped and refrigerated. Or, before you add the top crust to the pie, use small cutting molds like miniature cookie cutters or

ASK BUBBY

Do I have to vent a double-crust pie?

Yes, because otherwise it can balloon up or burst open when the steam starts to form inside the pie. You can also use a pie bird—a decorative ceramic or metal vent that fits into the top crust—to sing the steam out.

the large end of pastry tube tips to make a pattern. If the pie requires a well-sealed top (like an apple pie), keep the open areas to a minimum—use slits instead—or your fruit will dry out. You can make a lattice top crust with juicy fruit pies such as cherry or blueberry. If the design you have in mind involves a lot of cutaways, cut the well-chilled crust on a layer of parchment, center it over the filled pie, and carefully slide the crust onto the filling.

To place a pie bird in your pie (see page 329) cut an X in the center of the top crust and nestle the base in securely.

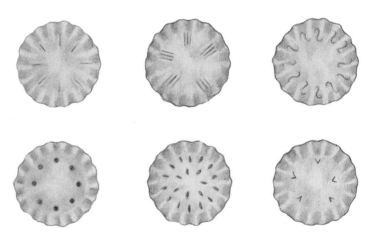

Lattice Crusts

Lattice pies are often used to showcase a beautifully colored, juicy fruit. Mix up a batch of double-crust pastry pie dough and line the pie plate with the bottom layer of dough. Refrigerate. Roll out the second round as you would for a double crust. Chill it for 10 minutes. Using a very sharp knife, a pizza cutter, or a wavy ravioli cutter, cut parallel strips at ¾-inch intervals (you can use a ruler or just wing it).

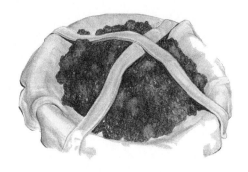

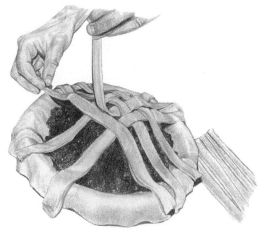

To build the lattice, lay the longest strips across the middle of the filled pie to form an X.

Lay the next two longest strips parallel to the strip that lies under the X, on either side of it. Switch directions and do the same for the other strip, weaving them over and under the larger strips in a basket-weave pattern. Repeat until the surface of the pie has been fully draped with it. Or, you can place one layer of strips on top of the filling and then place the other layer across them without weaving. You may need to thin out some of the lattice strips where they overhang and overlap at the crust edge before you roll it up, lest your crimped edge get too bulky.

Optional Finishing Touches for a Double-Crust Pie

A double-crust pie needs nothing more than a vent or two, but sometimes it's nice to add a little something for flavor, function, or beauty. Choose only one option and add it just before the pie goes in the hot oven.

SUGAR. Right before baking, you can sprinkle the top crust with a little sugar to give the fully baked crust a nice, sugary, slightly caramelized crackle. If you're working with a very tall pie like a Mile-High Apple Pie, flick a little bit of water on the crust (to help the sugar stick to it) and then sprinkle it with sugar. Bake immediately.

CREAM AND SUGAR. Using a pastry brush, brush heavy cream very lightly over the top crust and then sprinkle it with sugar. This gives a nice subtle sheen to the golden-brown crust and the sugar makes it sweeter. Typically, we prefer to use this one exclusively for lattice crusts or the biscuit crust on cobblers because it can seal a flaky crust too thoroughly.

HONEY. Use a squeeze bottle or honey spoon to drizzle honey lightly over the top crust. The honey design will take on the-quality of a drawing as it bakes; it gets a shade darker than the crust. We use it for sweet or savory apple or quince pies. This is especially good at the crust's edge, where the honey gathers and bakes into the pastry.

EGG WASH. Whisk an egg with a table-spoon or two of cold water and brush a light coat over the crust with a pastry brush. It produces a high-gloss sheen on the finished crust. This is recommended for savory pies or pastries as a means to hold sesame seeds, poppy seeds, or herbs in place.

Baking Pies in Quantity

If you are making more than six pies at a time, you'll want to change your methods. To make the dough, use a food processor to cut the butter into the flour but, as always, add the water by hand. If

ASK BUBBY

My crust is falling down. It looks like it's melting off the edge. Why?

When a crust doesn't set up correctly or hold its structure, there are a number of questions to ask. Was the dough cold enough when it went into the oven? Was the oven temperature high enough to set the crust quickly? Did you add more fat than the recipe called for? Was the dough too wet? If there's a lot of movement in the dough, too much water is often the culprit. Practice is the best teacher.

you are making a lot of dough, you should divide it into smaller batches to add the water. Form the dough into 6-ounce balls for 9-inch crusts (tennis ball size), wrap tightly with plastic wrap, and refrigerate for at least half an hour.

You can mix the pie dough a day or two in advance to save time. It is good for the dough to chill, rest, and relax. Pastry pie dough will hold in the refrigerator, in balls wrapped tightly in plastic wrap, for up to two days. Refrigerated dough that looks slightly gray is too old and should be thrown away.

Freezing dough can be a practical measure if you have two events a week apart, but in general, it's preferable to make up dough fresh because the freezer only diminishes the quality. If you freeze dough, take care to pack it well in extra layers of plastic wrap and put it inside a well-sealed plastic bag to prevent it from taking on added moisture or getting freezer burn. Thaw frozen dough in the refrigerator for twenty-four hours before you need it. Thawed dough can feel wet. Use a little more flour when rolling it out to help balance the moisture.

Prerolled, Prechilled Crusts

If you have a few double-crust pies to assemble, roll out and chill all your dough in advance—up to an hour or two ahead of time—so that your filling doesn't sit for too long once it's mixed together. If fruit for the pie filling is allowed to sit in a bowl with the sugar, the sugar will macerate the fruit and make the filling soupy. If you roll out rounds in advance, you can refrigerate them stacked like pancakes on a wide baking sheet with parchment, waxed paper, or plastic wrap between each layer. Wrap the stack and baking sheet completely with plastic wrap so the crusts won't dry out, and refrigerate them. Because crusts are more prone to drying out once rolled, only prepare them this way shortly before you plan to use them.

Cinnamon and Sugar Scrap Buddies

After rolling out the dough, you have some spare edges. Don't throw them away! Use this recipe to make an easy, excellent snack. This is a great project for kids and a good way to ensure that your children will treat you to pies in your old age. These can be baked at any oven temperature alongside your pie.

Kids love 'em.

3 tablespoons sugar
1 teaspoon cinnamon
Pastry pie dough trimmings

Mix up the cinnamon and sugar and then choose one of the following methods:

Teaching Aspiring Young Pie Bakers: Take your scraps of dough and let the youngsters mush them together into a ball or two. Let them roll them out again until the pieces are reasonably flat. (You can buy small rolling pins for kids.) Place their creations on a parchment-lined cookie sheet and let the kids sprinkle them with cinnamon and sugar. Bake at 375°F for 5 to 10 minutes, or until they're golden brown. Cool and serve. (The dough will get overworked but the treats will still taste very good. The point is to give kids a chance to play and be comfortable working with dough.)

Snails for the Aesthetically Minded Child: Lay the scraps flat and brush them with a touch of melted butter. Let the kids sprinkle them with cinnamon and sugar and help them roll the thin scraps up like a jellyroll and cut them into tiny cinnamon buns. Place the buns spiral side up on a parchment-lined baking sheet and bake at 375°F for 5 to 10 minutes, or until they're golden brown. Cool and serve.

Flaky Pastry Crusts

Bubby's All-Butter Pastry Pie Dough

An all-butter crust takes finesse to mix and handle because butter gets soft quickly at room temperature. Keeping a butter crust cold takes more attention, but pays off in flavor and flakiness. Its versatile flavor complements and accentuates other flavors in much the same way that a pat of butter and a pinch of salt do in the filling. It's often our first choice at home because it goes very well with any single- or double-crust fruit pie, savory pie, or cream pie.

8- TO 10-INCH SINGLE CRUST

4 to 5 tablespoons ice cold water

1½ cups all-purpose flour

¼ teaspoon salt

8 tablespoons (1 stick) cold unsalted butter

8- TO 10-INCH DOUBLE CRUST OR 12-INCH SINGLE CRUST

5 to 6 tablespoons ice cold water

2 cups all-purpose flour

½ teaspoon salt

11½ tablespoons cold unsalted butter

12-INCH DOUBLE CRUST

½ cup ice cold water

3 cups all-purpose flour

½ teaspoon salt

1 cup (2 sticks) cold unsalted butter

Measure out the water for the crust (with a bit of extra water in the measure in case you need a touch more) and then add ice cubes. Chill it in the freezer.

Measure out the flour (unsifted) by leveling off dry measuring cups, and add the flour to large bowl. Add the salt to the flour and give it a quick stir to combine evenly.

Use cold butter, measure out the amount you need, and then coat the cold, solid stick with the flour in the bowl. Using a dough scraper or a long butcher knife, cut the butter lengthwise in half, and then lengthwise in quarters, coating each newly cut side with flour as you go. Dice the butter into ¼-

inch cubes (or 1-inch sticks if using a food processor).Break up any pieces that stick together and toss them all to coat them with flour. (If it is a warm day, chill this mixture briefly in the freezer before continuing.)

HAND METHOD: Using a pastry cutter, press the blades through the mixture, bearing down repeatedly like you would to mash potatoes. Repeat this gesture until the largest pieces of fat are the size of shelling peas and the smallest are the size of lentils (none smaller). Do not get overenthusiastic here: this size range makes for excellent flakiness. Rechill if necessary.

FOOD PROCESSOR METHOD: Add the flour, salt, and butter mixture to the food processor and pulse it a few times. Do not use the continuous ON setting for pastry. To get the fat to cut in evenly you must stop and angle the entire food processor to give its contents a jostle by shaking and tilting it every couple of pulses. Pulse the mixture until the larger fat pieces are the size of shelling peas and the smallest fat pieces are the size of lentils. Do not overmix. Watch closely—it typically takes less than 10 quick pulses to get there. If you have a few bigger chunks of butter in a mixture that is otherwise perfect, dump the mixture into a large bowl and cut the bigger chunks down to size by hand with a pastry cutter so that the whole mixture remains consistent for flakiness. Transfer the fat and flour mixture to a bowl and chill it. Do not use the food processor to add the water to a pastry crust. Always mix in the water by hand.

When adding the water, begin with a fully chilled flour and fat mixture and ice cold water. Be judicious, even stingy, with the water. Do not add all the water at once; it must be dispersed into the mixture incrementally. Add

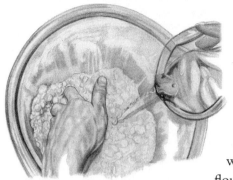

water two or three tablespoons at first, quickly tossing the mixture with your hands after each addition with light upward motion to distribute the water evenly throughout it. Work the dough as little as possible.

Continue adding little bits of water at a time. When there are no floury bits anymore—just little comet-like cobbles that don't quite cohere—slow down and sprinkle or flick water in at this point. One drop can make the difference and bring it all together. The balance can shift quickly from crumbly to wet.

To test the dough for consistency, lightly pat together some dough the size of a tennis ball. If the ball crumbles apart or has lots of dry-looking cracks in it, the dough is still too dry; let it break apart. Add a drop or two of water to the outside of the ball and work it just a little. If it holds and feels firm and supple, mop up any remaining crumbs with the ball—if they pick up easily, the dough is probably wet enough. If they fall back into the bowl, you might need a touch more water. The pastry should be just a little bit tacky when you touch it.

Wet dough may seem easier to work, but because the extra water overdevelops the gluten it makes a really tough crust. If your pie dough is stretchy (glutinous) and quickly retracts when you roll it out, chances are you have added more water than you need and your pastry is over-worked. If your dough is quite sticky, soft, and wet, it is better to pitch it and start over.

Dough can feel like it's holding together because the butter is melting. If at any point the dough ceases to feel cool to the touch or the butter pieces feel melty, soft, and warm, put the whole mixture in the freezer until it's cooled down again—about 10 minutes. It's impossible to gauge the water ratio accurately if the fat is melting into the flour.

If you're making a single crust, shape the dough into one round ball with your hands. If you're making a double crust, divide the dough into slightly uneven halves and shape each half into a ball—the larger of which will be for the bottom crust, the smaller ball for the top. Cover each ball tightly with plastic wrap and refrigerate it for at least half an hour to relax and slow the gluten development and rechill the fat. In practical terms, this cold rest makes the dough easier to roll out. For instructions on rolling out dough, see "Rolling and Shaping" on page 11.

Why is my fully baked pie crust shrinking?

If your pie crust shrinks while it is baking, chances are the gluten in the dough was overworked. Was the dough wet and stretchy? Ease off on the water the next time you mix your dough. Did you work the dough for a long time, either during the mixing process or while rolling it out? You may need to pause and rechill the dough more frequently to allow the gluten to relax. Another possibility is that your pie crust may have needed more of a chill before it went into the oven.

Basic Butter and Shortening Pastry Pie Dough

The butter gives this crust flavor and the shortening makes the dough a little easier to work with because of its higher melting temperature. It's an appealing choice for economy and convenience, and its forgiving nature makes it an easy dough to work with in production baking. This dough is a good choice for fried pies because it holds up so well and has good buttery flavor.

8- TO 10-INCH SINGLE CRUST
4 to 5 tablespoons ice cold water
1½ cups all-purpose flour
¼ teaspoon salt
5 tablespoons cold unsalted butter
3 tablespoons cold shortening

8- TO 10-INCH DOUBLE CRUST
OR 12-INCH SINGLE CRUST
5 to 6 tablespoons ice cold water
2 cups all-purpose flour

¼ teaspoon salt
7 tablespoons cold unsalted butter
4 tablespoons cold shortening

12-INCH DOUBLE CRUST
½ cup ice cold water
3 cups all-purpose flour
½ teaspoon salt
10 tablespoons cold unsalted butter
6 tablespoons cold shortening

Follow directions for Bubby's All-Butter Pastry Pie Dough on page 23.

To use lard or shortening, chop it into ¼-inch pieces (1-inch pieces for food processor method) and add them to the flour. Break up any pieces that stick together and toss them all to coat them with flour. (If it is a warm day, chill this mixture briefly in the freezer before continuing.)

LARD PASTRY PIE DOUGH

L ard is a very dense, pure fat. A little bit goes a long way. The ratio of flour to fat is greater in a lard crust: five parts flour to just one part lard (a butter crust is three to one). Crusts made with high-quality lard have a delicious, savory flavor and a light, flaky texture. They are recommended for a wide range of savory pies or hearty winter fruit pies, like apple and quince. They are not suitable for sweet berry pies or cream pies because the pronounced flavor of the crust makes an overwhelming, unflattering companion.

For instructions on rendering lard, see page 45.

8- TO 10-INCH SINGLE CRUST
3 to 4 tablespoons ice cold water
1½ cups all-purpose flour
¼ teaspoon salt
5 tablespoons cold lard, cubed
(see page 6)

8- TO 10-INCH DOUBLE CRUST
OR 12-INCH SINGLE CRUST
About ½ cup ice cold water

2½ cups all-purpose flour
½ cup cold lard, cubed
¼ teaspoon salt

12-INCH DOUBLE CRUST
½ cup ice cold water
3 cups all-purpose flour
9½ tablespoons cold lard, cubed
½ teaspoon salt

Follow directions for Bubby's All-Butter Pastry Pie Dough on page 23.

To use lard or shortening, chop it into ¼-inch pieces (1-inch pieces for food processor method) and add them to the flour. Break up any pieces that stick together and toss them all to coat them with flour. (If it is a warm day, chill this mixture briefly in the freezer before continuing.)

Savory Garlic Pastry Crust

Mix any kind of pastry dough and chill it. Before you line a pie plate with dough, cut a clove of garlic in half and rub the cut surface of the garlic over the interior surface of the pie plate. Discard the garlic and proceed to line the pie plate with dough. This variation would be good with lamb, beef, or chicken pies.

Sour Cream Pastry Pie Dough

This crust is easy to mix but a little more fragile to roll out and crimp than an all-butter or lard crust. The addition of sour cream makes this dough exceptionally delicious, rich, and tender. It's our favorite for an open-faced fruit pie topped with a sweet buttery crumble, such as in our Whiskey-Apple Crumble Pie (page 108). You can make Sour Cream Pastry by hand or in a food processor. We prefer the latter. However, this dough is not suitable for a double-crust pie because it's too fragile.

1 cup all-purpose flour	8 tablespoons (1 stick) cold unsalted butter
Pinch salt	½ cup very cold sour cream

Measure the flour and salt into a food processor. Give a quick pulse to mix. Cut the butter into 1-inch pieces and add them to the flour. Pulse until the butter is cut down to the size of shelling peas. Add the sour cream and pulse just until the dough forms a mass. Remove the dough, form it into a ball, and wrap it in plastic. Refrigerate it at least 30 minutes before rolling.

Roll the dough to fill an 8- to 10-inch pie plate (see pages 11 to 14). The dough will be a little moist and a little fragile. You may need to use more flour than usual when rolling it out, and a touch on your fingers when crimping the edges. Chill the formed crust well again before filling the pie.

Nut Pastry Pie Dough

MAKES ONE 8- TO 10-INCH SINGLE CRUST

One of the first pies Bubby's made was a banana cream pie with a walnut pastry crust. Nut crusts are versatile, tender, and flavorful cookie-like crust—you could make a peanut pastry crust for a Chocolate Pudding Pie or Bubby's Original Peanut Butter–Chocolate Pie, a walnut pastry crust for a Banana Cream Pie, a pecan pastry crust for a Pumpkin Pie, an almond pastry crust for a Pear Pie, or a hazelnut pastry crust for a Banana-Mocha Cream Pie. A pistachio pastry crust is particularly good with savory custard pies like the Goat Cheese Pie with Pomegranate Molasses (page 167) or Fig and Prosciutto Pie (page 169) or any of the pudding pies in Chapter 8. You can make this crust by hand or with a food processor. With a food processor, it is incredibly easy to mix and even easier to press into the pan with your fingertips. It's nearly foolproof—the perfect crust for bakers who view pie dough with trepidation. Nut Pastry Pie Dough crusts are almost always par-baked or blind-baked first before the filling is added.·

½ cup finely chopped, raw, unsalted nuts (almonds, hazelnuts, pistachios, pecans, walnuts, peanuts, or macadamia nuts)

¾ cup all-purpose flour

¾ teaspoon sugar

⅛ teaspoon salt

1½ tablespoons cold unsalted butter, diced

1 large egg, lightly beaten

FOOD PROCESSOR METHOD: In a food processor fitted with the metal blade, pulse the nuts, flour, sugar, and salt until just combined. Add the butter and egg and pulse until the dough balls on the blades. Remove the dough and shape it into a ball. Wrap it tightly with plastic wrap and refrigerate for at least 30 minutes.

HAND METHOD: Put the nuts in a medium bowl with the flour, sugar, and salt. Mix well. Cut in the butter with a pastry cutter until the mixture resembles dry cookie dough. Mix in the egg to moisten the dough. Shape the dough into a ball. Wrap the dough tightly with plastic wrap and refrigerate for at least 30 minutes.

Store nut crust dough up to 3 days in the refrigerator or 2 weeks in the freezer.

FORMING THE CRUST: Remove the ball of dough from the refrigerator 5 minutes before you want to use it. Put the dough in the center of a pie plate. Using your fingertips and thumbs, evenly work the lump of dough out along the bottom and up the edges of the plate. Dough often collects at the place where the plate angles up—push at these corners to help you even out the dough to about ⅛ inch overall. The edge of this pie crust is not rolled. To crimp it, you need to evenly amass dough near the lip of the plate and then crimp it using your fingers as instructed on page 14. Wrap and refrigerate the crust for at least 20 minutes before blind-baking.

PAR-BAKING AND BLIND-BAKING: Preheat the oven to 350°F. (Nut crusts are par-baked at a slightly lower temperature than pastry crusts since the nuts are more prone to burning.) Uncover the thoroughly chilled crust. Dock the bottom and sides with a fork. Nestle parchment paper or foil inside your crust and fill it with dried beans or pie weights. (If you're using aluminum tins, you can rest an extra one on top for this.) Par-bake the crust for 15 minutes. Remove the parchment and weights and bake the crust for 10 minutes more, until it looks dry, blonde, and blistered. The bottom of the crust will look partially cooked and there may still be some translucency to the dough.

To fully blind-bake the crust, increase the time that you bake it without the parchment and weights to 15 minutes, or until it is golden brown. Check on it from time to time during the first few minutes after returning it to the oven. If the crust starts to balloon up, you can lightly pat it down with your hand or a clean dish towel (yes it's hot, but just move quickly) and then prick the ballooning area with a fork and return it to oven. Cool the shell completely before adding the pie filling.

Short Dough for Tarts

Also known as pâte sucrée in French, this dough should only be used for tarts. It is too dense and cookie-like in texture for a regular single- or double-crust pastry pie. However, it makes a sweet, shortbread-like base for any French-style fruit tart with a layer of custard topped by a layer of fresh fruit. Short crust is very similar in properties to a nut crust, so you can just push any breaks together with your fingers.

1½ cups all-purpose flour	2 egg yolks
1 tablespoon sugar	2 tablespoons ice cold water
¼ teaspoon salt	
12 tablespoons (1½ sticks) cold unsalted butter	

FOOD PROCESSOR METHOD: Pulse the flour, sugar, salt, and butter as you would for a pastry crust (see page 8) but leave the mixture in the food processor. Whisk the yolks and water together and add them. Pulse the food processor just until the dough cobbles up. Remove the dough, wrap it in plastic, and refrigerate it.

HAND METHOD: In a medium bowl, mix the flour, sugar, and salt, and then cut in the butter as you would for a pastry crust (see page 8). Whisk the yolks and water together and add them. Stir until they are combined evenly with the dough. Wrap the dough in plastic and refrigerate it.

Store it for up to 1 week in the refrigerator or 1 month in the freezer.

FORMING THE CRUST: This dough can be pushed out like nut dough or rolled out as you would a pastry crust (see page 11). Transfer it into a tart pan with a removable bottom. Short crust is much less pliable than basic pastry, and can be tricky to roll onto a pin; on the other hand, it is easier to fix when it breaks. Ease it in gently, lifting the edges to help it settle all the way into the corners of the tart pan without forcing or stretching the dough. Press the dough against the perimeter of the tart pan. When it's perfectly shaped to the pan, roll a rolling pin across the top edge of the tart tin to cut the excess crust off. Refrigerate it for at least 20 minutes, then dock the crust on the sides and bottom walls with the tines of a fork.

PAR-BAKING AND BLIND-BAKING: Most recipes that call for short crusts require either a par-baked or blind-baked crust. Preheat the oven to 425°F. Dock the bottom and sides of the chilled crust with a fork. Nestle parchment paper or foil inside your crust and fill it with dried beans or pie weights. Par-bake the crust for 10 to15 minutes. Remove the parchment and weights and bake the crust for 10 minutes more, until the crust looks dry, blonde, and blistered.

To fully blind-bake the crust, par-bake it for 15 to 20 minutes. Remove the parchment and weights and bake the crust for 3 to 5 minutes more, or until it is a pale golden brown. Cool the shell completely before filling it.

Sweet Crumb Crusts

Homemade Graham Crackers

MAKES ABOUT 2½ CUPS CRUMBS; ENOUGH FOR A SINGLE CRUST

Known as "the poet of bran and pumpkins" in the 1830s, Sylvester Graham was a Presbyterian minister with strong opinions about health reform. Fresh air, clean water, regular tooth-brushing, vigorous exercise, homemade whole-grain bread, vegetarianism—these were some of the finer points he made about good health. But he also preached abstinence from alcohol, caffeine, and all forms of sexual desire, coaching married couples to curtail their activities to just once a month for better health. Graham preached the merits of a whole wheat and molasses cracker he invented that came to be known as a graham cracker. At Bubby's, our form of Graham-style fanaticism manifests in our enthusiasm for making things from scratch. Homemade Graham Crackers make a crust that is far superior in taste to one made with store-bought grahams of any kind.

1½ cups whole wheat flour	4 tablespoons (½ stick) unsalted butter, softened
¾ cup all-purpose flour	
¾ teaspoon salt	6 tablespoons sugar
½ teaspoon baking soda	1 egg, well beaten
2 teaspoons water	¼ cup honey

Preheat the oven to 350°F.

In a food processor, combine the whole wheat flour, all-purpose flour, and salt, and pulse once or twice to combine. Set aside.

Dissolve the baking soda in the water, then set aside. In the bowl of an electric mixer, cream the butter, sugar, and egg until they are light and fluffy. Add the honey and baking soda mixture, and mix until incorporated. Add the flour mixture gradually, scrape down the sides of the bowl occasionally, and mix just until uniform.

Line 4 baking sheets with parchment paper. Divide the dough into 4 lumps. On a generously floured surface (use all-purpose), roll out the dough, 1 lump at a time, to ⅛ inch thick. Cut the dough into approximately 4 x 4-inch sections, so that they will be easy to flip with a spatula during baking. Place the sections on a baking sheet 1 inch apart and roll out the rest of the crackers in the same way. Dock each cracker several times with a fork.

Bake the crackers for 8 minutes, then flip them over (the underside should be lightly browned). Bake for another 6 to 8 minutes, until the other side is lightly browned. Turn the oven off and open the oven door. Loosen the crackers with a spatula, snack on a few, and let the remaining dry out in the oven for 2 more hours.

Pulse the crackers in a food processor until they are fine- to medium-sized crumbs. Store the crumbs in an airtight container until needed. If you do not plan to use them within a couple of days, store the container of crumbs in the freezer.

GRAHAM CRACKER CRUST

A Graham Cracker Crust is a delicious complement to any number of cream, custard, or ganache pies like Key Lime Pie (page 254), Peanut Butter–Chocolate Pie (page 252), and Eskimo Pies (pages 296 to 297). Because the sweet brown-sugary crumbs cling so deliciously to the filling, they are also recommended for glazed fruit pies like the Fresh Blueberry Pie (page 71). This crust is best for fully thickened fillings, as it quickly gets soggy when subjected to juicy fillings. We strongly recommend baking this crust before filling it, though some recipes forgo par-baking. The flavor of a graham crust improves noticeably with baking and the heat firms up the crust.

1½ cups Graham Cracker crumbs (page 34)	Pinch salt
3 tablespoons sugar	5⅓ tablespoons unsalted butter, melted

In a large bowl, mix the crumbs, sugar, and salt. Add the butter and stir until evenly combined. (You don't need to worry about overworking a crumb crust.)

Press this mixture into an 8- to 10-inch pie tin with your fingers, striving to make the distribution and thickness (⅛ inch) of the crumb crust as even and compacted as possible. If you're using an aluminum tin and you have a spare, press the spare tin on top of the crumb crust and put pressure on the top tin to make the crumbs more compact. Remove the second aluminum tin. Refrigerate the crust for 30 minutes.

Preheat the oven to 350°F. Bake the crust for 8 minutes uncovered, until it begins to smell good and is lightly browned near the crust edge. Cool at room temperature and refrigerate (or freeze for an ice cream pie) before filling.

HOMEMADE GINGERSNAPS

MAKES ABOUT 3 CUPS CRUMBS; ENOUGH FOR
TWO 9-INCH SINGLE CRUSTS

The spicy ginger and sticky molasses make these cookies a good candidate for a crumb crust. You can also use this recipe to make one Gingersnap Crumb Crust and snack on the remaining cookies.

---

2 cups all-purpose flour

1 tablespoon baking soda

1½ teaspoons cinnamon

1½ teaspoons ground ginger

1 teaspoon ground cloves

¼ teaspoon salt

12 tablespoons (1½ sticks) unsalted butter, softened

1 cup sugar

1 cup molasses

1 large egg

In a large bowl, mix together the flour, baking soda, cinnamon, ginger, cloves, and salt.

With an electric mixer, cream the butter and sugar until light and fluffy. Add the molasses and egg. Mix just to combine the ingredients. Add the dry ingredients and mix until the batter is smooth. If you are making individual cookies, shape the dough into a log about 2 inches in diameter. Wrap it well and chill completely. If you're only making the cookies for the crumbs, chill the dough in the bowl instead.

Preheat the oven to 375°F. Slice the dough into ⅛-inch slices and place them 1 inch apart on parchment-lined baking sheets. Bake them for 12 minutes, until the cookie bottoms are golden brown. To bake the dough for crumbs, roll out one big ⅛-inch cookie between 2 sheets of parchment, remove the top sheet, and bake for approximately 15 minutes, or until the cookie smells good and the bottom is golden brown (it doesn't matter if you have to break it up to check it).

Cool the cookies on a wire rack, uncovered, and allow the cookies you intend to use for crumbs to dry out overnight.

    To make crumbs, put about half of the cookies in a food processor and process until the crumbs are fine. Another method for making crumbs is to toss the cookies in a resealable plastic bag and press the air out before sealing. Roll over the bag of cookies with a rolling pin until the crumbs are fine. Measure out 1½ cups for a single crust. Eat the remaining cookies or crumb them for another crust. The crumbs keep well in an airtight container in the freezer for a couple of months.

Gingersnap Crumb Crust

A gingersnap crust pairs very well with Buttermilk Pie with Fresh Berries (page 257), Key Lime Pie (page 254), and most ice cream pies (page 295). We recommend baking this crust before filling it. The flavor of a gingersnap crust improves and the heat firms up the crust.

1½ cups Gingersnap crumbs (page 37)

3 tablespoons sugar

Pinch salt

4 tablespoons (½ stick) unsalted butter, melted

In a large bowl, mix the crumbs, sugar, and salt. Add the butter and stir until evenly combined. (You don't need to worry about overworking a crumb crust.)

Press this mixture into an 8- to 10-inch pie tin with your fingers, striving to make the distribution and thickness (⅛ inch) of the crumb crust as even and compacted as possible. If you're using an aluminum tin and you have a spare, press the spare tin on top of the crumb crust and put pressure on the top tin to make the crumbs more compact. Remove the second aluminum tin. Refrigerate the crust for 30 minutes.

Preheat the oven to 350°F. Bake the crust for 8 minutes uncovered, until it begins to smell good and is lightly browned near the crust edge. Cool at room temperature and refrigerate (or freeze for an ice cream pie) before filling.

Homemade Chocolate Cookies

MAKES ABOUT 3 CUPS; ENOUGH FOR TWO 9-INCH SINGLE CRUSTS

These cookies are outstanding crumbed in our Chocolate Crumb Crust. The cookies would also be a nice addition to a Sweetie Pie (page 298). Use only the middle and upper racks of the oven when baking these; the bottom of the cookies will burn easily if they are on the lower shelf.

1½ cups all-purpose flour	11 to 12 tablespoons (1½ sticks) unsalted butter, softened
¾ cup unsweetened Dutch-process cocoa	1¼ cups sugar
1¼ teaspoons baking powder	1 large egg
⅛ teaspoon salt	½ teaspoon vanilla extract

Sift together the flour, cocoa, baking powder, and salt; set aside. With an electric mixer, cream the butter and sugar until light and fluffy. Add the egg and vanilla and mix until incorporated. On low speed, gradually add the dry ingredients, mixing well after each addition. Shape the dough into a 2-inch-diameter log. Wrap it well and chill completely—at least two hours.

Preheat the oven to 375°F. Slice the dough into ⅛-inch slices and place them 1 inch apart on parchment-lined baking sheets. Bake them for 8 to 10 minutes, until they smell good and remain firm when lifted with a spatula. Or, if you're only making the cookies for the crumbs, roll out one big ⅛-inch cookie between 2 sheets of parchment, remove the top sheet, and bake the dough for 15 minutes, until it smells good and portions of the cookie remain firm when lifted with a spatula. Cool the cookies on a wire rack, uncovered, overnight or until they are completely dry and wafer-like.

Use a food processor to crumb the cookies. Or, put the cookies in a resealable plastic bag and press the air out before sealing. Roll over the bag of cookies with a rolling pin until they form fine crumbs. Crumbs keep well in an airtight container in the freezer for up to a couple of months.

CHOCOLATE CRUMB CRUST

This rich, buttery, double-chocolate crust is a great choice for ice cream pies or cream pies. Melted chocolate is added to the crumbed Homemade Chocolate Cookies, giving body and flavor to the crust. Chocolate shavings can be made by hand-grating the chocolate or by grating it with a food processor. This crust is not baked and should only be used for cold or frozen fillings because of the melted chocolate in it.

2 cups Homemade Chocolate Cookie crumbs (page 40)

3 ounces bittersweet chocolate, finely grated

Pinch salt (optional)

3 tablespoons unsalted butter, melted

In a medium bowl, combine the crumbs, chocolate shavings, and salt (if using). Pour the butter over them. The butter will melt the chocolate into the chocolate crumbs. Stir well.

Press this mixture into a 8- to 10-inch pie tin, distributing the crumbs to form an ⅛-inch-thick crust. If you're using an aluminum tin and you have a spare, press the spare tin on top of the crumb crust and put pressure on the top tin to make the crumbs more compact. You can leave the tin in place until you are ready to use the crust. If you are not using nesting aluminum tins, just cover the crumb crust with plastic wrap and press and compact the crust with your fingers. Refrigerate the crust loosely covered (or freeze for an ice cream pie) before filling.

CHOCOLATE-PEPPERMINT CRUMB CRUST

Grind peppermint candy in a food processor until finely crushed to make ¼ cup. Add it to a Chocolate Crumb Crust during the mixing stage. Wowee! This crust puts a nice spin on an ice cream pie.

NUT CRUMB CRUST

Finely chopped nuts combined with any of our homemade cookie crumbs make a delicious variation on a crumb crust. We like to use our Candied Pecans (page 314) mixed with Homemade Graham Cracker crumbs (page 34) to make an extra flavorful crust for Viola's Sweet Potato Pie (page 134). Variations on this crust with any nut/cookie combination are good with pudding pies, custard pies, and ice cream pies.

½ cup Candied Pecans or Walnuts (page 314) or any kind of finely chopped nuts

1 cup Graham Cracker crumbs (page 34), Homemade Chocolate Cookie crumbs (page 40), or Gingersnap Cookie crumbs (page 37)

3½ tablespoons unsalted butter, melted

Pinch salt

Make and cool the Candied Pecans (page 314); this can be done days in advance. Combine the cookie crumbs and whole nuts in a food processor. Pulse until the nuts are fine but still visible. Or, if making by hand, chop the nuts very fine and combine them in a bowl with the cookie crumbs. Add the butter and mix briefly. (You don't need to worry about overworking a crumb crust.)

Press this mixture into an 8- to 10-inch pie tin with your fingers, striving to make the distribution and thickness (⅛ inch) of the crumb crust as even as possible. If you're using an aluminum tin and you have a spare, press the spare tin on top of the crumb crust and put pressure on the top tin to make the crumbs more compact. Remove the second aluminum tin. Refrigerate the crust for 30 minutes.

Preheat the oven to 350°F. Bake the crust for 8 minutes uncovered, until it begins to smell good and is lightly browned near the crust edge. Cool at room temperature and refrigerate loosely covered (or freeze for an ice cream pie) before filling.

BREAD CRUMB CRUST

MAKES ONE 8- TO 10-INCH SINGLE CRUST AND 1 CUP TOPPING

This crumb crust forms a tasty and practical base for our sticky Spring Vegetable Risotto Pie (page 163). Because the risotto is quite heavy and filling, a light, flavorful crust is in order—just something to help the filling release from the pan. We also use it as a topping to keep the pie from drying out too much in the oven. Use a cheese grater or the grater attachment on a food processor to grate the bread crumbs. A similar topping is used for the Paella Pie (page 165).

3 cups stale French or Italian bread crumbs	6½ tablespoons unsalted butter, melted
1 cup coarsely grated Parmesan cheese	½ teaspoon salt

Combine the crumbs and cheese and sprinkle them with the butter and salt to taste. Stir. Set aside 1 cup of the mixture and pour the remaining into a 9-inch pie plate. Form a crust by pressing this mixture into the plate, working the crumbs with your fingers until they are evenly distributed.

Preheat the oven to 325°F. Bake the crust, uncovered, for 12 to 15 minutes to develop the flavor. A hot precooked filling can be added to the hot crust when it comes out of the oven.

Fill the prepared crust and sprinkle the reserved topping evenly over the filling. This topping should be baked according to the pie recipe you're using, or for just a few minutes to brown it.

HERBED PASTRY CRUST

Add 1 tablespoon of chopped fresh rosemary or 1 teaspoon of fresh thyme to the flour before cutting the fat into the All-Butter Pastry Pie Dough, the Basic Butter and Shortening Pastry Pie Dough, or the Lard Pastry Pie Dough.

Sharp Cheddar Cheese Pastry Crust

MAKES ONE 9-INCH SINGLE CRUST

This nutty, piquant farmhouse Cheddar crust is delicious with meat pies, vegetable pies, and apple pies. Farmhouse Cheddar has more fully developed flavors than the mass-produced commercial Cheddars, which tend to be fairly bland and rubbery. The recipe can be made with any firm cheese—Gruyère, Swiss, Parmesan, Manchego, Monterey Jack (with dried chilies). If you are using a drier cheese like Parmesan, you may want to use just half a cup and increase the butter to 12 tablespoons.

1⅓ cups all-purpose flour

½ teaspoon salt

Pinch cayenne pepper

8 tablespoons (1 stick) cold unsalted butter, cubed

¾ cup grated extra-sharp Cheddar (Farmhouse)

3 tablespoons ice cold water

FOOD PROCESSOR METHOD: In a food processor, combine the flour, salt, and cayenne and pulse in the butter until it is the size of peas. Sprinkle in the grated cheese and pulse twice. Add the ice water and pulse until the dough cobbles up. Remove the dough and wrap it in plastic. Refrigerate it at least 30 minutes before using.

HAND METHOD: Measure the flour, salt, and cayenne into a medium bowl. Cut in the butter. Stir in the cheese. Sprinkle in the ice water and work the dough into a ball by kneading it lightly. Wrap the dough in plastic and refrigerate it at least 30 minutes before using.

Par-bake or blind-bake (if the master recipe calls for it) according to the directions on page 15.

HOT WATER PASTRY CRUST

This dough is the polar opposite of most pie pastry—it's made with hot ingredients and the pie is made up while the dough is still supple and warm. The lard gives the dough its solid structure. The result is a hearty, dense, flavorful pastry good for pasties (traditional British savory pies) and small meat pies like Pork Pie Hats. For recipe and instructions, see page 185.

How to Render Lard

If the lard you buy is the consistency of shortening, it has already been rendered. If it is in chunks, it needs to be rendered before you can use it for pie dough. Rendering, simply put, is the process of melting fat to extract it and separate it from its storage cells and their surrounding tissue. Use leaf lard or caul fat. If you are using caul fat that has been stored in brine, rinse it off in cold water and pat it dry with paper towels. Chop up the fat fairly finely so that it breaks down easily. Melt it slowly over very low heat to prevent it from browning, either covered in a heavy pan on the stovetop, or in a roasting pan in a slow oven. Heat the lard until it is almost entirely liquid and the solid bits are crispy and small—anywhere from one to four hours. Strain the melted lard through cheesecloth or a fine sieve. Store the strained lard in an airtight container in the refrigerator. It's worthwhile to do this in quantity. Chunks of lard render around two thirds of their weight; i.e., five pounds of fat yields about three pounds rendered lard. Chill completely before using lard in a pastry crust. Tightly covered, lard keeps for months in the refrigerator and years in the freezer. Other animal fats (duck, goose, etc.) can also be rendered using this method, but render and store each kind of fat separately.

A FRUIT PIE PRIMER

"Fine fruit is the flower of commodities." It is the most perfect
union of the useful and the beautiful that the earth knows. Trees
full of soft foliage; blossoms fresh with spring bounty; and, finally,
fruit, rich, bloom-dusted, melting, and luscious.

—ANDREW JACKSON DOWNING
(quoting Ralph Waldo Emerson)

It has always been Bubby's philosophy to keep the food we make simple, fresh, and pure. Fruit pies offer the perfect opportunity to incorporate all of those elements under one crust. The
fruit should be the finest, and the sauce it
forms should be, as the Reverend Henry
Ward Beecher wrote so eloquently, ". . .
the merest drip of candied juice along
the edges, (as if the flavor were so good
to itself that its own lips watered!) of a
mild and modest warmth, the sugar sug-
gesting jelly, yet not jellied. . . ."

Farm Fresh Fruit: Seasonality and the Farmer's Market

The best fruit pies begin with the best local fruit in season. Before refrigeration, trucking, and supermarkets, pies were made with whatever could be harvested from fields, orchards, gardens, and nearby woods—rhubarb, gooseberries, blackberries and apples—and were patterned by nature's cycle, not the supermarket. Pies made from fruits out of season came from "put up" jars of preserved fruit conserved back when the harvest was in full swing. Modern hothouse fruit production has made it less and less apparent what is really in season locally.

To obtain the best, freshest, most flavorful, naturally ripened fruit, and to understand the full range of what's in season where you live, you should get in the habit of making regular visits to your local farmer's market. Quality is worth waiting for; act in harmony with the season and take each bounty it has to offer.

At Bubby's, we have a long-standing relationship with the farmers at the local market at Union Square, though there is also a Saturday market in Tribeca that we are fond of, too. We love the Union Square farmer's market because it's open four days a week, and it is the most extensive New York City farmer's market, offering the largest variety, and the most farm stands with which to compare quality and prices. To find the best produce, we stroll through the whole market to survey the choices, smell and taste as we go, inquire about prices (quantity discounts when we're buying a lot), and make mental notes about who has the best of what. The best-looking fruit is not necessarily the best-tasting fruit. Tasting it is key—most vendors will give you a modest sample of a fruit in plentiful supply. Engage farmers in conversation; they have a great wealth of knowledge to share with you for the asking. Growing years have their own character—an exceptionally wet spring makes certain plants thrive and others stall out. Farmers can educate you about what to expect and when to expect it; teach you how to store and handle produce; and sometimes even give a tip or two on how to prepare it. Curiosity is seldom rebuffed, even amidst the brusque hustle-bustle of New York.

Generally, the first week a new fruit appears, its price is highest. We often use that week to experiment and dream about the pies we'll produce when abundance starts to drive the prices down in the thick of that fruit's season. For the thrifty, there are occasionally good deals to be made by going at the end of the market day, when farmers are packing up their wares. Be resourceful—seek out the slightly bruised ripe peaches for a deep discount.

However, we don't always get to pick and choose our timing based on what the harvest dictates—there are birthdays, events, and holidays that call for pies at times when there's no obvious produce at the height of its glory. It's still possible to make an outstanding pie with frozen fruit or supermarket fruit—it may take some planning ahead to ripen fruits prior to baking them, or a little more lemon juice or sugar to punch up the flavor.

Composing Pies: Things to Consider

You have a lot of leeway with the quantity of fruit you use for a pie— anywhere from 3 to 6 cups, depending on your fruit, its supporting ingredients, and your pie plate. Think about how full you want your pie to be and about how the particular fruit cooks down when baked. Is it a hard, dense fruit like a quince, which will not reduce much in size, or a soft, wet fruit like a strawberry, which will cook down a great deal? If your fruit is really juicy and your tin quite small, you might have a big wasteful mess once the filling starts cooking and spilling over. If you have the same scenario with a nice firm apple in a Mile-High Apple Pie, you'll get a high crust and a perfectly full but well-baked filling. Along the same lines, you can pile up an apple-blackberry pie higher than a blackberry pie because of the water content difference in the fruits inside.

Take into consideration the intensity of flavors of the filling to be used— although we do like an ample pie, more is not always better. Take the Raspberry–Black Currant Pie (page 79, for example. Its exquisite flavor is best appreciated in a thinner layer, a smaller mouthful, as a shallow pie or ample tart. The same is true of Concord Grape Pie (page 101)—the intensity of the dark flavorful grape is powerfully good but best experienced in modest proportion to the flaky double crust, maybe with a dollop of crème fraîche nearby. Imagine what you want a bite of your pie to taste like.

A glazed pie is ideal for fruits that have a better taste and texture uncooked. If you want a high raspberry pie, you might want to consider making an open-faced pie that uses a cooked raspberry sauce glazed over fresh raw raspberries. The raw raspberries won't release their juices when glazed, and thanks to the thick glaze, they can be piled to the heavens.

Thickening Fruit Pies

How were those early fruit pies thickened? Nineteenth- and early twentieth-century recipes draw from a fine assortment of whatever might have been handy—most often some crumbs, or an egg yolk (perhaps with a little cream or bread crumbs, too), cornstarch, or flour. The pies with egg yolk often used the remaining white to make a meringue topping. The 1941 edition of *The Settlement Cookbook* (their motto: "The Way to a Man's Heart") advises the following, "If fruits are very juicy, brush lower crust with unbeaten egg white or sprinkle with bread, cake, or cracker crumbs." There are also frugal pies—mock apple pie is an extreme example, where cracker crumbs (the thickener) fill an entire pie in lieu of apples—that were created to replace or extend what the cupboard lacked.

Even the same kind of fruit can vary in how juicy it is—on the large scale, from the early harvest to late harvest, and on the more individualized scale of ripeness. Environment plays a part too—a wet, hot growing season in Georgia produces a big, juicy peach completely different from a small, sweetly concentrated peach grown in the desert Southwest. Know as much as possible about the fruit you want to use so that you can plan accordingly.

A GOOD RULE OF THUMB FOR 9-INCH PIES FOR 4-6 CUPS FRUIT

Super-Juicy Fruits	Juicy Fruits	Modest–Firm	Dry
Strawberries	Apricots	Rhubarb	Quince
Gooseberries	Plums	Pears	
Currants	Nectarines	Apples	
Sour Cherries	Peaches		
Blackberries	Raspberries		
Concord Grapes	Blueberries		
Figs			
3+ Tbsp thickener (minimum amount)	2+ Tbsp thickener (minimum amount)	1+ Tbsp thickener (minimum amount)	None

We tend to use flour for all fresh fruit except berries (which take quick-cooking tapioca) and glazed pies (which take cornstarch). All thickeners have advantages and disadvantages; the most important challenge—no matter which thickener you use—is to try to get just the right amount for the fruit at hand, to achieve a concentrated, flavorful sauce that clings to the fruit. Try them all in turn and decide which suits your taste and particular pie best.

ALL-PURPOSE FLOUR, unbleached, is one of the mildest, slowest, most stable thickeners. It's particularly good in tandem with butter inside an apple, pear, or peach pie. A flour-thickened sauce baked slowly in a pie forms a flavorful, slightly opaque sauce with the fruit juices and sugar. Once flour reaches the optimum temperature, it is quite stable; continued heat does not harm it. It's particularly recommended for peaches, apples, pears, and firm-fleshed fruits. Flour and butter are sometimes cooked together to make a roux, the thickener of choice in Cajun and Creole sauces, étouffées, and soups. We use a blonde roux as a thickener for the sauces in a number of our savory meat pies.

CORNSTARCH, a corn-based thickener, forms a translucent sauce. Cornstarch is ideal for fruit sauces cooked only on the stovetop, and particularly for glazed fresh fruit pies. It is flavorless, silky in texture, and thickens a liquid at boiling point; if overcooked, it can give diminished returns, undoing the work it has done. Its power is also substantially weakened if it is paired with an acidic, tart sauce like that of a sour cherry. In excess it can form the gloppy, gel-like filling found in many store-bought pies.

Tapioca is a root-based thickener made from the cassava plant. It comes in a number of forms: flour, flakes (instant tapioca), and pearls (also called pellets). Only some of them are suitable for pie—flakes or flour. Tapioca flakes need to soften and swell a little in fruit juices (about 5 minutes) or they can wind up as crunchy as pebbles on top of the fruit in a lattice pie. When properly cooked, they contribute an interesting texture of their own: soft little gelatinous bubbles. Tapioca produces a clear, glossy sauce and doesn't impart a starchy flavor. Tapioca flour is also a very good option; it has the good characteristics of flake tapioca but the smooth texture of cornstarch.

Why's my pie so dry?

If it is a single-crust pie, it may be that a top crust or topping is needed to seal in the filling to steam it. This is often the case with apples, quince, and other firm-fleshed fruits. It's also the case if your fruit is dry and underripe—this can be true of stone fruits like peaches, apricots, and plums. One way to work around this problem, if you really don't want to cover your pie, is to coat the fruit in butter and sugar and either sauté it or roast it briefly in a hot oven. (See pages 93 and 120 for roast-ripening fruit.) Let the fruit cool, and then use it in the filling as usual. Another way to manage the situation is to poach the fruit before baking it in an open-faced pie. This strat-egy is often used with pears. For more information on poaching, see page 117. A third suggestion for those who really want an open-faced pie from a firm-fleshed fruit is to try the Apple-Caramel Upside-Down Pie (page 110). (But don't adapt this recipe to a juicy fruit or you'll have upside-down soup!) Some fruits, like quince, have lots of natural pectin and will thicken their own sauce. If a double-crust pie is too dry, it's most likely that it didn't get hot enough for the ingredients to release their juices and mix properly with the thickener. This can be the case with underripe fruit, which takes longer to break down than juicy, ripe fruit.

Tapioca works well for red currant or sour cherry pie because it is undeterred by acidity. It's also good for bramble berries. The texture of the tapioca is so similar to the drupelets of these fruits. Tapioca becomes less effective the longer it's cooked, so take care not to overbake pies thickened with tapioca.

EGGS are seldom used to thicken fruit pies, but they are used in custard pies, cream pies, pecan pies, ice cream, and in savory quiche pies. Eggs are discussed in more detail in the context of these recipes.

Sweeteners

Sugar macerates fruit; that is, it draws out the liquids and forms a flavorful syrup with the juices. The more sugar you use, the more thickener you'll need. Sugar makes sour fruits like red currants, sour

ASK BUBBY

Why is my room-temperature pie runny?

If you cut into your room temperature pie and it's too runny, you may need to adjust your thickener choice, quantity, or your baking method in the future. Thickeners are not created equal, and you may be making the wrong choice for your filling. Or, you may need a touch more next time. (Erring on the side of more thickener is not categorically better unless you like a thick, gloppy pie, like many store-bought fruit pies.) Another possibility is that the pie filling didn't get hot enough inside the pie to engage the thickener. Was it making slow, thick bubbles when you removed it from the oven? That is the ideal for proper thickening.

cherries, gooseberries, and rhubarb palatable and delicious in a pie; it complements and accentuates fruits with more of their own natural fruit sugars. White refined sugar is recommended for delicate-tasting fruits, as it doesn't overwhelm them. Moist light brown sugar, with its mild caramel-like flavor (from molasses) can be a subtle addition of flavor, as in the Whiskey-Apple Crumble Pie (page 108); dark brown sugar has a bittersweet molasses bite that adds a depth of flavor integral to a brown betty. We avoid corn syrups (high fructose corn syrup): it is highly processed, cloying, and unhealthy. More healthful sweeteners like honey, maple syrup, and molasses may be used with calculation; they impart distinctive flavors and work best with autumn fruits and nuts. Dry-fleshed fruits like apples and quinces absorb the juices they cook in and are good candidates for honey; maple syrup does well in conjunction with eggs in a nut pie; molasses makes Apple Pandowdy especially delicious. To cut down on sugar, combine sour fruits with sweet fruits. The classic example of this is a Strawberry-Rhubarb Pie (page 68).

Flavor Heighteners

> Ye are the salt of the earth.
> —MATTHEW 5:13

SALT—just a pinch—heightens and focuses the flavors of a sweet or savory filling or crust. We use fine sea salt for making most of our crusts and sweet fillings because it dissolves well, though we'll sometimes use kosher salt for stews and such. Rock salt is best suited for salting the ice in a hand-cranked ice cream maker.

CITRUS—juices and zest—are used to keep fruit colors and flavors bright. The acid in citrus juice prevents cut fruit from browning. Some old-fashioned pies use vinegar in this capacity. Zest can sometimes render the filling slightly bitter, so go light on it.

BUTTER enriches and complements the saucy juices in a pie filling, and it works in tandem with the thickeners. If a pie with butter in the filling chills down too much, the butter will solidify into beads; you may need to reheat the pie in a hot oven to melt the butter back into the filling.

SPICES, EXTRACTS, LIQUEURS: Sometimes we'll throw in a pinch of this or that spice, a dash of almond extract, real vanilla bean, or a flavored liqueur—they add interesting dimensions to the flavor of a fruit pie but should not overpower or upstage the integrity of the fruit's natural flavors. Our recipes are meant to be suggestive, especially in this area. If you're a beginner, stick to the recipe at first. If you already have firm opinions about how you want a sour cherry pie flavored but need to consult a tried-and-true recipe for ratios and methods, have at it. Experiment and achieve what *you* think tastes good in a pie.

Fruit Pie Craft: A Well-Built Pie

Different varieties of fruit pies are assembled in much the same way. Though the logic might not be apparent at first glance, follow this sequence for a flaky bottom and top crust in support of a well-composed fruit filling. This pattern helps you develop good habits that yield dependable results. You'll find that if you change the sequence, problems are likely to crop up. We've tried to make the reasons why apparent. As with dough making, an ounce of prevention is worth a pound of cure. Pies, especially fruit pies, invite improvisation within a structure. This is the basic structure for a fruit pie:

1. Mix the pastry dough—whether a single or a double crust—and chill it, tightly covered. (See more detail in Chapter 1, pages 8 to 11.)

2. Prepare and cut the fruit. Transfer it to a large bowl. If there is lemon juice in the filling and the fruit is prone to browning, toss the fruit with it.

3. Wait until you're ready to put the filling inside the pie before you toss the fruit with the sugar and other dry ingredients. If you wait until the last minute to mix the fruit up and put it in the crust, the bottom crust gets a chance to set in the hot oven before the bulk of the fruit juices hit it. The sugar macerates or "sweats" the fruit—the less they touch before they go into the oven, the better. Tapioca is an exception, it must soften up in the juices first.

4. Roll out the pastry bottom crust and line a pie tin with it. If it is a single crust, roll and crimp the edge; if it is a double crust, wait—leave the dough that overhangs the edge alone. Refrigerate it.

5. Roll out the second ball of dough for the top crust and leave it on the counter. (Sometimes this top crust is a crumble, crisp, or lattice pastry top. If so, follow recipe.)

6. Gently toss the fruit with the filling ingredients lightly as you would a salad—just try to distribute your thickener throughout. Use your hands (or a couple of wooden spoons). Taste the sauce to check flavors. Adjust if necessary.

7. Transfer the filling to the cold pastry-lined pie tin. When filling a pie, don't pack it down; let the filling mound up a little in the middle and tumble where it will. It will cook down.

8. Dot the fruit filling with a little butter if the recipe calls for it (unless it has already been added melted to the filling).

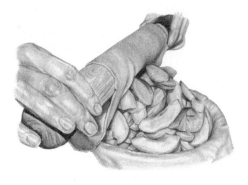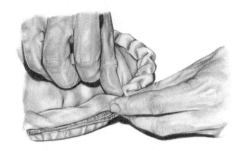

9. Top the fruit with the top crust. Trim the dough's edge; roll the edge and crimp it (see pages 16 to 17).

10. Preheat the oven to 450° and chill the whole pie in the refrigerator. Chilling the pie before baking helps ensure that the fat in the crust is cold and distinct, resulting in pastry that is flaky and light. Waiting to preheat the oven helps keep the kitchen and the pie dough optimally cool during mixing and rolling.

11. Cut vent slits in the top crust, put the pie on a lipped baking sheet to catch stray juices during baking, top the crust as you like (see page 17), and pop it in the oven.

12. It's usually best to start the pie in a hot oven (450°F) in order to set the crust, which helps achieve a flaky top crust and a crisp bottom crust. Set a timer for 7 minutes. When the time's up, take a look. If you have an oven light, peek through the oven window. Watch for the pastry to lose its glossy, wet, doughy look. The surface of the dough should look dry and crustlike, lightly blistered (much like a little friction

blister you'd get on your hand), quite blonde, and with faint tinges of golden brown. Learn what to look for—the time it takes is irrelevant (check your oven's accuracy with an oven thermometer if you're not achieving much after 20 minutes). If your nose is dependable, you can replace the timer with your sense of smell. It should begin to smell good, like a baked pie.

ASK BUBBY

Butter is dripping off the crust and smoking up my oven.

Use a lipped baking sheet with parchment on it. The butter will still smoke a little, but less than if it hits the oven floor. The same is true of the filling juices.

ASK BUBBY

The Bubble and Brown Method

If the visible juices are bubbling nice and slow through the pie vents, it means that the thickeners in the fruit filling have hit the boiling point inside the pie and are doing their sauce-making best with the butter and fruit juices. Those slow, thick bubbles wherever juices are visible show you that the fruit filling is fully cooked and richly thickened. Perky, quick bubbles from thin, juicy sauce indicate that the pie needs more time.

13. Turn the oven down to medium-high (375°F) to allow the internal temperature of the filling to warm up slowly. Let the filling bake uninterrupted for a nice long stretch—at least 30 minutes. Take notice again when your pie begins to smell fragrant. Fruit pies bake at different rates—even the same kind of fruit, depending on its water content, its ripeness, its sweetness, how it's been handled, and its chemistry with the other filling ingredients—so it's best to learn what to look for and let the *pie,* not the clock, show you when it's good and ready. What should the pie show you? Two things: bubble and brown.

A crust tastes best when it's golden brown—this doesn't mean blonde with tinges of golden brown, it means a full beautiful golden brown. Although the crust is already flaky and set up early on, the fat gets more flavorful and the sugar sprinkled on top caramelizes slightly as the crust browns. The most intense and delicious crust flavors develop in the last five minutes of baking.

One of the reasons to bake a pie at two temperatures—450°F briefly to set the

crust, and 375°F to slowly cook the filling—is that a crust rarely browns too
quickly at the lower temperature. (This
is the most common method, but occasionally our recipe instructions advise
otherwise.) If your crust is optimally
browned before your filling is ready, turn
the temperature down to 350°F and wait
it out until the contents of the pie are
ready too. If your filling is bubbling nice
and thick but your crust is still pale and
blonde, you can bump the temperature
up to 425°F so that it browns the surface
of the pie aggressively. If you learn what
to look for and can adapt your approach,
you'll get consistently great results, no
matter how much your pies vary.

ASK BUBBY

*Why do my pies take longer to
bake than most recipe times?*

You might have a slow oven, that is,
the internal temperature doesn't
match the dial setting. Test it with a
good-quality oven thermometer. You
can have your oven professionally re-
calibrated or just set the temperature
dial higher accordingly. You might
need to preheat it longer. If the oven
door is opened every five minutes, it
also lowers oven temperature. Peek
less and use your sense of smell
more.

Cooling Fruit Pies

Allow time for your fruit pie to cool down thoroughly before serving. If
you're impatient and cut into it straight from the oven, or before it is properly cooled, the hot filling juices—no matter how perfectly thickened—
will gush to form a lake where a slice has been prematurely removed,
upsetting the filling balance of the entire pie. Pie crust can be just warm to
the touch, while the filling may still be quite hot inside. Pie fillings thicken
as they cool. Wait at least a couple of hours—preferably three or four—before cutting into a pie. Early morning, when it's cool and quiet, is a good
time to make pies; they'll have ample time to set up by dinner.

Serving Sizes

Generally, a 9-inch fruit pie yields between six and eight slices. A generous
slice of fruit pie makes a fine breakfast, whereas a slender slice of pie might

be preferable after a hearty dinner. If the filling is very rich or intense in flavor, you may want to cut as many as twelve slices from a single pie. The first piece of pie often leaves a pie tin with reluctance; many bakers call this one the cook's. If you find serving yourself first impolite, just discreetly set it aside and serve your dinner companions with the second, third, and fourth pieces.

Pie Transport

Peterboro Basket Co. makes a two-tier pie basket that make traveling with pies easy (see Equipment).

If you're transporting a pie in the car, you can also nestle it into a big iron skillet lined with a dishtowel if you don't have a passenger who can hold it while you drive. If you're carrying a pie somewhere on foot, wrap it loosely in breathable cloth for transport. Don't cover it up tightly if it is still warm or it will steam the pastry, ruining the crisp crust. A fully cooled pie travels best.

Some pies are harder to transport than others—chilled or layered pies like Mile-High Lemon Meringue are the least amenable to travel. Heed advance cooling and set-up instructions carefully if you have to travel with cold pies. You can travel with a meringue pie, but if you are driving a considerable distance, use a chilled cooler with plenty of support and bracing for the pie. Refrigerate it promptly when you arrive at your destination.

Storing Fruit Pies

Refrigeration makes pastry crust soggy and should be avoided. In general, only refrigerate a pie if it contains animal products (excepting all fats, butter, and the tiny bit of egg, milk, or cream used to paint a top or bottom crust). For instance, a meat or custard pie is best refrigerated for safety. Double-crust pastry needs to breathe in order to remain light and flaky. A "pie safe" (see page 323), if you are lucky enough to come across one these days, is ideal for storing pies at room temperature. The screen or perforated tin windows allow the pastry to breathe and keep pie predators—insects, rodents, pets (but not people)—at bay.

Double-crust fruit pies should be stored uncovered at room temperature—or, if there are flies around, with a light breathable covering like a clean cotton tea towel. If the room temperature is very hot—upper 90s and higher—the heat can dramatically accelerate spoilage. In this case, refrigeration is definitely a lesser evil. Even inside the refrigerator, let the pastry breathe (uncovered). If you're worried about refrigerator odors permeating your pie crust, take the time to clean your malodorous refrigerator. To store a meringue pie, you might strategically place several toothpicks sticking up from the meringue and drape plastic wrap over the toothpicks, then press the plastic wrap right up against the cut face of the pie to keep it from forming a skin.

Reheating Fruit Pies

To rejuvenate pies when refrigeration or humid weather or time has dampened your crust's crisp: Heat the pie at 350°F (5–7 minutes for a slice, 20 or so minutes for a whole pie). You can also "dowdy" a pie if it is losing its appeal. To see how that's done, turn to page 216.

A microwave does more damage than good in reheating a pie. It transmogrifies the texture of the crust in ways that make it seem both steamed and tough. Glazed fresh fruit pies, like Fresh Blueberry Pie or Fresh Strawberry Pie, should only be served cold or at room temperature.

Chapter 3

SPRING AND SUMMER FRUIT PIES

There is greater relish for the earliest fruit of the season.
—MARCUS VALERIUS MARTIALIS, Roman poet (38–103 A.D.)

Rhubarb

When you see the first signs of crocuses blooming outside, it is time to start looking for rhubarb, the earliest spring "pie plant." In New England, rhubarb was once called "spring fruit"; in *The Frugal Housewife* it's called a Persian apple. Its availability in cool March or April marks the true beginning of the spring pie season. However, rhubarb is not a fruit, but rather a prolific vegetable stalk related to sorrel and buckwheat. It looks like embarrassed celery, blushing deep hues of pink and red.

Pick garden rhubarb early in the morning when it's still cool and full of moist, night air because it will be firmer than the sun-wilted rhubarb of late afternoon. When selecting rhubarb at the market, look for firm, slender stalks. Avoid thick, limp, or slimy-ended stalks. It's rarely sold with its huge leaf attached nowadays, but if so, discard it—the leaves are full of toxic levels of oxalic acid. Store rhubarb in the refrigerator and use it as soon as possible (within a day or two) so that it doesn't wilt or deteriorate. Early tender rhubarb needs little preparation—rinse it, trim off the ends, and slice the stalks crosswise in ½- to ¾-inch pieces. As the rhubarb season progresses, the stalks keep coming but they get thicker, tougher, and need to be peeled. To peel the fibrous outer strands, nip them between your thumb and the edge of a paring knife at the cut end of the stalk and pull away—the strands will come free of their own accord all the way down the length of the stalk. Make your way around the stalk this way until it is fully peeled. Slice really fat stalks a little smaller—into ¼-inch pieces—thinner in proportion to their girth.

Rhubarb's sour wallop rivals that of a lemon, so it is often paired with sweeter fruits—such as strawberries, raspberries, or blueberries. Rhubarb varies in flavor and texture over the course of the harvest season. You may need to adjust the sugar quantity to reflect your rhubarb at hand; taste it before baking to check. Rhubarb season starts well before the summery fruits it's often paired with and lasts through midsummer if the rhubarb plant is picked from regularly. Especially if you're growing rhubarb, it's good to have a bunch of delicious uses for it—all manner of rhubarb pies below, the Rhubarb Buckle (page 212) we make at Bubby's, and warmly spiced Rhubarb Crisp (page 200)—to ride out its harvest and make the best use of this prolific plant.

RHUBARB CUSTARD PIE

This pie's gentle, lofty, custard filling tastes faintly of nutmeg and potently of rhubarb. This treasured recipe comes from Jen's Grandma Adeline, who, as a young girl growing up on a Nebraska farm, was given the nickname "Sour Rhubarb" by her family—in part due to her ornery personality and in part due to her funny habit of snacking on rhubarb stalks straight from the garden. Adeline's pie is now in Bubby's repertoire and it sure moves fast in the spring. Because this pie has a custard base, it is best made as a single-crust pie.

Pastry for a 9-inch single-crust pie, crimped and chilled in pie tin, such as Bubby's All-Butter Pastry Pie Dough (page 23), Basic Butter and Shortening Pastry Pie Dough (page 27), or Sour Cream Pastry Pie Dough (page 29)

3 generous cups (1½ pounds) rhubarb, cut into ½-inch pieces

1¾ cups sugar

3 tablespoons all-purpose flour

2 large eggs, lightly beaten

1 tablespoon unsalted butter, melted and cooled

½ teaspoon ground nutmeg

Preheat the oven to 375°F. In a large bowl, add the sugar, flour, eggs, butter, and nutmeg and mix just until combined. Spread the cut rhubarb in the chilled uncooked pastry shell and pour the liquid mixture over it. Give it a little jiggle to settle it in evenly.

Bake the pie for 45 minutes, or until the center looks cooked and does not jiggle when the pie is nudged (do not use a two-temperature bake for this because it's a custard pie). Cool the pie almost to room temperature before serving.

This pie is really best served on the day it is baked but will keep for 3 days, loosely covered in the refrigerator.

DINAH'S RASPBERRY-RHUBARB PIE

MAKES ONE 9-INCH DOUBLE-CRUST PIE

J en's mom made this pie for the family year after year with rhubarb from the garden.

Because the spring rhubarb season barely overlaps the mid- to late-summer raspberry season, frozen raspberries are often the best choice for this pie.

Pastry for a 9-inch double-crust pie, chilled, such as Bubby's All-Butter Pastry Pie Dough (page 23), or Basic Butter and Shortening Pastry Pie Dough (page 27)

1½ cups sugar, plus extra for sprinkling on the top crust

3 tablespoons quick-cooking tapioca flakes

1 tablespoon all-purpose flour

⅛ teaspoon salt

1 tablespoon unsalted butter, melted

1 cup frozen raspberries

3 cups (1½ pounds) rhubarb, cut into ½- to ⅓-inch pieces

½ teaspoon fresh-squeezed lemon juice

⅛ teaspoon almond extract

In a medium bowl, mix the sugar, tapioca, flour, salt, and butter. Add the raspberries and toss them well. Let the mixture stand for 15 minutes to macerate the fruit and soften the tapioca. Stir in the rhubarb and let the mixture stand another 5 minutes while you roll out the dough.

Roll out the pastry and line a 9-inch pie tin with the bottom crust. Roll out the remaining dough for the top crust. Rechill the pastry if necessary.

Preheat the oven to 450°F.

Add the lemon juice and extract to the fruit filling and stir. Pour the fruit into the bottom crust and cover it with a lattice (see page 18) or top crust. Trim and crimp the crust; chill the pie for 10 minutes in the freezer. Cut vent slits in the top crust (no need if it's a lattice) and sprinkle the crust lightly with sugar.

Bake the pie on a lipped baking sheet for 7 to 10 minutes, or until the crust looks dry, blistered, and blonde. Turn the oven down to 375°F and bake at least

30 minutes more, or until the crust is golden brown and visible juices are thickened and bubble slowly through the lattice or the slits in the top crust.

Cool the pie completely before cutting, at least a few hours. Serve it at room temperature. Store the pie uncovered at room temperature in a pie safe or cover the pie with a layer of cheesecloth (so that the pastry can breathe) up to 3 days.

> Doubtless God could have made a better berry, but doubtless God never did.
>
> —DR. WILLIAM BUTLER,
> seventeenth-century English writer

Strawberries

The strawberry, a member of the rose family, is the first true fruit and the second consolation that much-awaited spring offers pie bakers after a long winter. Its botanical name, *Fragaria,* means "fragrance" in Latin. A strawberry is the only fruit with its seeds on its outside—up to 200 per berry! The first big wave of fresh local strawberries comes in June after months of only rhubarb, so you can imagine how strongly it signals the onset of summer. Our local homegrown strawberries are smaller but have twice the flavor of the cosmetically perfect, bland hothouse berries available year-round in the grocery stores. Strawberries bruise easily and should be handled lightly. Prepare them as soon after they are picked as possible—they will not improve in flavor, only deteriorate. Refrigeration (during shipping or at home) dulls their flavor.

Strawberry-Rhubarb Pie

MAKES ONE 9-INCH DOUBLE-CRUST PIE

It's a serendipitous and practical combination: Sour rhubarb heightens the flavor of the strawberries, while the berries add flavorful natural fruit sugars to the rhubarb.

Pastry for a 9-inch double-crust pie, chilled, such as Bubby's All-Butter Pastry Pie Dough (page 23) or Basic Butter and Shortening Pastry Pie Dough (page 27)

3 cups strawberries, halved or thickly sliced

3 cups (1½ pounds) rhubarb, cut into ½- to ⅓-inch pieces

1 cup sugar, plus extra for sprinkling on the top crust

4½ tablespoons all-purpose flour

1 teaspoon orange zest

⅛ teaspoon salt

2 tablespoons unsalted butter, cubed

Roll out the pastry and line a 9-inch pie tin with the bottom crust. Roll out the remaining dough for the top crust. Rechill the pastry if necessary.

Preheat the oven to 450°F.

In a large bowl, combine the strawberries, rhubarb, sugar, flour, zest, and salt. Mix the ingredients briefly by tossing them as you would a salad. Scrape the fruit into the pastry-lined pie tin. Dot the fruit with the butter and cover it with the top crust. Trim and crimp the crust; chill the pie for 10 minutes in the freezer. Cut vent slits if not using a lattice and sprinkle the top crust lightly with sugar.

Bake the pie on a lipped baking sheet for 10 minutes, or until the crust looks dry, blistered, and blonde. Turn the oven down to 375°F, and bake for at least 30 minutes more, or until the crust is golden brown and visible juices are thickened and bubble slowly through the slits in the top crust.

Cool the pie completely before cutting it, at least a few hours. Serve it at room temperature. Store the pie uncovered at room temperature in a pie safe or cover the pie with a layer of cheesecloth (so that the pastry can breathe) up to 3 days.

FRESH STRAWBERRY PIE IN A CHOCOLATE CRUMB CRUST

MAKES ONE 8- TO 10-INCH SINGLE-CRUST PIE

Bubby's makes this stunning open-faced pie every June to show off flavor-packed fresh strawberries at their best. A small portion of the berries is cooked down to make a flavorful, deep ruby sauce to glaze the rest of the fresh berries. The resulting taste is bright and intensely lovely next to the dark Chocolate Crumb Crust, especially when served with homemade ice cream or a dollop of homemade Crème Fraîche (page 303). This is a really good way to showcase fresh local strawberries when they're available.

---

1 recipe Chocolate Crumb Crust, chilled in pie tin (page 41)

Crème Fraîche (page 303)

GLAZE

2 cups ripe strawberries

3 tablespoons Cointreau, Grand Marnier, or fresh-squeezed orange juice

1 teaspoon orange zest (optional)

⅓ cup sugar

3 tablespoons cornstarch

1 cup water

2 tablespoons balsamic vinegar

Pinch salt

4 cups ripe but firm strawberries

One day in advance, make the Crème Fraîche. At least 2 hours before assembling the pie, make the crust and chill.

TO MAKE THE GLAZE: Put the strawberries (use any especially ugly ones here in the sauce), Cointreau, and zest in a saucepan over low heat. Simmer for 5 minutes and then mash the berries with the back of a spoon (if you want a more refined sauce, you can purée it at this point). Simmer the mixture on low, uncovered, for 15 minutes more, until the sauce resembles a saucy jam.

Combine the sugar and cornstarch in a bowl and whisk in the water gradually until smooth. Add this to the sauce and cook, stirring constantly, simmering over medium heat 1 to 2 minutes until it is boiling very lightly. When the opacity goes out of the sauce, and it looks shiny and steamy, remove it from the heat and whisk in the vinegar and salt. Chill the sauce until it is cool to the touch but not cold. (The temperature is important—the fresh strawberries will release lots of juice if they contact a hot or even warm sauce, and you'll get strawberry soup, not strawberry pie. If the sauce gets overly cold, it's hard to fold in the berries.)

Clean and trim the strawberries (if they are small, leave them whole; if they are large, halve or quarter them). Fold them into the cool sauce and pour it all into the chilled crust. The consistency will be quite thick. Chill for 2 hours to let it set up before serving.

Serve the pie cold with Crème Fraîche. This pie is best the day it is made, but can still be served the next day. Keep it refrigerated, loosely covered with plastic wrap.

Blueberries

Blueberries come from a diverse family of berries, most of which are native to North America. Many varieties of *Vaccinium* with wonderful names were found in homesteader pies and desserts, among them cranberries, farkleberries or bilberries (also known as sparkleberry, trackleberry, whinberry, blaeberry, myrtle blueberry, and whortleberry), lingonberries or cowberries, and huckleberries. There are two predominant kinds of blueberries: the rarer wild low-bush blueberries native to Maine, Quebec, and Newfoundland are smaller and more expensive but have a more intense flavor than the cultivated high-bush blueberries that are harvested mid-April through October from California up through Newfoundland, with the peak of the season in July. Blueberries, especially wild ones, are remarkably high in antioxidants: they're good for you and tasty, too.

Fresh Blueberry Pie with Crème Fraîche

This glazed open-faced blueberry pie combines the best of two worlds: the tanginess of raw blueberries and the concentrated sweetness of a simmered sauce. It is inspired by Rose Levy Beranbaum's lovely recipe. Serve it with a dollop of homemade Crème Fraîche (page 303) or one scoop of Vanilla or Buttermilk Ice Cream (pages 272 and 274).

Pastry for a 9-inch single-crust pie, crimped and chilled in pie tin, such as Bubby's All-Butter Pastry Pie Dough (page 23), Basic Butter and Shortening Pastry Pie Dough (page 27), Graham Cracker Crust (page 36), or Gingersnap Crumb Crust (page 39)

1 cup Crème Fraîche (page 303)

4 cups blueberries, sorted and cleaned

½ cup plus 2 tablespoons water, divided

2 tablespoons cornstarch

½ cup sugar

2 tablespoons fresh-squeezed lemon juice

One day in advance, make the Crème Fraîche. If using a pastry dough, fully blind-bake the crust (see page 15) until it is golden brown; set aside to cool. For a crumb crust, follow recipe instructions.

Place 3 cups of the blueberries in a large bowl and set aside. Place the remaining cup of blueberries in a saucepan with ½ cup of the water and bring to a boil. Simmer the berries for 3 to 4 minutes, until they are cooked and liquidy. Smash any remaining berries with a spoon.

In a separate bowl, mix the cornstarch and remaining 2 tablespoons of water until smooth. Add the cornstarch slurry, sugar, and lemon juice to the sauce and stir until the sauce is boiling lightly, the starchy cloudiness disappears, and the sauce thickens to a shiny blue-black, about 2 minutes. Pour the hot sauce over the fresh blueberries and stir gently until all of the berries are coated. Pour the blueberries into the pie shell and let the pie set up for 2 hours at room temperature.

The pie is best served the day it's made, with a dollop of Crème Fraîche on the side. Store the pie uncovered in the refrigerator up to 3 days.

BAKED BLUEBERRY PIE

Bubby's double-crust Baked Blueberry Pie has been a cherished member of our family since we started selling pies in the summer of 1990. Blueberries have a long season; we start making this pie in mid-April and stop making it when they are out of season in the United States.

Pastry for a 9-inch double-crust pie, chilled, such as Bubby's All-Butter Pastry Pie Dough (page 23) or Basic Butter and Shortening Pastry Pie Dough (page 27)

5 cups blueberries, sorted and cleaned

¾ cup sugar, plus extra for sprinkling on the top crust

¼ cup cornstarch

2 tablespoons fresh-squeezed lemon juice

1 teaspoon Cointreau or other orange liqueur (optional)

1 lemon, zested

½ teaspoon ground cinnamon

Pinch salt

Tiny pinch ground cloves

3 tablespoons cold unsalted butter

Roll out the pastry and line a 9-inch pie tin with the bottom crust. Roll out the remaining dough for the top crust. Rechill the pastry if necessary.

Preheat the oven to 450°F.

In a large bowl, combine the blueberries, sugar, cornstarch, juice, Cointreau (if using), zest, cinnamon, salt, and cloves. Toss the fruit until the filling evenly coats it. Scrape the filling into the bottom crust, dot the filling with the butter, and cover it with the second crust. Trim and crimp the crust; chill the pie for 10 minutes in the freezer. Cut vent slits in the top crust and sprinkle it lightly with sugar.

Bake the pie on a lipped baking sheet for 10 to 15 minutes, until the crust looks dry, blistered, and blonde. Turn the oven down to 375°F, and bake for at least 30 minutes more, until the crust is golden brown and visible juices are thickened and bubble slowly through the slits in the top crust.

Cool the pie completely before cutting, at least a few hours. Serve it at room temperature. Store the pie uncovered at room temperature, up to 3 days.

BLUEBARB PIE

MAKES ONE 9-INCH DOUBLE-CRUST PIE

This recipe can be adapted to make blackberry-rhubarb pie or almost any kind of berry-rhubarb pie by substituting an equal measure of other berries for the blueberries. Rhubarb, like lemon, heightens other flavors, and this pie tastes like a tart blueberry pie. We make this pie when the last of the good rhubarb overlaps with the forefront of the blueberry harvest.

Pastry for a 9-inch double-crust pie, chilled, such as Bubby's All-Butter Pastry Pie Dough (page 23) or Basic Butter and Shortening Pastry Pie Dough (page 27)

3 cups blueberries, sorted and cleaned

3 cups (1½ pounds) rhubarb, cut into ½- to ⅓-inch pieces

1 cup sugar, plus extra for sprinkling on the top crust

⅓ cup all-purpose flour

1 lemon, zested and juiced

Pinch salt

3 tablespoons unsalted butter, melted

Roll out the pastry and line a 9-inch pie tin with the bottom crust. Roll out the remaining dough for the top crust. Rechill the pastry if necessary.

Preheat the oven to 450°F.

In a large bowl, combine the blueberries, rhubarb, sugar, flour, zest, juice, salt, and melted butter. Lightly toss the fruit and filling ingredients and set aside.

Scrape the filling into the bottom crust and cover it with the second crust. Trim and crimp the crust; chill the pie for 10 minutes in the freezer. Cut vent slits in the top crust and sprinkle it lightly with sugar. This pie is particularly beautiful if small round vent holes are stamped in the top crust (see page 17)—when the blueberry juice spills out it looks like a blueberry.

Bake the pie on a lipped baking sheet for 10 minutes, or until the crust looks dry, blistered, and blonde. Turn the oven down to 375°F, and bake for at least 30 minutes more, or until the crust is golden brown and visible juices are thickened and bubble slowly through slits in the top crust.

Cool the pie completely before cutting, at least a few hours. Serve it at room temperature. Store the pie uncovered at room temperature, up to 3 days.

The Bramble Family: Raspberries & Blackberries

The luscious bramble fruits—raspberries, blackberries, loganberries (a cross between the two), dewberries, cloudberries, and many variations on blackberries—such as marionberries and ollalieberries—mark summer's irrevocable arrival. Brambles belong to the genus *Rubus* and are in the same family as the strawberry. They're aggregate fruits, which means that they're composed of small jewel-like units called "drupelets." Avoid getting these berries wet—only wash them if they look or feel dirty, and if so, just rinse them under running water—don't soak them, lest they get soggy and waterlogged.

BLACKBERRY PIE

D ark and lustrous, this Blackberry Pie has undertones of orange. Blackberries can vary in sweetness a good deal, so sample your filling to make sure you have enough sugar—you may need more. You may also use less if the berries are very sweet.

Pastry for a 9-inch double-crust pie, chilled, such as Bubby's All-Butter Pastry Pie Dough (page 23) or Basic Butter and Shortening Pastry Pie Dough (page 27)

4 cups blackberries

¾ cup sugar, plus extra for sprinkling on the top crust

2 tablespoons quick-cooking tapioca flakes

1 tablespoon orange zest

Pinch salt

3 tablespoons unsalted butter, cubed

Roll out the pastry and line a 9-inch pie tin with the bottom crust. Roll out the remaining dough for the top crust. Rechill the pastry if necessary.

Preheat the oven to 450°F.

In a large bowl, gently toss the blackberries with the sugar, tapioca, zest, and salt. Scrape the filling into the bottom crust, dot the filling with the butter, and cover it with the second crust. Trim and crimp the crust; chill the pie for 10 minutes in the freezer. Cut vent slits in the top crust and sprinkle it lightly with sugar.

Bake the pie on a lipped baking sheet for 10 minutes, or until the crust looks dry, blistered, and blonde. Turn the oven down to 375°F, and bake for at least 30 minutes more, or until the crust is golden brown and visible juices are thickened and bubble slowly through slits in the top crust.

Cool the pie completely before cutting, at least a few hours. Serve it at room temperature. Store the pie uncovered at room temperature, up to 3 days.

Currants

Currants and gooseberries, members of the genus *Ribes,* are perfectly at home in pies and jams. Red currants grow in luminous red clusters that resemble delicate champagne grapes. The small seedy berries are remarkable for their brightly tart flavor and radiant beauty in jellies, pies, and pastry. Their albino family members, white currants, are quite similar but lower in acidity. There's also a variety of pink currants, a cross between red and white currants. To de-stem the currant clusters quickly before use, freeze them for half an hour and you'll be able pull all of the berries perfectly intact from their stems in one sweep. Currants are typically sold perfectly ripe in late June and early July in New York—they can be harvested at leisure because once ripe, they hold on the plant that way up to four weeks.

June 21.—Here I am, on the west bank of the Hudson, 80 miles north of New York, near Esopus, at the handsome, roomy, honeysuckly-and-rose-embower'd cottage of John Burroughs. The place, the perfect June days and nights, (leaning toward crisp and cool) the hospitality of J. and Mrs. B., the air, the fruit, (especially my favorite dish, currants and raspberries, mixed, sugar'd, fresh and ripe from the bushes—I pick 'em myself) . . . .

—WALT WHITMAN,
"Happiness and Raspberries," 1892

RASPBERRY–RED CURRANT PIE

MAKES ONE 9-INCH DOUBLE-CRUST PIE

Ruby red, seedy in texture, and potently flavored, this pie is full-on summer. We get our currants from the farmer's market in July. Unless we're making a pie straightaway, we'll put them on baking sheets in the freezer until they are frozen solid. At that point, they're very easy to strip off their stems. Store stemmed currants in the freezer in sealed plastic bags until needed. This recipe can be made with frozen or fresh fruit.

Pastry for a 9-inch double-crust pie, chilled, such as Bubby's All-Butter Pastry Pie Dough (page 23) or Basic Butter and Shortening Pastry Pie Dough (page 27)

3⅓ cups red raspberries

2½ cups red currants, stemmed

1¼ cups sugar, plus extra for sprinkling on the top crust

5 tablespoons quick-cooking tapioca flakes

1 tablespoon fresh-squeezed lemon juice

2 tablespoons cold unsalted butter, cubed

Roll out the pastry and line a 9-inch pie tin with the bottom crust. Roll out the remaining dough for the top crust. Cut tiny currant-sized circles (vent holes) in the rolled-out top crust with a cake decorating cone tip. Rechill the pastry if necessary.

Preheat the oven to 450°F.

Sort through the berries and currants to remove any stems and duds. Put them in a bowl and add the sugar, tapioca, and lemon juice. Mix the fruit very gently, scrape it into the bottom crust, and dot the filling with the butter. Lay the top crust over the pie. Trim and crimp the crust; chill the pie for 10 minutes in the freezer. Sprinkle the crust lightly with sugar.

Bake the pie on a lipped baking sheet for 10 minutes or until the crust looks dry, blistered, and blonde. Turn the oven down to 375°F, and bake for at least 30 minutes more, or until the crust is golden brown and visible juices are thickened and bubble slowly through slits in the top crust.

Cool the pie completely before cutting, at least a few hours. Serve it at room temperature. Store the pie uncovered at room temperature, up to 3 days.

Black Currants

Black currants look and are shaped like a matte blue-black doppelganger of the blueberry. They have a taste utterly unique among berries—something like a blackberry and cherry crossed with a basil plant. Next to rosehips, black currants contain some of the highest levels of vitamin C in the fruit world—four times that of an orange. They make a delicious pie berry, one also at home in savory dishes, particularly with duck or lamb. Black currants are well known in Europe in jams, juices, and in cassis, a French black currant liqueur. In the United States, black currants can be hard to find. They were banned from cultivation here up until 1966 because they served as an alternate host for white pine blister rust, a disease that affected white pine trees cultivated for timber. Some states still ban cultivation; as a result, many Americans are still unfamiliar with black currants. They are grown primarily in New York and Michigan. To get them in your area, request them in July or, better yet, encourage a farmer at market to plant some. Black currants are not to be confused with dried currants, made from Zante currants, which are not currants at all, but small seedless grapes.

Raspberry–Black Currant Pie

MAKES ONE 9-INCH DOUBLE-CRUST PIE

The black currants lend a savory note—a subtly herbal flavor to the raspberries. You're only likely to find them at farmers' markets; if you do, buy them up and make this pie and Black Currant Sauce (see variation on Raspberry Sauce, page 312) to put up. Black currants from market can also be frozen for use later.

Pastry for a 9-inch double-crust pie, chilled, such as Bubby's All-Butter Pastry Pie Dough (page 23) or Basic Butter and Shortening Pastry Pie Dough (page 27)

4 cups red raspberries

1⅔ cups black currants, stemmed

¾ cup sugar, plus extra for sprinkling on the top crust

¼ cup quick-cooking tapioca flakes

1 lemon, juiced

Pinch salt

2 tablespoons unsalted butter, cubed

Roll out the pastry and line a 9-inch pie tin with the bottom crust. Roll out the remaining dough for the top crust. Rechill the pastry if necessary.

Preheat the oven to 450°F.

Rinse and sort through the berries and currants to remove any stems and duds. Put the fruit in a bowl and add the sugar, tapioca, lemon juice, and salt. Mix the fruit very gently, scrape the filling into the bottom crust, and dot it with the butter. Lay the top crust over the pie. Trim and crimp the crust; chill the pie for 10 minutes in the freezer. Cut vent slits in the top crust and sprinkle it lightly with sugar.

Bake the pie on a lipped baking sheet for 10 minutes, or until the crust looks dry, blistered, and blonde. Turn the oven down to 375°F, and bake for at least 30 minutes more, or until the crust is golden brown and visible juices are thickened and bubble slowly through slits in the top crust.

Cool the pie completely before cutting, at least a few hours. Serve it at room temperature. Store the pie uncovered at room temperature for up to 3 days.

Fresh Raspberry and Sugared Currant Pie

MAKES ONE 9-INCH SINGLE-CRUST PIE

R adiant fresh raspberries in a red currant glaze are a beautiful backdrop to a delicious layer of sugared fresh black currants. It's a modestly filled pie bursting with flavor. Superfine sugar can be made at home by putting white sugar in a food processor and grinding it down so it's finer than granulated but coarser than confectioners sugar.

Fully blind-baked crust for a 9-inch single-crust pie, such as Bubby's All-Butter Pastry Pie Dough (page 23), Basic Butter and Shortening Pastry Pie Dough (page 27), Nut Pastry Pie Dough (page 30), or any crumb or cracker crust (pages 34 to 42) (Do not prebake a Chocolate Crumb Crust.)	4 cups red currants, stemmed
	1½ cups sugar
	¼ cup water
	2 tablespoons cornstarch
	1 teaspoon cassis liqueur
	1 cup black currants, stemmed
	½ cup superfine sugar (see note)
	4 cups red raspberries

Cook the red currants and sugar in a saucepan over medium heat, uncovered, for 15 minutes, until the currants are bubbly and juicy. Strain the juices through a fine-mesh strainer, pressing the fruit to extract remaining juice. Discard the seeds. Return the juices to the pan over medium heat to reduce to 1½ cups, about 20 minutes. While it cooks, whisk the water and cornstarch together until smooth and then whisk the mixture into the fruit juice. Stir continuously over the heat, until the sauce is boiling lightly, the cloudiness clears, and the red is bright and translucent, about 2 minutes. Remove the pan from the heat and cool the sauce to room temperature.

In a medium bowl, whisk 1 tablespoon of the red currant sauce with the cassis. Toss the black currants with it and then roll them in a shallow dish of superfine sugar, shaking the dish back and forth so the currants are coated entirely. Handle them as little as possible. Set the sugared currants aside. Fold the raspberries into the red currant sauce, and then scrape the mixture into the pie shell. Sprinkle the candied black currants over the top with a spoon or a gentle hand.

Refrigerate, uncovered, for at least 30 minutes before serving, until the filling is fully set when jiggled. Serve slender slices because this is a powerfully flavored pie. Store the pie in the refrigerator for up to 5 days.

Gooseberries

There are several thousand varieties of plump translucent gooseberries in the *Ribes* genus. Gooseberries arrive at market shortly after the red currants first appear, typically midsummer. They're about one-inch round or oblong berries a little larger than a table grape, with a delicately curling pale green stem. They range in color from plum red to lime green to yellow or white. The mildest red ones taste a little like a tart kiwifruit, but the green ones are more sour than rhubarb. Like rhubarb, gooseberries are not typically served raw. Although kiwifruit is also known as Chinese gooseberry, true gooseberries and kiwis are not related. One of the dictionary definitions of gooseberry is "a silly person." A gooseberry fool, an English dish made with double cream stirred into stewed gooseberries, inspired the following poem by Edward Lear from *The Book of Nonsense:*

> There was an Old Person of Leeds,
> Whose head was infested with beads;
> She sat on a stool,
> And ate gooseberry fool,
> Which agreed with that person of Leeds.

GOOSEBERRY CRUMBLE PIE

MAKES ONE 9-INCH SINGLE-CRUST PIE

Gooseberries require more thickener than the average berry because they are juicier. Even though tapioca would be a good choice for such an acidic fruit (see page 52), we like the consistency of this pie best with flour. The sweet crumble contrasts the tartness of the filling. Add ¼ cup more sugar if using the tarter green gooseberries.

Pastry for a 9-inch single-crust pie, crimped and chilled in pie tin, such as Bubby's All-Butter Pastry Pie Dough (page 23), Basic Butter and Shortening Pastry Pie Dough (page 27), or Sour Cream Pastry Pie Dough (page 29)

CRUMBLE
1½ cups all-purpose flour
12 tablespoons (1½ sticks) cold unsalted butter

⅓ cup sugar
½ teaspoon ground cinnamon
Pinch salt

FILLING
4½ cups gooseberries
1 cup sugar
⅔ cup all-purpose flour
Pinch salt
1 cup heavy cream, whipped, to serve with pie (optional)

TO MAKE THE CRUMBLE: Combine the flour, butter, sugar, cinnamon, and salt in a food processor and pulse until the mixture resembles bread crumbs. Or, if you are working the crumble by hand, cut the butter into the flour with a pastry cutter and finish by rubbing in the butter with your fingertips until it resembles bread crumbs, then stir in the sugar and other ingredients. Refrigerate the crumble until needed.

Preheat the oven to 450°F.

Pinch the stems off the gooseberries and then measure the sugar, flour, and salt on top of them in a mound. Toss the fruit filling, scrape it into the chilled pie shell, and sprinkle the crumble topping evenly over it.

Bake the pie on a lipped baking sheet for 7 to 10 minutes, or until the crust edge looks dry, blistered, and blonde. Turn the oven down to 350°F, and bake for at least 30 minutes more, or until the crumble is pale gold, the crust edge is golden brown, and visible juices are thickened and bubble slowly at the edge of the crumble.

Cool the pie completely before cutting, at least a few hours. Serve it at room temperature with whipped (see page 302) or plain heavy cream poured over it. Store the pie uncovered at room temperature, up to 3 days.

Blue Goose Pie

MAKES ONE 9-INCH DOUBLE-CRUST PIE

Like Bluebarb Pie (page 73), sweet mellow blueberries offset another tarter ingredient here. It's common practice to truncate "blueberries" to "blue" and "gooseberries" to "goose."

Pastry for a 9-inch double-crust pie, chilled, such as Bubby's All-Butter Pastry Pie Dough (page 23) or Basic Butter and Shortening Pastry Pie Dough (page 27)

2 cups gooseberries

2 cups blueberries

⅔ cup sugar, plus extra for sprinkling on the top crust

4 tablespoons quick-cooking tapioca flakes

½ lemon, juiced

1 tablespoon lemon zest

Pinch salt

Roll out the pastry and line a 9-inch pie tin with the bottom crust. Roll out the remaining dough for the top crust. Rechill the pastry if necessary.

Preheat the oven to 450°F.

Pinch the stems off the gooseberries and sort through all the berries, discarding any duds. In a medium bowl, toss the berries with the sugar, tapioca, juice, zest, and salt. Scrape the filling into the bottom crust and cover it with the second crust. Trim and crimp the crust; chill the pie for 10 minutes in the freezer. Cut vent slits in the top crust and sprinkle it lightly with sugar.

Bake the pie on a lipped baking sheet for 7 to 10 minutes, or until the crust looks dry, blistered, and blonde. Turn the oven down to 375°F, and bake for at least 30 minutes more, until the crust is golden brown and visible juices are thickened and bubble slowly through slits in the top crust.

Cool the pie completely before cutting, at least a few hours. Serve it at room temperature. Store the pie uncovered at room temperature for up to 3 days.

Sweet Cherries

Sweet cherries are best eaten raw, as a snack. Baking only dulls them; glazing them in a fresh fruit pie (see Fresh Strawberry Pie, page 69, for ideas) is agreeably good but they shine brightest just as they are, perfect.

Sour Cherries

Sour cherries, on the other hand, make it to heaven in a pie. (Sours can be eaten fresh too, if you're inclined, but be warned—they speed the digestion along at an alarming pace.) Ninety percent of sour cherries are grown in Michigan and are pitted and frozen in a light sugar syrup for pies year-round. But while that four- to six-week window is open between the end of June and the end of July, we leap at the chance to bake with the fresh local New York sour cherries. The most common sour cherry, the Montmorency or "cherry pie cherry," is a bright, icy red cherry with pale gold flesh and a gold pit. Late in the sour cherry season, another great sour cherry, the Balaton, joins it. The Balaton cherry is Hungarian in origin; it has only been grown in the United States since the mid-1980s. It is deep burgundy throughout, with a smaller pit, and its bountiful juice is the color of ruby port.

If you are picking your own cherries, wait until they're fully ripe—they won't ripen off the tree. Refrigeration (as ever, eat or bake with fruit as soon as possible after picking) will not harm cherries, sweet or sour. If you plan to make just one fresh sour cherry pie every year, it's worth investing in a hand-operated Cherrymat cherry-pitting machine for the next decade's worth of pitting (see Equipment and Source Reference, page 321). You might consider buying one with your circle of friends and sharing it. It works quickly and effectively (26 pounds an hour!), cleans easily, and will save you hours of slow labor. There are handheld cherry/olive pitters that will work in a pinch, but at a snail's pace and accompanied by significant hand cramps. Sour cherries are sometimes prone to small white worms inside, so keep an eye out for them as you pit, and discard any cherries that have them.

SOUR CHERRY–ALMOND CRUMBLE PIE

MAKES ONE 9-INCH SINGLE-CRUST PIE

Almonds are in the *Prunus* genus with cherries, and they complement each other well. Technically, the part of the almond that we eat is the seed and the hard shell around it is the fruit. If you're buying nuts in bulk, smell them—they should smell sweet and nutty, not sharp or bitter or rancid. The same holds true of almond flour, available at most Middle Eastern markets. Almond flour can also be made at home in a food processor. The temperature for this pie is lower and the baking is slower than usual because the crumble browns so easily.

Pastry for a 9-inch single-crust pie, crimped and chilled in pie tin, such as Nut Pastry Pie Dough made with almonds and a high crimped edge (page 30), or Bubby's All-Butter Pastry Pie Dough (page 23), Basic Butter and Shortening Pastry Pie Dough (page 27), or Sour Cream Pastry Pie Dough (page 29)

FILLING

4 cups sour cherries, pitted

1¾ tablespoons quick-cooking tapioca flakes

½ cup sugar

3 tablespoons unsalted butter, melted

1 teaspoon lemon zest

ALMOND CRUMBLE

2 cups almond flour or 1 pound blanched almonds

½ cup sugar

1 teaspoon ground ginger

¾ teaspoon salt

3 tablespoons cold unsalted butter

If using a pastry dough, par-bake the crust (see page 15) until it is blistered and blonde; set aside to cool. For a crumb or cracker crust, do not prebake it.

In a large bowl, combine the cherries with the tapioca so that it has a chance to soften. Set aside.

TO MAKE THE CRUMBLE: If making your own almond flour, mill small batches of blanched almonds in a spice grinder until fine textured (about the consistency of buckwheat flour). Don't overprocess or it will become almond butter. A spice mill works better than a full-sized food processor because it grinds the nuts more consistently. Measure out 2 cups almond flour and re-frigerate any excess for another recipe. Mix the flour with the sugar, ginger, and salt. Cut the butter into the dry ingredients until the mixture clumps up to form gravel-sized lumps, then chill this mixture.

Preheat the oven to 350°F.

Toss the cherries with the sugar, butter, and zest. Scrape the cherry filling into the crust, and sprinkle the crumble evenly onto the cherries.

Bake the pie on a lipped baking sheet for 1 hour, until the fruit is bubbling nice and slow around the edges and the crumb is pale gold. Be patient, it could take longer. If the crumble begins to brown too much, loosely rest foil on top of the pie.

Cool the pie completely before cutting, at least a few hours. Serve it at room temperature. Store the pie uncovered at room temperature, up to 3 days.

> I gave my love a cherry
> That has no stone,
> I gave my love a chicken
> That has no bone,
> I gave my love a baby
> That's no cryin'.
> How can there be a cherry
> That has no stone?
> How can there be a chicken
> That has no bone?
> How can there be a baby
> That's no cryin'?
> A cherry when it's buddin',
> It has no stone.
> A chicken in the eggshell
> It has no bone.
> A baby when it's sleepin'
> Is no cryin'.
> —OLD APPALACHIAN SONG

Sour Cherry Lattice Pie

Sour cherry season starts around the end of June, a little before the Fourth of July, making this stunning pie the perfect choice for the holiday celebration. For most of July, it's possible to make fresh sour cherry pies with local cherries, and we take full advantage, cycling through all our favorite sour cherry pie recipes. If you make even one of these every year, invest in a cherry pitter (see page 321). We keep this Bubby's favorite on the menu year-round with the high-quality frozen sour cherries we get from Michigan—the Sour Cherry Belt of our nation. If you're working with frozen sour cherries, thaw the cherries two hours before they are needed. When they're ready, combine them with the tapioca.

Pastry for a 9-inch double-crust pie, chilled, such as Bubby's All-Butter Pastry Pie Dough (page 23) or Basic Butter and Shortening Pastry Pie Dough (page 27)

5½ cups sour cherries

¼ cup quick-cooking tapioca flakes

¾ cup sugar, plus extra for sprinkling on the top crust

4 tablespoons (½ stick) unsalted butter, melted

1 teaspoon lemon zest

½ teaspoon almond extract

Pinch salt

Pit the cherries into a bowl and combine them and the juice they create with the tapioca so that it has a chance to soften.

Roll out the pastry and line a 9-inch pie tin with the bottom crust. Roll out the remaining dough for the top crust. Rechill the pastry if necessary.

Preheat the oven to 450°F.

Add the sugar, butter, zest, extract, to the cherries. Toss briefly and fill the bottom crust with the mixture. Cover it with a lattice top crust (see page 18) or any variation on a top crust design. Trim and crimp; chill the pie for 10 minutes in the freezer. Sprinkle the top lightly with sugar.

Bake the pie on a lipped baking sheet for 10 minutes, or until the crust looks dry, blistered, and blonde. Turn the oven down to 375°F, and bake for at least 30 minutes more, or until the crust is golden brown and visible juices are thick and bubble slowly through the lattice top crust.

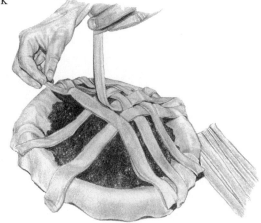

Cool the pie completely before cutting, at least a few hours. Serve it at room temperature. Store the pie uncovered at room temperature, up to 3 days.

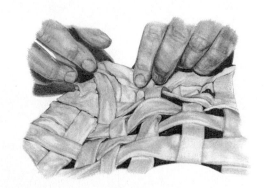

Apricots

A ripe apricot is truly a glorious thing to behold—its delicate, muted hue of orange makes the most sensual persimmon seem garish; its perfume is as concentrated as a whole apricot tree in bloom; and its skin is as soft to the touch as the down on a newborn baby's head. Select plump fragrant fruit without a trace of green. Allow it to soften before using—either at room temperature or in a paper bag, until it is just on "the brink of viability." The Latin name for apricot, *praecoquus,* means "early ripening."

The apricot exists on the brink of viability.
—WAVERLY ROOT

APRICOT–SOUR CHERRY PIE

This pie is outstanding with Hungarian-variety Balaton sour cherries—late-season sour cherries, deep burgundy throughout with a smaller pit. They are smaller than Bing cherries but about the same hue; tasting one should clear up any confusion—they're plenty sour enough to distinguish themselves. This recipe, like many, is authored by the growing seasons—apricots and Balatons are at the height of their season by mid-July, making it hard to pass up one or the other at the farmer's market. Pure laziness—the other mother of invention—also plays a part, adding apricots cuts down on the labor of cherry pitting. The flavors and colors of these two fruits complement each other beautifully, so a lattice top or a variation thereof is recommended to show off the filling a bit.

Pastry for a 9-inch double-crust pie, chilled, such as Bubby's All-Butter Pastry Pie Dough (page 23) or Basic Butter and Shortening Pastry Pie Dough (page 27)

1½ pounds (3 cups) sour cherries

3 tablespoons quick-cooking tapioca flakes

1½ pounds apricots, halved or quartered (3 cups)

1 cup packed light brown sugar

Extra (white) sugar for sprinkling on the top crust

3 tablespoons unsalted butter, melted

1 tablespoon lemon zest

1 teaspoon salt

1 teaspoon almond extract

Pit the cherries into a bowl and combine the fruit and the juice they create with the tapioca so that it has a chance to soften.

Roll out the pastry and line a 9-inch pie tin with the bottom crust. Roll out the remaining dough for the top crust. Rechill the pastry if necessary.

Preheat the oven to 450°F.

Add the apricots, sugar, butter, zest, salt, and extract to the cherry filling. Scrape the filling into the bottom crust and cover it with the second crust. Trim and crimp the crust; chill the pie for 10 minutes in the freezer. Cut vent slits in the top crust (if not using a lattice) and sprinkle it lightly with sugar.

Bake the pie on a lipped baking sheet for 10 minutes, or until the crust looks dry, blistered, and blonde. Turn the oven down to 375°F, and bake for at least 30 minutes more, or until the crust is golden brown and visible juices are thickened and bubble slowly through the slits in the top crust.

Cool the pie completely before cutting, at least a few hours. Serve it at room temperature. Store the pie uncovered at room temperature, up to 3 days.

Peaches

Peaches, like apricots and plums, are members of the Rosaceae family. They are classified as clingstone or freestone according to how tightly their flesh clings to its pit. As one might expect of something covered in soft, velvety down, peaches bruise rather easily, and their flesh is averse to tropical extremes and severe cold climates. Our recipes can be made with any flavorful variety of yellow or white ripe peach.

Wishing to be friends is quick work, but friendship is a slow-ripening fruit.

—ARISTOTLE

We all want the perfect peach, but not many of us go directly to the tree for this marvel—juicy, yielding, concentrated, and warm from the sun. More and more stone fruits leave their branches reluctantly these days—underripe—to head to market. You can hardly blame the farmer for keeping time on his side—a perfectly ripe peach bruises easily. By picking it when it's mature—full-color and full-size but still firm—the farmer's banking on the ripening arc of the peach. Stone fruits continue to ripen and develop more complex flavors, change color, and improve in texture after they've been picked.

Your local farmer only has to take the mature fruit from the field to the farmer's market or store—a short distance in comparison to long-trucked produce—and won't need to pick the fruit green or gas it beforehand. (A tiny amount of ethylene gas occurs naturally in most fruits and vegetables, but when ethylene's artificially piped into a "ripening room," the gas stimulates underripe fruit to start acting ripe. Of course, ethylene doesn't compare to the sun and time itself.) Find the fruit with the most intoxicating fragrance, one that looks deeply colored and feels heavy for its size (sugar weighs more than water). Ask for a sample (many stores will cut a sample too). If it's delicious, buy some promptly and tell all of your friends where they can be found. Mealy peaches should be avoided entirely—unlike slightly underripe peaches, they will only get worse.

If you need to hasten the ripening process for a day or half a day before you plan to bake a pie, put underripe stone fruit in a paper bag, close it up, and store it in a room temperature (not hot) place to ripen. Check on its progress once or twice a day—the fruit can change rapidly on a hot summer day—and remove it from the bag when it nears ripeness. If the fruit is still a little too firm when you need to bake the pie, just slice the fruit extra thin.

A refrigerator can be used as a stopgap to delay spoilage of ripe fruit, but it will deaden the fruit flavors. It's better to buy and use the fruit when it's almost perfectly ripe.

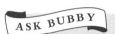

Roast Ripening Peaches, Apricots, and Nectarines

If you have just returned from the store with underripe fruit and only have an hour or so before you need to start baking pies, slice the fruit in half and open it up. You can leave the stone in. Coat the fruit (with peels left on) in melted butter and sprinkle it lightly with sugar. Roast in a 375°F oven for approximately 15 minutes. This concentrates the fruit flavors and softens the texture quite persuasively. If you sample some, it should taste like ripe fruit. Let the fruit cool and then continue preparing it for baking as you would a ripe, fresh piece of fruit.

Peach–Vanilla Bean Pie

MAKES ONE 9-INCH DOUBLE-CRUST PIE

Bubby's regular diners clamor for the first slice of peach pie each summer. These folks become particularly enthusiastic when the first New Jersey peaches—fuzzy and perfumed—show up at the market. Our local peaches rival any that ride up in trucks from down South. Although Georgia peaches are good in the South, there's really nothing as juicy and sweet as a local Jersey peach when you're in New York. Look for the best local fruit in your area for this pie. The light brown sugar gives the peaches a caramelized flavor reminiscent of a brown betty. The tiny black flecks of vanilla bean, cinnamon, and cardamom punctuate the bright peach flesh and give it a fragrant, warmly spiced flavor. Real vanilla bean is much preferred, but if you can't locate one, you can substitute vanilla extract.

Pastry for a 9-inch double-crust pie, chilled, such as Bubby's All-Butter Pastry Pie Dough (page 23) or Basic Butter and Shortening Pastry Pie Dough (page 27)	¼ cup all-purpose flour
	1 lemon, zested and juiced
	Pinch salt
	Pinch ground cinnamon
1 vanilla bean, split lengthwise, or 1 teaspoon vanilla extract	Pinch ground cardamom
	Tiny pinch ground cloves
3 pounds peaches, peeled (see page 97) and quartered	3 tablespoons cold unsalted butter, cubed
¾ cup packed light brown sugar	Sugar, for sprinkling on the top crust

Roll out the pastry and line a 9-inch pie tin with the bottom crust. Roll out the remaining dough for the top crust. Rechill the pastry if necessary.

Preheat the oven to 450°F.

Scrape the fine black seeds from the center of each vanilla bean half by running a knife blade along the cut face of the pod on a cutting board. Be thorough and get all of the gummy inside of the vanilla bean on the knife. In a large bowl, combine the vanilla seeds with the peaches, sugar, flour, lemon zest and juice, salt, cinnamon, cardamom, and cloves. Mix the fruit filling lightly, as little as possible, to just get the ingredients dispersed. Scrape the filling into the bottom crust, dot the top of the fruit with the butter, and cover it with the second crust. Trim and crimp the crust; chill the pie for 10 minutes in the freezer. Cut vent slits in the top crust and sprinkle it lightly with sugar.

Bake the pie on a lipped baking sheet for 7 to 10 minutes, or until the crust looks dry, blistered, and blonde. Turn the oven down to 375°F, and bake 30 minutes or until the crust is golden brown and visible juices are thickened and bubble slowly through slits in the top crust.

Cool the pie completely before cutting, at least a few hours. Serve it at room temperature with a scoop of vanilla ice cream on the side to enhance the flavor. Store the pie uncovered at room temperature, up to 3 days.

Why is my bottom crust soggy?

If your fruit macerates (releases juice when it comes into contact with sugar) too long before you fill your pie with it, it can make it more difficult to achieve a crisp bottom crust. To prevent this, wait until the very last minute to mix the cut fruit with the sugar and other ingredients.

Also, a hot oven in the beginning is crucial to a well-set bottom crust. A crisp, flaky crust results from the way in which the dough is prepared and the initial high heat that reaches it in the oven. Is your oven as hot as the dial indicates? Some pans conduct heat better than others. Ceramic is particularly slow, whereas dark metals and Pyrex are good conductors. Wait to cut into your pie until it is fully cooled or the hot juices will form a big lake no matter how perfectly thickened the pie is.

White Peach Crumble Pie

T he delicately perfumed flavors of the white peach preside in this pie—we just added a crumble to complement their texture. White peaches are more perfumed than yellow peaches, which is why we've toned all other flavors down to showcase their unique flavor. It's important to follow the mixing instructions closely—if the peaches macerate in the sugar before going into the pie, or if the fruit sits around in the bottom crust before being baked, the bottom crust will be soggy.

Pastry for a 9-inch single-crust pie, crimped and chilled in pie tin, such as Bubby's All-Butter Pastry Pie Dough (page 23), Sour Cream Pastry Pie Dough (page 29), or Basic Butter and Shortening Pastry Pie Dough (page 27)

CRUMBLE

1 cup all-purpose flour

8 tablespoons (1 stick) cold unsalted butter

3 tablespoons packed light brown sugar

Pinch ground cinnamon

Pinch salt

FILLING

3 pounds white peaches, peeled (see page 97)

¾ cup packed light brown sugar

¼ cup all-purpose flour

½ teaspoon ground cinnamon

Pinch or two salt

TO MAKE THE CRUMBLE: Combine the flour, butter, sugar, cinnamon, and salt in a food processor and pulse until the mixture resembles bread crumbs. Or, if you are working the crumble by hand, cut the butter into the flour with a pastry cutter and finish by rubbing in the butter with your fingertips until it resembles bread crumbs, then stir in the sugar and other ingredients. Refrigerate the crumble until needed.

Preheat the oven to 450°F.

Slice the peaches into a large bowl and measure out the sugar, flour, cinnamon, and salt on top of the fruit. Toss gently until the filling is evenly dispersed. Scrape the peaches into the prepared bottom crust and distribute the crumble topping evenly on top of it. Chill pie for 10 minutes in the freezer.

Bake the pie on a lipped baking sheet for 10 minutes, or until the crust looks dry, blistered, and blonde. Turn the oven down to 350°F, and bake for at least 30 minutes more, or until the crust is golden brown and visible juices are thickened and bubble slowly through the crumble topping.

Cool the pie completely before cutting, at least a few hours. Serve it at room temperature. Store the pie uncovered at room temperature, up to 3 days.

How to Skin a Peach

Peach skin can be left on the peach if you like the texture in your pie, but if you prefer to peel them, here's how. Scalding ripe peaches makes the skin separate and slip from the flesh with very little waste involved. (If the peaches are underripe, it won't work so smoothly. In that case, it's better to peel them with a vegetable peeler and roast-ripen them before using (see page 93).

Bring a big pot of water to a boil. Cut a shallow X on the bottom of each peach. Prepare a bowl or basin of ice water in the sink. When the pot of water comes to a boil, drop the peaches in. Count to ten and take one out with a slotted spoon. If the skin slips off very easily from the corner of the X that you cut on the bottom, continue on to the next step. If your test peach is not ready, return the peach to the boiling water and repeat the test with another peach.

Once the skin slips easily, remove the peaches with a slotted spoon, and submerge them in the basin of ice cold water. Slip off the skins, starting with the bottoms scored by the X. If the skin still doesn't come off easily, drop the reluctant peach back in the hot water a few seconds more and try again. Once peeled, put the peaches in a bowl, slice them, and cover them with plastic wrap. If the peaches will be waiting around for long time (over half an hour), squeeze a little lemon juice on them to keep them from browning.

BLUEBERRY-PEACH PIE

MAKES ONE 9-INCH DOUBLE-CRUST PIE

B ubby's has been serving up this pie from its earliest days as a pie shop. This is a "veh-reh Suuth-n paah," soothing and jammy, dark violet, and mellow.

Pastry for a 9-inch double-crust pie, chilled, such as Bubby's All-Butter Pastry Pie Dough (page 23) or Basic Butter and Shortening Pastry Pie Dough (page 27)

1½ pounds peaches, peeled (see page 97) and cut in sixths

2 cups blueberries

¾ cup packed light brown sugar

¼ cup all-purpose flour

1 lemon, zested

½ lemon, juiced

½ teaspoon vanilla extract

Pinch salt

3 tablespoons cold unsalted butter, cubed

Sugar, to sprinkle on top crust

Roll out the pastry and line a 9-inch pie tin with the bottom crust. Roll out the remaining dough for the top crust. Rechill the pastry if necessary.

Preheat the oven to 450°F.

In a large bowl, layer in the peaches, blueberries, sugar, flour, lemon zest and juice, vanilla, and salt. Mix the fruit filling lightly, as little as possible, to get the ingredients just dispersed. Scrape the filling into the bottom crust and dot the top with the butter. Cover it with the second crust. Trim and crimp the crust; chill the pie for 10 minutes in the freezer. Cut vent slits in the top crust and sprinkle it lightly with sugar.

Bake the pie on a lipped baking sheet for 10 minutes, or until the crust looks dry, blistered, and blonde. Turn the oven down to 375°F, and bake for at least 30 minutes more, or until the crust is golden brown and visible juices are thickened and bubble slowly through slits in the top crust.

Cool the pie completely before cutting, at least a few hours. Serve it at room temperature. Store uncovered at room temperature, up to 3 days.

AUTUMN AND WINTER PIES

How many times it thundered before Franklin took the
hint! How many apples fell on Newton's head before he
took the hint! Nature is always hinting at us. It hints
over and over again. And suddenly we take the hint.

—ROBERT FROST

A utumn at Bubby's is full of anticipation of the fruits of the harvest:
the multitude of apples and pears, the last of the blackberries, and,
perhaps most of all, the reappearance of our Pumpkin Pie with Caramel
Sauce and Candied Pecans (page 127)—a pie that is always brought back on
the very last day of October, for Halloween and stays on the menu through
Christmas.

To experience the fullness and fruition of the growing year coming to a
close, make the trek out to a pick-your-own orchard. Look around your
immediate environs, too—there is a staggering quantity of fruit that goes
unpicked in untended fruit trees and vines. Just be sure to ask permission to
harvest it and share your take in thanks or pies. It's fun to take children on
the harvest outing. Or, go to the farmer's market to pick your apples there.

Making pie crust in the fall is easier than in summer. Unlike the dog days
of summer, cool hands, cool houses, and cool surfaces are cooperative, and
fewer dough chilling intervals are necessary. It's lucky that the nation's

biggest pie-eating day occurs on Thanksgiving, when the days are invariably hospitable to pie dough.

Concord Grapes

Concord grapes are native to North America. They ripen in late fall, and should be picked or purchased perfectly ripe—dark velvety purple with a fine silvery powder. Discard any burst or shriveled grapes and store them in clusters in the refrigerator, unwashed, wrapped in tissue paper or paper towels. Rinse and sort grapes before using. Concords are the only variety of grape we use for pies. Concords have a thick skin and a viscous, seedy interior. They are laborious to prepare, but taste them and you'll see why it's worth it: You'll encounter intoxicating childhood tastes—grape juice and jelly—and the more adult taste of a heady, musky wine.

The most pungent grape flavor is in the bluish purple skin; the translucent juicy pale green interior clings tenaciously to a clutch of seeds. The pulp slips from the skin very easily if the grape is squeezed between the thumb and forefinger. Separating the seeds from the pulp is a bit more challenging: cook the pulp and seeds with sugar on the stovetop until the pulp breaks down and becomes liquid enough to strain (see more on this in the following recipe). The skins on their own are too toothy to use without the extracted pulp, so we use mixture of the two elements. We also determined that it helped the flavor and consistency of the pie filling to purée a portion of the skin to add to the rest of the slipped skins and pulp in the filling.

Concord Grape Pie with Crème Fraîche

This pie is a lot of work, but when finished, it is like eating a slice of autumn, capturing the essence of Concord grapes.

Pastry for a 9-inch double-crust pie, chilled, such as Bubby's All-Butter Pastry Pie Dough (page 23), Basic Butter and Shortening Pastry Pie Dough (page 27), Sour Cream Pastry Pie Dough (page 29), or Short Dough For Tarts (page 32)

2 scant pounds (3½ cups) whole Concord grapes

¾ cup sugar, plus extra for sprinkling on the top crust

6 tablespoons all-purpose flour

2 tablespoons unsalted butter, melted

2 tablespoons fresh-squeezed lemon juice

½ teaspoon ground cinnamon

¼ teaspoon salt

1 cup Crème Fraîche (page 303)

Rinse the grapes and allow them to dry while you mix the pastry.

Slip the skins off the grapes by pinching the contents (pulp and seeds) into one bowl; drop the skins, separately, into another bowl. The skins should slip off willingly, as if they've had the very thing in mind themselves. Simmer the seedy greenish pulp and the sugar over medium-low heat until it gets juicy and bubbly and breaks down. Look for the point when the seeds separate easily from the pulp. If they don't yield, cook them a little longer. Strain the mixture through a fine-mesh strainer to separate the seeds from the pulp. Discard the seeds.

Measure ⅓ of the skins into the pulp and run the mixture through a food mill or food processor. Add the remaining skins whole for an intensely grapey taste—the most potent flavor resides in the skin. Cool down the grape mixture until it is completely cold, about 2 hours.

Roll out the pastry and line a 9-inch pie tin with the bottom crust. Roll out the remaining dough for the top crust. Rechill the pastry until you're ready to fill the pie.

Preheat the oven to 450°F.

Combine the grape mixture with the flour, butter, juice, cinnamon, and salt. Stir. Pour the soupy fruit mixture into the bottom crust. Cut vent holes in the top crust *before* placing it over the pie (the soupy filling will spurt though if you cut it post-assembly). Trim and crimp the crust; chill the pie for 10 minutes in the freezer. Sprinkle the top lightly with sugar.

Bake the pie on a lipped baking sheet for 10 minutes, or until the crust looks dry, blistered, and blonde. Turn the oven down to 375°F, and bake for at least 30 minutes more, or until the crust is golden brown and visible juices are thickened and bubble slowly through slits in the top crust.

Cool the pie completely before serving, at least a few hours. Serve each slice with a dollop of crème fraîche. Store the pie uncovered at room temperature, up to 3 days.

Bring a concertina after sunset under the apple trees.
Let romance stutter to the western stars, "Excuse . . . me. . . ."
—CARL SANDBURG, *Cornhuskers*, 1918

Apples

All apples trees are descended from their wild, sour little cousins the crab-apples, according to the *Oxford Dictionary of Food*. Crabapples are the only apple that might fairly be called "wild." In order to increase the size, sweetness, and fleshy edible portion of the crabapple, humans have intervened with nature since the second century BC to aggressively interbreed this fruit by grafting scions (young branches) onto crabapple rootstock to create new varieties.

American apple varieties developed differently from European varieties because of the method of propagation—seeds (pips) from Europe were cultivated and interbred with native American crabapple trees. Most species we now call heirloom American apples are the inventions of the early or mid–nineteenth century grow-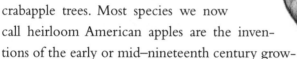ers, though there are new apple species coming into being all the time. There are currently between 7,000 and 8,000 named varieties in the world.

The apple pie is often considered the measure of a worthwhile pie pantry. And a great apple pie is dependent upon great apples. The best apples for pie vary from place to place, and opinions about the best apples for pie often vary from baker to baker. The most widely available commercially produced apple well suited to pie is the bright green Granny Smith; its tart, firm flesh has good body when baked. However, it would be a shame to use supermarket variety apples at the height of apple harvest. In New York State, the Macoun or Cortland are some of our favorites for double-crust pies, and Opalescent works well for open-faced apple pies . . . but we're always tasting and baking with varieties that spring up at the farmer's market.

Look for crisp, firm flesh, and a tart, full flavor. Ask the grower for samples and recommendations for good pie apples. Tasting the apples before you buy them is a great way to know you're going home with quality fruit. Be aware that "a good cooking apple" might mean good for applesauce, not for pie. Very juicy apples may require a pinch more thickener.

The pie bakers we've surveyed recommend the following tart, crisp, firm-fleshed apples for pie: Macoun, Cortland, Belle de Boskoop, Mutsu, Northern Spy, Greenings, Newton Pippin, Winter Banana, Ginger Gold, Rome, Baldwin, Spitzenberg, Gravenstein, Bramley's, Liberty, York, Enterprise, Russet, Golden Russet, Haralson, Spartan, and Braeburn (but there are many delicious varieties beyond this short list).

The point in the growing season and in the life of a given apple's arc of ripeness varies. When you buy a Winesap, it might be perfectly tart, crisp, and firm—the Rolls-Royce of apples—but after a week or two, that same apple may have changed into a sweeter, softer apple that has more in common with a McIntosh. Ideally, you bake with the finest selection of apples, but if you need to work with a softer apple, here's one way to think about it:

When you're baking an apple pie, the first, high-temperature bake is to achieve a light flaky top and bottom crust; the second, moderate-temperature bake is to fully cook and thicken the filling. If you are working with a riper, tender apple (as in the case of the two-week-old Winesap above), it helps to think of a ripe apple as a par-baked, "almost there" apple during the second phase. You can shorten your baking time; it will need a nudge, not a push, to finish baking. Look for thickened bubbles to make sure your interior has cooked enough to thicken.

If an apple is mealy, don't waste your effort—go buy more or make a different kind of pie.

Mix varieties of apples in a pie—a mixture of Northern Spy and Cortland apples with one McIntosh apple added in for sweetness is lovely—to get extra dimension and interest from a range of flavors and textures. Factor in how different apples behave during baking. For example, a single McIntosh will get nice and saucy around a majority of Newton Pippins—a good calculated effect since the tart Newton Pippins have more body when cooked and benefit from the addition of a single sweeter, saucier apple. Imagine how the reverse proportions would prove to be a problem— underbaked slices of Newton Pippin adrift in a sea of McIntosh applesauce. Tender apples suitable for the "just one sweet, saucy apple thrown in" configuration include McIntosh, Golden Delicious, Fuji, Wealthy, Empire, Jonagold, and Jonathan apples.

Apples are best used fresh from the tree, but they will keep very well in cold storage after the harvesting season ends. The saying "one bad apple spoils the bunch" is actually true, especially if the apples are packed tightly against one another. For optimum longevity, apples should be stored in a cool, dry place with good air circulation (apple farmers store at 32° all year long). A cool pantry is best; a refrigerator will help prevent spoilage but may dull the flavors.

Apples with a thin, tender peel (think Golden Delicious or Yellow Transparent apples) do not need to be peeled before being baked in a pie. It is advisable to peel ruddier, thick-skinned apples like Russets because the skins will remain tough, even fully baked. Taste the peel to decide if you like its texture and flavor. There are plenty of apples where you could go either way, according to your own personal preference. Some cooks enjoy the added texture. You can use a vegetable peeler or a paring knife to peel the fruit—whichever is most comfortable to you.

If you have lots of apples on your hands every autumn, we recommend investing in a slightly fancier apple-peeling tool that clamps onto a counter (see Equipment and Source Reference, page 322). It will impress and delight any child (or adult) who wants to be helpful. It not only peels your apples, it cores them too. All with the ease of reeling in a fish! It's an indispensable tool for production baking because it's fast and saves a lot of wear and tear on the hands (as anyone who has peeled huge batches of apples can testify)—and even the youngest family members will fight over who gets to help peel the apples first.

> To appreciate the wild and sharp flavors of these October fruits, it is necessary that you be breathing the sharp October or November air. What is sour in the house a bracing walk makes sweet. Some of these apples might be labeled, "To be eaten in the wind."
>
> —HENRY DAVID THOREAU

MILE-HIGH APPLE PIE

MAKES ONE 9-INCH DOUBLE-CRUST PIE

At Bubby's, we make this pie "mile high" by piling the apples up much higher than the tin is deep. It's a mountain of a pie with more fruit in it than most. While baking, the apples cook down some but the crust remains sculptural, curvaceous, and high. We'll use local Macouns (alone) from the farmer's market if they're available. Sautéing the apples in butter first is a good step for hard fruits and works well for this pie because it makes the apples a little more compact at the outset. The process also stops the apples from turning brown, so you end up with a really white filling.

Pastry for a 9-inch double-crust pie, chilled, such as Bubby's All-Butter Pastry Pie Dough (page 23), Basic Butter and Shortening Pastry Pie Dough (page 27), or Lard Pastry Pie Dough (page 28)

3½ pounds apples

4 tablespoons (½ stick) unsalted butter

¾ cup sugar, plus extra for sprinkling on the top crust

3 tablespoons all-purpose flour

1 tablespoon fresh-squeezed lemon juice

1 teaspoon salt

1 teaspoon ground cinnamon

¼ teaspoon ground nutmeg

Pinch ground cloves

Roll out the smaller batch of pastry and line a 9-inch pie tin with the bottom crust. Roll out the remaining large ball of dough for the top crust. Rechill the pastry if necessary.

Peel, core, and slice the apples ¼ to ½ inch thick (to get about 7 cups). In a large sauté pan, melt the butter and sauté the apples for 2 to 3 minutes, until the outer edges get slightly soft. Remove from heat. In the pan, measure the sugar, flour, butter, lemon juice, salt, cinnamon, nutmeg, and cloves on top of the apples, but do not stir until they are ready to go into the pie or they will get too soupy.

Preheat the oven to 450°F.

When you're ready to proceed, toss the apples with the other filling ingredients. Because this pie is so tall, mounding up the apples takes a little finesse. Scrape the apple filling into the bottom crust until the pie reaches average height, then add the remaining apples by the handful, using your free hand to steady the mound.

Cover it with the second crust. Trim and crimp the crust; chill the pie for 10 minutes in the freezer. Cut vent slits in the top crust and sprinkle it very lightly with water and then sugar. Because the top crust slope is so steep, you need to flick a little water at it to keep the sugar from rolling off and caking at the crust edge when you sprinkle it on.

Bake the pie on a lipped baking sheet for 10 minutes, or until the crust looks dry, blistered, and blonde. Turn the oven down to 375°F, and bake for at least 30 minutes more, or until the crust is golden brown and visible juices are thickened and bubble slowly through slits in the top crust. With a pie this high, you can expect some runoff on the tray. Test apples for doneness by poking a wooden skewer down through the open vent slits of the top crust. Apples inside should

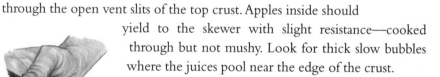

yield to the skewer with slight resistance—cooked through but not mushy. Look for thick slow bubbles where the juices pool near the edge of the crust.

Cool the pie completely before cutting, at least a few hours. Serve it at room temperature. Store the pie uncovered at room temperature, up to 3 days.

WHISKEY-APPLE CRUMBLE PIE

MAKES ONE 9-INCH SINGLE-CRUST PIE

This pie is comfort food at its best. The sweet pecan crumble complements the warmly spiced apples, which taste faintly of whiskey. The sour cream pastry offers a tender, tangy contrast. All in all, it just has irresistible chemistry. Opalescents, Cortlands, or Macouns all work well for this pie. If you choose to use harder, dense apples like Russets or Granny Smiths, they will need to be sautéed slightly longer before going into this loosely covered open-faced pie.

Pastry for a 9-inch single-crust pie, crimped and chilled in pie tin, such as Sour Cream Pastry Dough (page 29)

CRUMBLE

¾ cup all-purpose flour

6 tablespoons (¾ stick) cold unsalted butter

¼ cup packed light brown sugar

¼ cup sugar

½ teaspoon ground cinnamon

½ teaspoon salt

½ cup chopped pecans

FILLING

2 pounds tart, crisp apples

3 tablespoons unsalted butter

½ cup packed light brown sugar

2 tablespoons whiskey or bourbon

½ teaspoon ground cinnamon

Pinch ground cloves

Pinch ground nutmeg

Pinch salt

TO MAKE THE CRUMBLE: Combine the flour, butter, sugars, cinnamon, and salt in a food processor and pulse until the mixture resembles bread crumbs. Or, if you are working the crumble by hand, cut the butter into the flour with a pastry cutter and finish by rubbing in the butter with your fingertips until it resembles bread crumbs, then stir in the sugar and other ingredients. Add the pecans and refrigerate the crumble until needed.

Preheat the oven to 450°F.

Peel, core, and slice the apples about ¼ inch thick. In a large sauté pan over low heat, melt the butter and sauté the apples for 5 minutes, until the outer edges get slightly soft.

In the pan off the heat, measure the sugar, whiskey, cinnamon, cloves, nutmeg, and salt on top of the apples and toss gently until the apples are evenly coated. Scrape the filling into the bottom crust. Sprinkle the crumble evenly on top.

Bake the pie on a lipped baking sheet for 10 minutes, or until the crust looks dry, blistered, and blonde. Turn the oven down to 350°F, and bake for about 1 hour, until the crumble browns, the apples yield when pierced with a knife, and the juice is bubbling thickly at the edges of the pie.

Cool the pie completely before cutting, at least a few hours. Serve it at room temperature. Store the pie uncovered at room temperature, up to 3 days.

 ASK BUBBY

Why is my hot pie runny when I cut into it?

Most likely, you are cutting into your pie too soon. A hot pie will invariably be runny just because it's hot. If you allow it to cool at room temperature, the juices will slowly be reabsorbed into the fruit. Think of the way gelatin works: The heat activates the thickener and distributes it evenly but the cooling process is what actually allows it to set up. Pies are the same (regardless of the thickener used). Plan on 2 to 3 hours of cooling time before cutting a pie or it'll be too soupy—some pies take longer than others to cool—it just depends on how heat-retentive the ingredients are.

Good apple pies are a considerable part of our domestic happiness.
—JANE AUSTEN, 1815

APPLE-CARAMEL UPSIDE-DOWN PIE (TARTE TATIN)

Like a classic French Tarte Tatin, this pie is made in a heavy sauté pan and is built as follows: a base of flavorful caramel sauce, apple slices layered in methodically, sealed over with a layer of pastry crust. In the oven, the apples drink in the sauce and caramelize as they bake. Invert this pie and you'll find that the apples have turned a hue of glazed gold in their flowerlike spiral. The apples you use should be sturdy, flavorful, tart, and medium to firm, like a Winesap. Bosc pears or quince could also be added to the apples as a variation. Juicy fruits won't hold up and will get too saucy to work in this context.

Pastry for a 9-inch single-crust pie, chilled, such as Bubby's All-Butter Pastry Pie Dough (page 23), Basic Butter and Shortening Pastry Pie Dough (page 27), or Sour Cream Pastry Pie Dough (page 29)

CARAMEL

¼ cup water

½ cup sugar

2 tablespoons unsalted butter

Pinch salt

FILLING

3 pounds apples

2 tablespoons fresh-squeezed lemon juice

1 tablespoon lemon zest

½ cup sugar

Pinch salt

4 tablespoons unsalted butter

TO MAKE THE CARAMEL: Pour the water into a heavy saucepan, add the sugar, and clip a candy thermometer to the side of the pan. Don't stir, but give the pan a little shake if the sugar is above the waterline. Place the pan over high heat. When the sugar and water get hot and bubbly and the sugar lique-fies, turn the heat down to medium-high. Give the pan a gentle shake to keep the syrup moving and to prevent uneven browning—watch out for darker color around the edges or burning smells. The caramel should heat, at the very least, to a color resembling dark honey. If you like a bitter caramel, go darker, to a nice rich brown (380°F). Turn off the heat and add 2 tablespoons of butter and a pinch of salt. Stir well and pour the caramel into an ovenproof 10-inch sauté pan or 9-inch pie plate. This can be done several hours in advance and left out at room temperature.

Preheat the oven to 450°F.

Peel, core, and slice the apples about ¼ inch thick. They need to be as uniform as possible to make the floral spiral pattern when it is done. In a large bowl, combine the apples, juice, and zest. Toss well. Add the sugar and a pinch of salt. Stir well to combine. In a large sauté pan over medium-high heat, melt the remaining 4 tablespoons of butter. Sauté the apple mixture for about 3 minutes, stirring gently with a wooden spoon, until the outer edges get slightly soft. Cool them to room temperature.

To assemble the pie, select the prettiest, best-looking apple slices for the first layer—these will become the top face of the pie when it's flipped over. Starting from the center of the sauté pan with the caramel in it, overlap the apples in a spiral. Keep overlapping them in the same direction. When you have filled it to the outside edge of the pan, start another layer on top of it, working again from the center outward. After the third layer, you can just scatter the remaining apples on top.

Roll out the crust to a diameter slightly larger than your pan and lay it on top of the apples. Trim off any excess dough (more than a 1-inch overhang) and tuck the crust's edge under so that it hugs the edge of the fruit and the inside lip of the pan. This edge doesn't need to be crimped. Don't vent the crust or sprinkle sugar on this top crust—it will become the pie's bottom crust when it finishes baking and gets inverted.

Bake the tart for 15 minutes. Turn the oven down to 350°F and bake for 30 minutes more, until the apples are bubbly and the crust is golden brown.

Cool the tart for 5 minutes before inverting. To invert, select a platter larger than the pie. Run a sharp knife tip around the edge of the pan between it and the crust. Place the platter upside down on the top of the pie pan like a lid. Holding the two together tightly, quickly flip them over so that the pie is sitting on the platter. Remove the sauté pan, scraping any caramel out onto the tart with a spatula. Serve slices of this pie warm or reheat them for 10 minutes in a 325°F° degree oven. Store the pie in a manner that allows the pastry to breathe—either uncovered in a pie safe or covered with a light breathable cover, such as a pie screen, for up to 3 days.

Apple Pie with Black Pepper Blackberry Glaze

MAKES ONE 9-INCH SINGLE-CRUST PIE

Lustrous deep burgundy from the blackberry glaze on the surface, this intoxicating open-faced apple pie belies a creamy white interior. Its peppery fruit flavor hovers deliciously between sweet and savory, accented by ruby port and a hint of balsamic vinegar. Choose a flavorful mid-range apple—not the firmest, but sturdier than a McIntosh. We had good results with Opalescent apples; Cortlands would also work well.

Pastry for a 9-inch single-crust pie, crimped and chilled in pie tin, such as Bubby's All-Butter Pastry Pie Dough (page 23), Basic Butter and Shortening Pastry Pie Dough (page 27), Sour Cream Pastry Pie Dough (page 29), or Nut Pastry Pie Dough (page 30)

2½ pounds apples

2 tablespoons unsalted butter

3 tablespoons sugar

2 tablespoons fresh-squeezed lemon juice

1½ tablespoons all-purpose flour

1 tablespoon ruby port

½ teaspoon vanilla extract

½ teaspoon balsamic vinegar

¼ teaspoon freshly ground black pepper

¼ teaspoon salt

¼ teaspoon ground cinnamon

Pinch ground nutmeg

Pinch ground cloves

BLACKBERRY GLAZE

1 cup fresh or frozen blackberries

2 tablespoons sugar

Roll out the pastry and line a 9-inch pie tin with the bottom crust. Trim and crimp the crust; chill it.

Preheat the oven to 450°F.

Peel, core, and slice the apples about ¼ inch thick. In a large sauté pan over medium heat, melt the butter and sauté the apples for 2 or 3 minutes, until the outer edges get slightly soft. Add the sugar, lemon juice, flour, port, vanilla, vinegar, pepper, salt, cinnamon, nutmeg, and cloves and stir gently. Scrape the filling into the bottom crust.

Put the pie on a lipped baking sheet and cover the pie loosely with foil (because this pie is wide open, this step is necessary to keep the apples from drying out). Bake for 10 minutes, or until the crust looks dry, blistered, and blonde. Turn the oven down to 350°F, and bake for at least 30 minutes more, or until the apples are tender when tested with a knife and the crust edge is golden brown. If the apples are done but the crust is pale, remove the foil and bake 5 minutes more at 425°F.

Meanwhile, place the berries and sugar in a small saucepan, sprinkle a few drops of water on top to help get the berries cooking, and give the pan a shake. Put the pan over medium-low heat and cook the berries for 8 to 10 minutes, until they are juicy, breaking up the berries with a spoon. When the berries are broken down to a pulpy liquid, strain the liquid into a bowl, discarding the seeds. Return the juice to the pan and reduce over medium-high heat for about 15 minutes, until it thickly coats the back of a spoon. Cover until needed.

Cool the pie to room temperature before painting the top with the black-berry glaze or the apples will absorb too much of it. Then generously spoon it over the top of the apples and let it cool in the refrigerator for 30 minutes before serving. Store the pie in the refrigerator, lightly covered with waxed paper, for up to 4 days.

Stay me with flagons, comfort me with apples: for I am sick
with love. —SONG OF SOLOMON 2:5

An apple a day keeps the doctor away. —J. T. STINSON

GINGER-HONEY APPLE PIE

This pie is the perfect antidote to the winter cold season. It is good for what ails you. It has ginger and cayenne to calm the digestion and warm you up, and lemon and honey to soothe your throat. Combine them with the old "apple a day" adage, and you'll have the perfect cordial pie to bolster your health, or, at the very least, lift sagging spirits.

Pastry for a 9-inch double-crust pie, chilled, such as Bubby's All-Butter Pastry Pie Dough (page 23) or Basic Butter and Shortening Pastry Pie Dough (page 27)

1 cup good local honey, plus extra for drizzling over the top crust

2 tablespoons grated peeled fresh ginger

3 tablespoons unsalted butter

3 pounds tart, crisp apples (see page 104)

3 tablespoons all-purpose flour

3 tablespoons fresh-squeezed lemon juice

1 tablespoon lemon zest

1 tablespoon finely chopped candied ginger

½ teaspoon ground ginger

Pinch cayenne

Pinch salt

Roll out the pastry and line a 9-inch pie tin with the bottom crust. Roll out the remaining dough for the top crust. Rechill the pastry until the filling is ready.

Preheat the oven to 450°F.

In a small sauté pan over low heat, heat the honey and fresh ginger for 20 minutes, to infuse the honey with its the ginger flavor. Remove the pan from the heat and add the butter to melt it.

Peel, core, and slice the apples about ¼ inch thick. Measure the flour, lemon juice and zest, candied ginger, ground ginger, cayenne, and salt on top of apples. Toss the mixture to combine well. Add the honey mixture and stir gently.

Scrape the filling into the bottom crust and cover it with the second crust. Trim and crimp the crust; chill the pie for 10 minutes in the freezer. Cut vent slits in the top crust and drizzle the top lightly with honey.

Bake the pie on a lipped baking sheet for 10 minutes, or until the crust looks dry, blistered, and blonde. Turn the oven down to 375°F, and bake for at least 30 minutes more, or until the crust is golden brown and visible juices are thickened and bubble slowly through the slits in the top crust. Test the apples for doneness by poking a wooden skewer or small knife through the open slits in the top crust. They should be tender but not mushy.

Cool the pie completely (for at least 2 to 3 hours) on a cooling rack before cutting. Serve the pie at room temperature. Store the pie in a manner that allows the pastry to breathe—either uncovered in a pie safe or covered with a light breathable cover, such as a pie screen or a single layer of cheesecloth, for up to 3 days.

Honey

Varieties of honey vary considerably in color and are as specific and varied in flavor as the flowers at the bees' disposal. If you see local honey at the farmer's market, ask to taste and compare different kinds. Commercial mass-produced honey tastes pretty much the same because it contains many varieties, though it is typically mostly clover honey. For this pie, we prefer a lighter floral variety like linden or lavender honey.

> It is, in my view, the duty of an apple to be crisp and crunchable, a pear should have such a texture as leads to silent consumption. . . . The pear must be approached, as its feminine nature indicates, with discretion and reverence; it withholds its secrets from the merely hungry.
>
> —EDWARD BUNYARD,
> author of *The Anatomy of Dessert* (1929)

Pears

Pear cultivation progressed much faster than that of the apple; there were myriad varieties of cultivated pears even in classical times. Pears are not native to America; they originate from the area near Armenia and Azerbaijan and have been widely cultivated in Europe and Asia. Asian pears are round like apples, ginger colored, with an even covering of pale white freckles, and tend to be juicy, crisp in texture, and best eaten raw (not used for pies), hence the Korean proverb: "Eating pears cleans the teeth." European pears, as Bunyard observed, are buttery in texture and highly prized for desserts.

Look for flavorful, juicy, near-ripe pears for pie—Bosc, Bartlett, and Anjou are the most common. Ralph Waldo Emerson joked of the pear, "There are only ten minutes in the life of a pear when it is perfect to eat." Ripe is indeed a very narrow window for a pear, and because baking has a similar ripening effect on the pear, it's best to use near-ripe pears rather than perfectly ripe pears. Avoid using hard or crisp pears for baking—a buttery texture is preferable. If the only pears available are hard, they can be poached or encouraged to ripen more quickly in a paper bag, or expediently by roast-ripening (see page 120). Pears continue to develop flavor and sweetness after picking.

Calibrate the other filling ingredients to the pear: For sweeter pears, go light on sugar; for juicy pears, add an extra measure of thickener. Slice harder pears thinner and riper pears thicker. Because pears macerating in sugar practically spurt out their juices, wait until the very last second to mix the sugar with the pears. Too much liquid skews the balance of the filling in the direction of soupy and makes for a soggy bottom crust.

If you're going to poach some pears to make a tart, use a firm-fleshed variety like a Bosc because it holds up well. If you're making a sliced pear pie, use a sweeter, juicier, more flavorful near-ripe pear in season like a Bartlett or a Anjou. Pear pies, like pears, have "such a texture as leads to silent consumption" and are wonderful paired with ginger ice cream, caramel ice cream, or caramel sauce.

POACHED PEARS IN PORT

This method imbues the pears with port and cooks them to a velvety consistency. These pears make an excellent open-faced tart.

6 cups water	½ teaspoon ground cinnamon
2 cups red wine or port	Pinch salt
1 cup sugar	Pinch whole cloves
½ lemon or orange, juiced and set aside	1 vanilla bean, split in half lengthwise
	2 or 3 pounds pears

In a medium stockpot, combine the water, wine, sugar, lemon or orange juice, cinnamon, salt, cloves, and split vanilla bean. Bring the liquid to a low simmer for 30 minutes.

Peel the pears, but leave them whole, with their stems intact and add them to the simmering poaching liquid. If the poaching liquid doesn't cover them completely, add a little more water to the stockpot until it does. Poach them over medium-low heat for 10 minutes, covered, until they are tender when pierced through with a knife, but still slightly firm.

Cool the pears in their poaching liquid for at least 1 hour before using. They can be poached days in advance and stored in their poaching liquid in the refrigerator; this allows the flavors to develop even more.

Open-Faced Pear Pie with Red Currant Glaze

MAKES ONE 9-INCH SINGLE-CRUST PIE

Sweet, spicy, and best served warm the day it's baked. Bartlett pears are our favorite variety in this pie because their buttery texture bakes readily in an open-faced pie (whereas a Bosc would probably dry out unless it was poached beforehand).

Pastry for a 9-inch single-crust pie, crimped and chilled in pie tin, such as Bubby's All-Butter Pastry Pie Dough (page 23), Basic Butter and Shortening Pastry Pie Dough (page 27), Sour Cream Pastry Pie Dough (page 29), or Nut Pastry Pie Dough (page 30)

1 tablespoon fresh-squeezed lemon juice

2 pounds pears

¼ cup sugar

2 tablespoons all-purpose flour

2 tablespoons unsalted butter, melted

4 teaspoons cassis

¼ teaspoon ground cinnamon

Pinch ground cloves

Pinch salt

⅓ cup currant jam

Par-bake the crust (see page 15) and then turn the oven down to 350°F.

Pour the lemon juice in the bottom of a large bowl. Peel, halve, and core the pears with a melon baller, removing the stem and fiber, and slice them into the bowl, coating them with lemon as you go. In a separate bowl, mix together the sugar, flour, butter, cassis, cinnamon, cloves, and salt. Add it to the pears just before you want to bake the pie, mix gently, and then taste a pear slice. Add more sugar to taste, as needed. Scrape the filling into the bottom crust.

Put the pie on a lipped baking sheet and cover the pie loosely with foil (because this pie is wide open, this step is necessary to keep the pears from drying out). Bake for at least 30 minutes, or until the pears are tender when tested with a knife and the crust edge is golden brown.

Cool the pie for at least 1 hour. In a small pan, heat the jam until it is just melted—don't let it get too hot. Brush it generously over the pears. Serve the pie immediately or cool it completely. Store the pie uncovered at room temperature, up to 3 days.

Pear Pie with Caramel Sauce and Crème Fraîche

MAKES ONE 9-INCH DOUBLE-CRUST PIE

Rules of three! The sweet tender pears harmonize with tangy Crème Fraîche and rich Caramel Sauce. Bosc pears work well. Make the Crème Fraîche a day in advance.

Pastry for a 9-inch double-crust pie, chilled, such as Bubby's All-Butter Pastry Pie Dough (page 23) or Basic Butter and Shortening Pastry Pie Dough (page 27)

1 tablespoon fresh-squeezed lemon juice

1 teaspoon lemon zest

3 pounds pears

2 to 4 tablespoons sugar, plus extra for sprinkling on the top crust

1 tablespoon cornstarch

¼ teaspoon ground cinnamon

¼ teaspoon salt

Pinch ground cloves

2 tablespoons cold unsalted butter, cubed

1 cup Crème Fraîche (page 303)

1 recipe Caramel Sauce (page 309)

Roll out the pastry and line a 9-inch pie tin with the bottom crust. Roll out the remaining dough for the top crust. Rechill the pastry if necessary.

Preheat the oven to 450°F.

Pour the lemon juice and zest in the bottom of a large bowl. Peel, halve, and core the pears with a melon baller, removing the stem and fiber. Slice pears and place them in the bowl, coating them with lemon as you go. In a separate bowl, mix together 2 tablespoons of the sugar, the cornstarch, cinnamon, salt, and cloves. Add the sugar mixture to the pears just before you want to bake the pie, mix gently, and then taste a pear slice. Add more sugar to taste, as needed.

Scrape the filling into the bottom crust, dot the top with the butter, and cover it with the second crust. Trim and crimp the crust; chill the pie for 10 minutes in the freezer. Make vents in the top crust. We often make curved arc-shaped vents with a melon baller (our designation of pear pie at Bubby's). Sprinkle sugar lightly on top.

Bake the pie on a lipped baking sheet for 10 minutes, or until the crust looks dry, blistered, and blonde. Turn the oven down to 375°F, and bake for at least 30 minutes more, or until the crust is golden brown and visible juices are thickened and bubble slowly through the slits in the top crust.

Cool the pie completely before cutting, at least a few hours. Serve it at room temperature with Caramel Sauce and Crème Fraîche. Store the pie uncovered at room temperature, up to 3 days.

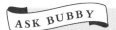

Roast-Ripened Pears

If your pears are too firm and you are in a pinch, preheat the oven to 375°F. Peel and slice the fruit in half. Scoop the seeds out with a melon baller and pull out the fibrous strands that connect to the stem. Coat the surface of the fruit in melted butter and sprinkle the entire surface of the pear lightly with sugar. Roast them on a parchment-lined baking sheet for about 15 minutes, until the fruit is tender but firm. Roast ripening concentrates the fruit flavors and softens the texture quite persuasively. If you sample some, it should taste like ripe fruit. Let the fruit cool and then continue preparing it for baking as you would a ripe, fresh piece of fruit.

CRANBERRY-PEAR CRUMBLE PIE

MAKES ONE 9-INCH SINGLE-CRUST PIE

The sweet walnut crumble is pleasing next to the creamy texture of baked pears, and the cranberries give the fruit filling a tart bite and a pink hue. This pie appears on our pie board at the restaurant come Thanksgiving time. Select pears that are ripe and smell good, but are not too soft.

Pastry for a 9-inch single-crust pie, crimped and chilled in pie tin, such as Sour Cream Pastry Pie Dough (page 29), Bubby's All-Butter Pastry Pie Dough (page 23), Basic Butter and Shortening Pastry Pie Dough (page 27), or Nut Pastry Pie Dough (page 30)

CRUMBLE
¾ cup all-purpose flour
6 tablespoons (¾ stick) cold unsalted butter, cubed
¼ cup sugar
¼ cup packed dark brown sugar
½ teaspoon ground cinnamon
½ teaspoon salt
½ cup chopped walnuts

FILLING
½ lemon, juiced
3 pounds ripe pears
1 cup fresh or frozen cranberries
¾ cup packed dark brown sugar
3 tablespoons full-fat sour cream
2 tablespoons all-purpose flour
½ teaspoon ground cinnamon
¼ teaspoon ground cloves
Pinch salt

Roll out the pastry and line a 9-inch pie tin with the bottom crust. Crimp and chill it.

Preheat the oven to 450°F.

TO MAKE THE CRUMBLE: Combine the flour, butter, sugars, cinnamon, and salt in a food processor and pulse until the mixture resembles bread crumbs. Or, if you are working the crumble by hand, cut the butter into the flour with a pastry cutter and finish by rubbing in the butter with your fingertips until it resembles bread crumbs, then stir in the sugar and other ingredients. Add the nuts and refrigerate the crumble until needed.

Pour the lemon juice in the bottom of a large bowl. Peel, halve, and core the pears with a melon baller, removing the stem and fiber, and slice them into the bowl, coating them with lemon as you go. In a separate bowl, mix together the cranberries, sugar, sour cream, flour, cinnamon, cloves, and salt. Add them to the pears just before you want to bake the pie, mix gently, and then taste a pear slice. Adjust seasoning and sugar to taste. Scrape the filling into the pie shell and sprinkle the top evenly with the crumble.

Bake the pie on a lipped baking sheet for 10 minutes, or until the crust edge looks lightly browned. Turn the oven down to 350°F, and bake for at least 30 minutes, or until the filling juices are bubbling slow and the crumble is brown.

Cool the pie on a cooling rack for at least 2 to 3 hours before serving. Serve the pie warm or at room temperature. Because this pie has sour cream in it, refrigerate it afterwards, lightly covered, for up to 3 days. Reheat the pie (see page 61) before serving.

LEMONY PEAR PIE

B right in flavor, and velvety in texture, this simple pie will lift your spirits on the winter day when you start to long for summer. Ripe Bartlett or Anjou pears are good in this pie.

Pastry for a 9-inch double-crust pie, chilled, such as Bubby's All-Butter Pastry Pie Dough (page 23) or Basic Butter and Shortening Pastry Pie Dough (page 27)

½ cup fresh-squeezed lemon juice

3 pounds pears

½ cup sugar, plus extra for sprinkling on the top crust

3 tablespoons all-purpose flour

1¼ teaspoons ground ginger

Pinch salt

Roll out the pastry and line a 9-inch pie tin with the bottom crust. Roll out the remaining dough for the top crust. Chill the pastry.

Preheat the oven to 450°F.

Pour the lemon juice in the bottom of a large bowl. Peel, halve, and core the pears with a melon baller, removing the stem and fiber, and slice them into the bowl, coating them with lemon as you go. In a separate bowl, mix together the sugar, flour, ginger, and salt. Add them to the pears just before you want to bake the pie, mix gently, and then taste a pear slice. Add more sugar to taste, as needed.

Scrape the filling into the bottom crust and cover it with the second crust. Trim and crimp the crust; chill the pie for 10 minutes in the freezer. Cut vent slits in the top crust and sprinkle it lightly with sugar.

Bake the pie on a lipped baking sheet for 10 minutes, or until the crust looks dry, blistered, and blonde. Turn the oven down to 375°F, and bake for at least 30 minutes more, or until the crust is golden brown and visible juices are thickened and bubble slowly through the slits in the top crust.

Cool the pie completely before cutting, at least a few hours. Serve it at room temperature. Store the pie uncovered at room temperature, up to 3 days.

Quince

Quince, a member of the rose family, resembles a curvaceous golden pear faintly perfumed of rose and honey. The skin is slightly waxy under a faint shadow of peach-like down. Its hard, astringent flesh is loaded with natural pectin that will thicken the juices of a pie without additional thickeners. When cooked, quince turns a lovely pink. Quince adapts well to both sweet and savory use, and is sometimes used in stews to tenderize the meat.

In Greek and Roman times, quinces were preserved in honey, hence the Roman name for quince, *melimelum,* meaning "honey apple." They figured into ancient Greek marriage ceremonies, as the quince was sacred to Aphrodite, the goddess of love. It's likely that the apples in the Song of Solomon are actually quinces. A female quince is called a quincess, and a male quince is called a quince apple.

Quinces are native to the area around the Caucasus Mountains on the border of Europe and Asia and have been cultivated around the world. Quince is sometimes found in the United States sold as *membrillo,* a Spanish garnet-colored quince paste served with Manchego cheese. The fruit shows up at the farmer's market around roughly October and can be found in stores through December. A Middle Eastern grocery is likely to carry them, since quinces are prized in the Middle East. In Australia, *quince* is slang for aggravate or annoy, as in, "You're getting on me quince!"

"An apple-pye with quinces—why quinces, when you know quinces are so dear?"

—HENRY FIELDING,
The Grub Street Opera, 1731

QUINCE-PEAR PIE

MAKES ONE 9-INCH DOUBLE-CRUST PIE

Quince marries well with a sweeter fruit like a pear, and the port picks up on both flavors harmoniously. This would be a good dessert after a hearty roast. Any variety of pear works well. This pie has no thickener because the pectin in the quince does it all.

Pastry for a 9-inch double-crust pie, chilled, such as Bubby's All-Butter Pastry Pie Dough (page 23) or Basic Butter and Shortening Pastry Pie Dough (page 27)

1 pound quinces

4 tablespoons (½ stick) unsalted butter

½ cup dried currants

2 pounds ripe pears

¾ cup sugar, plus extra for sprinkling on the top crust

¼ cup ruby port

½ teaspoon ground cinnamon

Pinch salt

Roll out the pastry and line a 9-inch pie tin with the bottom crust. Roll out the remaining dough for the top crust. Chill.

Pare, quarter, and core the quinces. Slice the quinces about ¼ to ½ inch thick. In a large sauté pan over low heat, melt the butter and sauté the quinces and currants for 5 to 10 minutes, until the quince slices are tender.

Preheat the oven to 450°F. Peel, halve, and core the pears with a melon baller, removing the stem and fiber, and slice them into a large bowl. Combine the pears with the quinces, currants, sugar, port, cinnamon, and salt and mix well. Scrape the filling into the bottom crust and cover it with the second crust. Trim and crimp the crust; chill the pie for 10 minutes in the freezer. Cut vent slits in the top crust and sprinkle it lightly with sugar.

Bake the pie on a lipped baking sheet for 10 minutes, or until the crust looks dry, blistered, and blonde. Turn the oven down to 350°F, and bake for at least 45 minutes more, or until the crust is golden brown and visible juices are thickened and bubble slowly through the slits in the top crust.

Cool the pie completely before cutting, at least a few hours. Serve it at room temperature. Store the pie uncovered at room temperature, for up to 3 days.

Sugar Pie Pumpkins

The sugar pie pumpkin is its own particular species—small, pale yellow outside and bright orange inside, fine-fleshed, and sweet. To prepare fresh pumpkin, halve the pumpkin lengthwise—stem to bottom—and remove and save the seeds, but leave the pulpy inner lining of brighter flesh they nest in—it's the sweetest part of the pumpkin. The seeds, known in Spanish as *pepitos,* can be washed, oiled, and seasoned with salt, cayenne, cumin, and a pinch of sugar and roasted in the oven at 325°F for snacks or used in a salad or soup.

A 1½-pound pumpkin yields about 2 cups of pumpkin purée; we'll typically opt for a 3-pounder to make two pies at a time, since it adds very little additional work. Chop up the pumpkin in chunks and boil it in unsalted water until tender. Drain very well. Remove the skin with a knife, discard the skin, and mash the flesh. Leftover cooked pumpkin can be stored in the refrigerator, covered, for up to a week (this is a good route if you need to stagger your pie baking for two different occasions during the holidays).

Some old bakers recommend the green-striped Cushaw for the same desirable attributes that the sugar pumpkins have. If the farmers at your market don't grow them, encourage them to try a crop the following year. Farmers are always responding to demand at the market—your request might benefit both the farmer and pie bakers the following year. Or try some in your garden. Butternut squash is also a good substitute if you want to work with fresh squash. Canned pumpkin with no extra additives is a perfectly good choice for pumpkin pie. It's easy to work with and has a nice texture.

Who does not thank for little will not thank for much.
—ESTONIAN PROVERB

Pumpkin Pie with Caramel Sauce and Candied Pecans

Pumpkin pie was also called "pumpkin pudding" in early "receipts" (an old word for recipe), even though it was made up with a bottom crust. That's because the filling is actually a custard, or pudding. Pumpkin pies can be made a day in advance at holiday times to relieve a little pressure from an overtaxed oven and cook. If you are making your pumpkin purée at home from a fresh pumpkin, it can be made up to a week in advance. This pie recipe is one of our most requested for the Thanksgiving holiday and is tried and true. The consistency is rich and dense like a cheesecake, pumpkiny, and not overly sweet. It's outstanding plain or with the toppings; the Caramel Sauce and Candied Pecans might seem like bells and whistles at first, but once you've had them with this pie, you might change your tune.

Par-baked crust for a 9-inch single-crust pie, crimped and chilled in pie tin, such as Bubby's All-Butter Pastry Pie Dough (page 23), Basic Butter and Shortening Pastry Pie Dough (page 27), Sour Cream Pastry Pie Dough (page 29), Nut Pastry Pie Dough (page 30), Graham Cracker Crust (page 36), or Gingersnap Crumb Crust (page 39)

1 tablespoon all-purpose flour

1 teaspoon ground cinnamon

1 teaspoon salt

Pinch ground nutmeg

2 cups fresh pumpkin purée or canned, unsweetened pumpkin

1⅓ cups heavy cream

3 large eggs

⅓ cup packed light brown sugar

⅓ cup sugar

1 tablespoon vanilla extract

2 tablespoons chopped candied ginger (optional)

1 recipe Caramel Sauce (page 309)

1 recipe Candied Pecans (page 314)

Preheat the oven to 325°F.

In a small bowl, combine the flour, cinnamon, salt, and nutmeg and set aside. In the bowl of an electric mixer, blend the pumpkin, cream, eggs, sugars, and vanilla until smooth. Add the dry ingredients and blend just until combined. Sprinkle the ginger in the par-baked pie shell and pour the filling on top.

Bake the pie on a lipped baking sheet for 50 to 55 minutes, or until just barely set in the center. Wiggle the pie gently to test its doneness—look for a center that jiggles but doesn't slosh. The retained heat in the custard will continue cooking the middle as the pie cools off. Don't overcook it or the texture won't be as silky. Cracks in a custard are signs of overcooking. A cracked custard is still quite edible, but not optimal.

Cool the pie completely on a cooling rack before cutting, at least a few hours, then refrigerate. Serve it cold with Caramel Sauce and Candied Pecans. Store the pie covered in the refrigerator for up to 3 days.

Pecans

Native to North America, hickory trees produce pecans, the subject of one of our favorite Thanksgiving pies. It's a wonder that the expression, "as American as apple pie" wasn't for pecan pie instead because pecans originated here. These relatives of the walnut are cultivated in the temperate southern United States and are harvested from October to December. Cracking their smooth, oblong shell reveals two sweet nutmeats encased in an intricate chamber. We make Nut Pastry Pie Dough (page 30), Nut Crumb Crusts (page 42), all manner of crumbles (page 195), and candied nuts (page 314) with them, but the following recipe is our favorite way to showcase them. Store pecans in a cool, dry, dark place, lest they go rancid.

PECAN PIE

This isn't one of those pecan pies with scarcely enough pecans to skim the surface. Nuts predominate here, bound by a flavorful combination of maple syrup and brown sugar custard with accents of orange, molasses, and rum. Since the day we opened, Bubby's has purchased Grade A golden maple syrup from our friends the Doerflers. They have a small maple farm just north of the New York/Canadian border. We have been invited every year to go up in spring to tap trees and help boil down the syrup. It's an amazing process, to see the watery sap cooking down to the thick, golden stuff we pour on pancakes. It certainly makes this pecan pie extra special.

Pastry for a 9-inch single-crust pie, crimped and chilled in pie tin, such as Bubby's All-Butter Pastry Pie Dough (page 23), Basic Butter and Shortening Pastry Pie Dough (page 27), Sour Cream Pastry Pie Dough (page 29), or Nut Pastry Pie Dough (page 30)

2 cups shelled pecan halves

1 cup packed light brown sugar

3 large eggs

½ cup maple syrup

2 tablespoons blackstrap molasses

1 tablespoon orange zest

1 tablespoon Cointreau or rum (optional)

1 teaspoon white vinegar

¼ teaspoon salt

If using a pastry dough, par-bake the crust (see page 15) until it is blonde and blistered; set aside to cool.

Turn the oven to 325°F.

Toast the pecans on a baking sheet for about 15 minutes, or until they are aromatic. Set aside to cool. Increase the oven temperature to 350°F.

In a large bowl, whisk together the sugar, eggs, syrup, molasses, zest, Cointreau or rum (if using), vinegar, and salt. Add the pecans. Stir gently. Fill the pie shell.

Bake the pie on a lipped baking sheet for 30 minutes, or until the filling is set in the center and doesn't jiggle when wiggled.

Cool the pie completely on a cooling rack before cutting, at least a few hours. Serve it at room temperature. Store the pie lightly covered in the refrigerator for up to 3 days.

MOCHA-PECAN PIE

Thanksgiving doesn't offer much in the way of desserts to appeal to the chocolate lover, so this recipe came about to scratch that itch (the recipe that follows this one will too). Imagine a moist pecan brownie with a hint of coffee (who doesn't need that after a turkey dinner?) in a light flaky pastry crust.

Par-baked crust for a 9-inch single-crust pie, such as Bubby's All-Butter Pastry Pie Dough (page 23), Basic Butter and Shortening Pastry Pie Dough (page 27), Sour Cream Pastry Pie Dough (page 29), or Nut Pastry Pie Dough (page 30)

1 cup pecan halves

¾ cup maple syrup

3 large eggs

½ cup grated bittersweet chocolate

2 tablespoons unsalted butter

2 tablespoons all-purpose flour

2 teaspoons instant espresso

Pinch salt

Parbake a 9-inch crust and then turn the oven down to 325°F.

Toast the pecans on a baking sheet for about 15 minutes, or until they are aromatic. Set aside to cool. Increase the oven temperature to 350°F.

Using an electric mixer or a whisk, blend the syrup, eggs, chocolate, butter, flour, espresso, and salt until smooth and light. Stir in the pecans by hand. Pour the mixture into the par-baked pie crust.

Bake for 30 to 40 minutes, until the filling is set but still moist—when a toothpick inserted comes out clean.

Cool the pie completely on a cooling rack before cutting, at least a few hours. Serve it at room temperature. Store the pie uncovered at room temperature, up to 3 days. (Even though this pie has eggs in it, like brownies, it can still be stored at room temperature.)

Pecan-Caramel-Chocolate Tart

MAKES ONE 10-INCH TART

Another alternative to plain pecan pie for Thanksgiving, this is a delight: a marriage of toasted pecans, burnt orange caramel, and bittersweet chocolate ganache with a hint of espresso. It's like a delicious turtle candy.

Fully blind-baked crust for a 10-inch single-crust pie, chilled, such as Short Dough for Tarts (page 32), Bubby's All-Butter Pastry Pie Dough (page 23), Basic Butter and Shortening Pastry Pie Dough (page 27), Sour Cream Pastry Pie Dough (page 29), or Nut Pastry Pie Dough (page 30)

3 cups pecan halves

GANACHE

3 tablespoons heavy cream

1 tablespoon sugar

1 teaspoon instant espresso powder

3 ounces bittersweet chocolate

1 recipe Caramel-Orange Sauce, warm (page 310)

Preheat the oven to 325°F.

Toast the pecans on a baking sheet for 10 minutes, or until aromatic. Set aside to cool.

TO MAKE THE GANACHE: In the top of a simmering double boiler over low heat, stir together the cream, sugar, and espresso powder. When evenly combined, add the chocolate and stir until melted and smooth. Turn the heat off, cover and keep warm until needed.

In a medium bowl, stir together the Caramel-Orange Sauce and pecans and fill the tart shell with the mixture. Even out the filling with a rubber spatula. Using a pastry bag with a fine tip, pipe the chocolate ganache onto the tart filling in a squiggly, random way. Allow about 20 minutes for the tart to set up before serving. This recipe works well made a day or two in advance.

Store the tart loosely covered at room temperature. It keeps for up to a week—longer than usual—because of its candy-like composition.

Sweet Potatoes and Yams

The tropical sweet potato, unrelated to the potato, is widely confused with the yam—and for good reason. Both sweet potatoes (native to the West Indies and southern United States) and yams (native to West Africa and Asia) are sweet-fleshed tubers that boast great species diversity. Both encompass varieties that vary considerably in size (there is one species of sweet potato the size of an adult man), shape (round, oblong, tapered, pointed), interior color (white, yellow, orange, purplish), and exterior texture and color (barklike, rough or smooth, pale or dark, brown or purple). We make this pie with a ginger-skinned variety with pale, starchy yellow flesh, but they are all good. The deeper the orange interior color, the more nutritious the tuber. Store sweet potatoes and yams in a cool dry place.

Viola's Sweet Potato Pie

MAKES ONE 9-INCH SINGLE-CRUST PIE

Viola Kuhn, a home cook from Gurdon, Arkansas, who makes a mean sweet potato pie, generously shared her family recipe with us. Viola is sort of like that talented relative who makes a particular pie better than everybody else but humbly professes that she does it exactly the same way. Thankfully, when we follow her recipe, ours tastes like hers.

Pastry for a 9-inch single-crust pie, crimped and chilled in pie tin, such as Bubby's All-Butter Pastry Pie Dough (page 23), Basic Butter and Shortening Pastry Pie Dough (page 27), Graham Cracker Crust (page 36), Nut Crumb Crust (page 42), Sour Cream Pastry Pie Dough (page 29), or Gingersnap Crumb Crust (page 39)

2 cups cooked mashed sweet potatoes

1 cup half-and-half

¾ cup sugar

½ cup packed light brown sugar

2 large eggs

2 tablespoons unsalted butter, melted

1 teaspoon vanilla extract

½ teaspoon salt

½ teaspoon ground cinnamon

¼ teaspoon ground nutmeg

Pinch ground cloves

If using a pastry dough, par-bake the crust (see page 15) until it is blonde and blistered; set aside to cool. For a crumb or cracker crust, do not prebake it.

Preheat the oven to 325°F.

In a large bowl, whisk together the mashed sweet potatoes with the half-and-half, sugars, eggs, butter, vanilla, salt, cinnamon, nutmeg, and cloves until relatively smooth. Pour the mixture into the pie shell.

Bake the pie on a lipped baking sheet for about 1 hour, or until just barely set in the center. Wiggle the pie gently to test its doneness—look for a center that jiggles but doesn't slosh. The retained heat in the custard will continue cooking in the middle as the pie cools off. Don't overcook it or the texture won't be as silky. Cracks in a custard are signs of overcooking. A cracked custard is quite edible, but not optimal.

Cool the pie completely on a cooling rack before cutting, at least a few hours, then refrigerate. Serve it cold. Store the pie covered in the refrigerator for up to 3 days.

COCONUT SWEET POTATO PIE

Substitute coconut milk for half and half. Use a pinch of cayenne pepper instead of cloves. Follow recipe above.

Mincemeat

In early American recipes, "mincemeat" most often refers to a rich combination of finely chopped "scraggy neck meat," cold steak, roast beef, or "corn meat" preserved with suet, dried fruit, nuts, spices, candied peel, and often brandy or cider. One crazy recipe we came across called for a cow's head split in two, soaked all night with two hog's heads, boiled tender tongue, and the *harslet* (or internal organs)—like hearts and livers. Indeed!

A mincemeat with meat is not a very hot ticket item in a restaurant these days, and the mention of it is often met with a hesitant, questioning, "Uh . . . well . . . what's in it?" response. Instead, we make an outstanding all-fruit mincemeat to use in tarts and small pies. Fashions in food do change, so if you are curious and want to try a meat mincemeat, the basic ratios *The Frugal Housewife* (1832) cookbook gives are: two pounds boiled beef, chopped fine; three quarters of a pound suet (their tip: "The suet is sweeter and better to boil half an hour or more in the liquor the beef has been boiled in; but few people do this"); one and a quarter pounds sugar; three pounds apples; two pounds currants; a gill of brandy; a quart of cider; an ounce of cinnamon; an ounce of cloves; and two nutmegs. Most recipes stress the importance of making the mincemeat mixture plenty wet. And all recommend topping off the mixture with something to preserve it, like a layer of molasses or suet or spirits.

Of meat shread into small pieces he makes a mince-meat, tidbits, jiggets. —J. A. COMENIUS, 1662

Bubby's All-Fruit Mincemeat

MAKES 10 CUPS; ENOUGH TO PUT UP, GIVE AWAY,
AND ENJOY IN MANY PIES (1 CUP MAKES 16 LITTLE 2-INCH PIES)

Irresistible, on the tart side of fruity, this outstanding meatless mince-meat ages gracefully, concentrating and improving in flavor. Use high-quality, unsulphured dried fruit from a shop that sells it loose, by the pound. Our mincemeat keeps well all winter in the refrigerator. Plan to make it at least two weeks in advance of its first use to allow time for the flavors to develop.

1 cup roughly chopped whole orange (skin and pulp minus seeds)

1 large tart apple, peeled, cored, and roughly chopped (about 1 cup)

1 cup ruby port

1 cup sugar

½ cup brandy

½ cup water

4 ounces dried apples

4 ounces dried cherries

4 ounces dried apricots

4 ounces dried peaches

2 ounces dried currants

4 tablespoons (½ stick) unsalted butter

1 ounce candied ginger

1 teaspoon ground allspice

½ teaspoon ground nutmeg

½ teaspoon ground cloves

½ teaspoon salt

Pinch cayenne

In a deep 6-quart saucepan, combine all of the ingredients. Cover the pan and set it over low heat to simmer. Cook the mixture for about 40 minutes, or until the dried fruit is nice and plump. Remove the pan from the heat and let the mixture cool completely.

Roughly chop the mincemeat in batches in a food processor so that there are still some pea-sized chunks in it. Store it, tightly covered, in the refrigerator for at least 2 weeks before using. This mincemeat keeps well refrigerated all winter and improves in flavor.

SMALL MINCE POCKET PIES WITH CLOTTED CREAM

MAKES SIXTEEN 2-INCH PIES

M ince pies are typically made up quite small on account of the potent flavors. These are small and round, about the size of a biscuit, with flavorful fruity mincemeat sandwiched between two thin layers of pastry. They are perfect for holiday parties—tangy, buttery, flaky—and meatless. The filling is best made at least two weeks in advance. They are excellent served with clotted cream from Devonshire (available at gourmet shops), mascarpone, or sweetened Crème Fraîche or whipped cream.

---

1 recipe Double-Crust Bubby's All-Butter Pastry Pie Dough (page 23), chilled

All-purpose flour, as needed

1 cup Bubby's All-Fruit Mincemeat (page 137)

2 tablespoons unsalted butter, cubed into 16 little cubes

Sugar, for sprinkling on the top crust

1 cup clotted cream (see page 304) or Crème Fraîche (page 303)

On a lightly floured work surface, roll out the dough and cut out 32 circles with a 2-inch biscuit cutter. Fill half of the circles with 1 teaspoon of mince-meat. Put a small dot of butter on top of each one. Lightly wet the edges, place another circle on top, and crimp the pies closed with a fork. Dock the top of each pie twice lightly with a fork and sprinkle it with sugar. Place the pies on a baking sheet lined with parchment. Freeze them for 10 minutes.

Preheat the oven to 450°F.

Bake the pies for about 20 minutes, or until golden brown. Serve them warm with a dollop of clotted cream or Crème Fraîche. Store them at room temperature, lightly covered, for up to 4 days. To refresh, heat briefly in a 350°F oven, until they smell good and are warm to the touch.

Raspberry-Tangerine Tart

MAKES ONE 10-INCH SINGLE-CRUST TART

Imagine fresh red raspberries painted with tangerine glaze nestled down into creamy tangerine curd inside a sweet cookie-like crust. Around Christmas time we make this gem-like tart with a homemade curd flavored with fresh tangerine juice (curd is a tart, smooth, almost pudding-like spread similar to what you might find inside a lemon jelly-roll); the raspberries aren't in season then, but they pair so beautifully with tangerines (which are) and we can't resist them. The crust, the curd, and the glaze can be made in advance. You could also substitute Lemon Curd (page 307) or another kind of berry—strawberries, blueberries, blackberries, etc.

Fully blind-baked crust for a 10-inch single-crust tart such as Short Dough For Tarts (page 32), Sour Cream Pastry Pie Dough (page 29), Graham Cracker Crust (page 36), Gingersnap Crumb Crust (page 39), Chocolate Crumb Crust (page 41)

TANGERINE CURD

1 cup fresh-squeezed tangerine juice

½ cup sugar

4 large egg yolks (about 2 fluid ounces)

4 tablespoons (½ stick) cold unsalted butter

Pinch salt

2 tablespoons tangerine zest

TANGERINE GLAZE

1 cup fresh-squeezed tangerine juice

¼ cup sugar

1 tablespoon tangerine zest

4 cups fresh raspberries

TO MAKE THE CURD: In a small nonreactive pan over low heat, reduce the tangerine juice down to about ⅓ cup. This should take 10 to 15 minutes. Set aside to cool. In another heavy non-reactive pan, beat the sugar and egg yolks with a whisk until well blended. Stir in the butter and reduced juice. Cook over medium heat, stirring constantly, until the sauce thickly coats the back of a spoon but is still liquid enough to pour. Stir in the salt and zest. Cool the curd, covered, in the refrigerator.

TO MAKE THE GLAZE: In a small non-reactive pan over low heat, slowly reduce the juice with the sugar to a glaze, stirring frequently. When ready, it should coat the back of a wooden spoon. Remove it from the heat and stir in the zest. Refrigerate until needed. Spread the cooled curd in the tart shell. Arrange the raspberries in concentric circles from the outer edge inward. Paint the berries with the cooled glaze. Refrigerate the tart for at least 30 minutes before serving.

The components can be prepared in advance, but this tart is best served the same day it is assembled. Store it in the refrigerator, lightly covered, for up to 3 days.

SAVORY PIES AND PASTRIES

During medieval times, a "huff paste" crust made of oil and water was used as a seal around meat as it cooked to preserve its juices and keep it tender. This primitive crust was tough and not really intended for consumption, though it was common for servants to gnaw on it. Similarly "trenchers," or hard pastry plates, served as a sort of edible dish. The crust improved when rendered meat fats and churned butter replaced oil in the pastry dough. Early recipes often just refer to the dough as "paste" or "rich paste." Historically, these hearty meat pies are scrappers, or dressed-up stews—delicious, filling, and good for home economics. With a meat pie, you can feed a whole table full of people by stretching out a small parcel of meat that might normally serve only two. It's also a good way to make use of leftover fish, meat, vegetables, and mashed potatoes . . . one night's leftover baked chicken and roasted vegetables can be remade into a pot pie with no love lost.

A stew is a stew. They feed it to prisoners and kings. Bubby's feeds both (or the New York equivalent) during the harsh New York City winters, when our customers take refuge from the icy winds whistling around Tribeca to duck into the restaurant and warm their bones with a steaming hot Chicken Pot Pie, or an herby potato and cheddar cheese–crusted Shepherd's Pie. Hearty savory pies embody all that is cozy and comforting about a home-cooked meal.

"Pot pie" was once a term used for either fruit or meat pies—meaning simply "cooked in a deep dish or pot"—but now refers primarily to meat pies. Pot pies typically are stews, made in a deep dish, either with or without a bottom crust

Meat cobblers and chili pies are essentially cousins of the casserole; they're deep-dish stews without a bottom crust, topped with peppery cheese scones or spicy cornbread. In a similar vein, shepherd's pies and tweed kettle pies are crustless underneath and are topped with a creamy top crust of mashed potatoes. Like the pot pies and shepherd's pies, our risotto pie or paella pie are hearty enough to be the mainstay of a dinner. Savory custard pies, quiche-like and light, are good brunch dishes when served with a salad. Pasties, empanadas, and knishes are the original fast-food meat pies, suitable travel fare, easily tucked in a pocket for lunch at sea, in the fields, or on the road.

Lard crusts work quite well with savory pies, as do crusts that employ a bit of fresh herbs or rendered fat (goose or duck) to infuse them with flavor (see page 6).

A Well-Built Chicken Stock

MAKES 5 TO 6 CUPS

Though there are countless approaches to stock making, in our conception, a well-built stock is composed of clean, peeled, quality ingredients cooked at the lowest possible simmer for several hours. We like to use chicken wings because they have lots of cartilage, which gives gelatinous body to the stock. The longer the stock will cook, the larger you cut the vegetables. We use this stock in a number of savory pies: Chicken Pot Pie (page 145), Paella Pie (page 165), and Shepherd's Pie (page 154).

5 pounds chicken wings	5 to 6 sprigs fresh thyme
2 cups chopped yellow onions	2 sprigs fresh tarragon
1½ cups chopped celery stalks (no leaves)	4 cloves garlic, peeled
	1 tablespoon pepper
4 cups chopped peeled carrots	2 bay leaves
5 sprigs fresh parsley	1 tablespoon kosher salt

Rinse the chicken wings in cold water and put them in an 8-quart stockpot.

Put the remaining ingredients in the pot in the order they are listed. This is important because as the stock cooks, this pile slowly settles down into the water. The ingredients on the top cook for a shorter time. Give the pan a little shake to settle all of the ingredients in the pot. Add cold water to the pot until it is 1 inch *below* the top surface of the vegetables.

Place the pan over low heat, uncovered, and let it attain a very subdued simmer—the slower the better. The vegetables will soon cook down below the water level. The surface will look serene with just an occasional bubble surfacing, very much like the occasional movement in a quiet pond. Do not stir or let the stock come to a boil—the slow, low simmer makes for clear stock and clean flavor. You'll have very little evaporation at such a low simmer. After the first hour or two of cooking, give the vegetables an occasional gentle prod with a wooden spoon if they are sitting up on top. Simmer the stock for 4 to 6 hours—the longer, the better.

Strain the stock through a fine-mesh sieve, pressing out all the liquid with a ladle or spoon, and discard the solids. Store the stock in a covered container in the refrigerator if using within 3 to 4 days. Otherwise, freeze it for up to 2 months. The layer of fat that forms on top of the cold stock helps preserve it, but should be pulled off before using the stock. Most of it will come off in one piece.

Save the schmaltz (chicken fat) in the freezer for another day. It's great in chopped liver.

CHICKEN POT PIE

This pie has plenty of tender shredded chicken and carrots, parsnips, potatoes, peas, and celery held in a creamy sauce made with chicken stock, buttermilk and fresh herbs, topped with a flaky, buttery layer of pastry (there's no bottom crust). You can make this pot pie with leftover chicken, pulled into strips. Don't chop or cube the chicken for this filling, or it will get a spongy texture. The stew is best made a day in advance so that it is fully chilled and the flavors have a chance to marry.

You could also use this filling to make a chicken cobbler with biscuits like the Lamb Cobbler (page 152).

Pastry for a 9-inch double-crust pie, chilled, such as Bubby's All-Butter Pastry Pie Dough (page 23), Basic Butter and Shortening Pastry Pie Dough (page 27), or Lard Pastry Pie Dough (page 28)

2 potatoes, peeled or unpeeled (your preference), ¼-inch dice

1 cup (2 sticks) plus 2 tablespoons unsalted butter, divided

2 cups onions, ⅛-inch dice

3 cups cooked chicken, shredded in 2 by ¼-inch strips and cleaned of all fat, skin, and sinew

2 large parsnips, peeled and cut into ½-inch dice

2 large carrots, peeled, and cut into ½-inch dice

1½ cups fresh shelling peas or petite frozen peas

1 cup sliced celery, ¼-inch

2 cloves garlic, minced

3 cups Chicken Stock (page xx)

1 heaping tablespoon chopped fresh thyme

1 cup all-purpose flour

½ cup buttermilk

1 tablespoon salt

1 teaspoon freshly ground black pepper

½ cup chopped fresh parsley

Put the diced potatoes in cold water so they don't turn brown as you prepare the other vegetables. Drain before using.

In a large pot over medium heat, melt 2 tablespoons of the butter and sauté the onions until they're translucent. Add the potatoes to the pot along with the chicken, parsnips, carrots, peas, celery, and garlic. Add the stock and thyme. Simmer, uncovered, for 30 minutes, until the vegetables are tender but not soft (they will cook more inside the pie in the oven).

MAKE A BLONDE ROUX: Melt the remaining 1 cup butter in a medium sauté pan over medium heat. Stir in the flour with a wooden spoon, smashing up any lumps. Continue stirring for a few more minutes, or until the roux has an even consistency and looks runny and bubbly. Remove it from the heat. (If it develops any color or scorches on the bottom, start the roux over.) Add the roux to the chicken stew mixture, stirring as you add it.

Add the buttermilk and let the whole thing simmer for 15 to 20 minutes, or until it has thickened slightly. Add the salt and pepper, taste, and adjust the seasoning as needed. Let the mixture cook for a couple minutes more, until it is a really thick stew. Remove it from the heat, add the parsley, and refrigerate, uncovered, until the stew is completely chilled, at least 2 hours, preferably overnight. (To get a light, flaky pastry top crust, the stew must be very cold when the crust is added and the pie goes in the oven.)

Roll out the pastry ⅛-inch thick to the shape of your dish. Rechill the pastry rounds, layered between parchment, until needed.

Preheat the oven to 450°F.

Line a pie plate with pastry and add the cold stew. Cover it with a pastry crust and cut vent slits. If you want a shiny finish, you can brush it with egg (see page 20).

Bake the pot pie on a lipped baking sheet for 8 to 10 minutes, or until the top crust blisters and loses its wet look. Turn the oven down to 350°F and bake for 30 to 40 minutes more, or until the filling is bubbly and the crust is golden brown. Cool for 10 to 20 minutes at room temperature before serving (the interior is quite hot). Store leftovers covered in the refrigerator for up to 2 days. Refresh in the oven before serving (see page 61).

Brandon's Steak and Guinness Pie

MAKES ONE 12-INCH DOUBLE-CRUST PIE

This recipe is from Ron's younger brother, Brandon Crismon, who made it for one of our pie socials. Use lard pastry for this pie for its slightly savory flavor and flaky texture—if you want to vary it, you could add fresh thyme or rosemary (see page 43). There's no need to use an expensive cut of steak in this English pie—a top round, chuck, or top sirloin will work well—because the meat stews so long it falls apart. The flour coating on the meat gives it a nice texture when browned and then later helps to thicken the stew. The stew is best made a day in advance so that it is fully chilled and the flavors have a chance to marry.

1 pound top round, chuck, or top sirloin, trimmed of fat and cut into 1-inch cubes	2 cups carrots, peeled and cut into ¼-inch dice
1 teaspoon salt	1½ cups diced fresh (or canned) tomato
½ teaspoon freshly ground black pepper	24 ounces Guinness or other dark stout beer
2 tablespoons all-purpose flour	1 tablespoon Worcestershire sauce
3 tablespoons vegetable oil	1 cup diced mushrooms (if using)
2 tablespoons unsalted butter	2 tablespoons chopped fresh thyme
2 cups diced yellow onions	½ cup chopped fresh parsley
2 cloves garlic, sliced	1 recipe Lard Pastry Pie Dough (page 28) for a 12-inch double-crust pie, chilled
3½ cups Idaho potatoes, peeled and cut into ¼-inch dice	

Season the meat with the salt and pepper and toss it in the flour to coat it. In a large, deep skillet, heat the oil over high heat until it is very hot, near smoking. Carefully add the meat and brown it on all sides. After it is crispy and nicely browned and seared, remove the meat from the pan to cool on a plate. Do not clean out the pan.

Turn the heat down to medium-high and add the butter. When it is melted, add the onions and garlic and sauté until they are translucent. Add the potatoes, carrots, and tomatoes. Stir until the mixture is simmering. Add the beer, thyme, Worcestershire, and mushrooms (if using) and turn the heat down to medium-low. Stir occasionally, simmering for 1 hour, until it reaches a thick stew consistency.

Remove the stew from the heat and season it with salt and pepper to taste. Add the parsley. Refrigerate the stew until it is fully cooled.

Roll out the pastry in rounds about ⅛ inch thick to fit a 12-inch round ceramic pie plate or a rectangular 3-quart dish. Line the dish with the bottom crust, and chill. Roll out the top crust, cut vents, and chill it on a baking sheet, covered.

Preheat the oven to 450°F.

Fill the dish with the stew and top it with the pastry crust. Roll and crimp the edge as you would for a double crust (see page 16).

Bake the pie on a lipped baking sheet for 8 to 10 minutes, or until the top crust blisters and loses its wet look. Turn the oven down to 350°F and bake for 30 to 40 minutes more, or until the filling is bubbly and the crust is golden brown. Cool for 20 minutes at room temperature before serving (the interior will be quite hot). Store leftovers covered in the refrigerator for up to 5 days. Refresh in the oven before serving (see page 61).

Todd's Beef Chuck Chili Pie

MAKES ONE 9 X 13-INCH OR 12-INCH PIE

This exquisitely flavored adobo chili features big chunks of stew meat. It's topped with a thin layer of our favorite cornbread and Cheddar cheese crust. Make this stew one day in advance to allow it to cool down and give its smoky, spicy flavors time to develop. This chili pie is amenable to both summer picnics (it's a bit heavy to carry, though!) and cold winter nights. Our friend Todd Griffin brought this delicious pie to one of our first pie socials and he was generous with his recipe. Serve it hot or at room temperature. Dried ancho chiles and canned chipotles are found in the ethnic food section of most supermarkets.

FILLING

¼ cup cumin seeds

10 dried chipotle chiles

6 dried ancho chiles

1 large head garlic

1 tablespoon salt

4 to 6 tablespoons water

8 tablespoons vegetable oil, divided

3 pounds beef chuck stew meat

1 tablespoon all-purpose flour

1 large onion, chopped

2 tablespoons cornstarch

2½ cups water

¼ cup fresh-squeezed lime juice

1 cup chopped fresh cilantro

CORNBREAD BATTER FOR CRUST

1½ cups plus 1 tablespoon cake flour or all-purpose flour

¾ cup plus 2½ tablespoons cornmeal

⅔ cup sugar

5 teaspoons baking powder

½ teaspoon salt

1⅓ cups milk (or 1 cup sour cream and ½ cup milk)

5 tablespoons unsalted butter, melted

1 large egg

1 cup sharp Cheddar cheese, grated

Lime wedges, for garnish

Chopped fresh cilantro, for garnish

Sour cream, for garnish

Preheat the oven to 350°F.

Put the cumin seeds in a skillet. Toast them on the stovetop over medium heat or in the preheated oven for about 15 minutes, until they smell toasted. Put the dried chipotles and anchos on a baking sheet and toast them in the oven for 10 to 12 minutes, or until they smell aromatic.

Meanwhile, peel the garlic cloves and finely chop the garlic. Add the salt to it and mash them together with a fork or by dragging the blade of a knife over the mixture until it is a smooth paste. Transfer it to a bowl and stir in 2 tablespoons of the oil.

Finely grind the toasted cumin with a spice mill or mortar and pestle. Remove the seeds and stems from the dried, toasted chiles and dispose of them (if you want a spicier pie, save some seeds and add them in the next step). Put the chiles in the bowl of a food processor and pulse until they are ground fairly small. Transfer them to a spice mill and grind them down to a powder. Transfer the chiles to a medium bowl and add enough water to make a thick paste—about 4 to 6 tablespoons.

Heat 4 tablespoons of the oil in a large, heavy saucepan over high heat. Put the meat in a large bowl and toss it with the flour. When the oil begins to smoke a bit, carefully add the meat and stir to coat it with oil. Brown it on all sides, then transfer it to a platter. Don't clean the pan.

Add the remaining 2 tablespoons of oil to the pan and then add the onions. Stir them occasionally over medium heat until they are translucent and beginning to brown a little. Add the garlic mixture and let it sizzle a little, then add about 2 tablespoons of water to the pan to deglaze it. Scrape up the *fond* (sticky meat bits) from the bottom of the pan to incorporate them in the sauce. Add the chile paste mixture and the cumin and stir. Put the beef back in the pan and add 2½ cups of water.

Simmer the meat for several hours, until it is tender and really falling apart. At this point, add the cornstarch and stir until it thickens the sauce. Transfer the stew to a container and refrigerate it overnight.

The next day, add the lime juice and cilantro to the cold stew and transfer it to a big baking pan, such as a 9 x 13-inch pan or a very large skillet.

Preheat the oven to 350°F.

TO MAKE THE CORNBREAD CRUST: Sift the flour, cornmeal, sugar, baking powder, and salt together. In a medium bowl, stir together the milk, butter, and egg until smooth. Mix the wet into the dry ingredients until just combined, then spoon the mixture onto the chili. It need not cover the surface uniformly. Sprinkle the cheese on top.

Bake the pie on a lipped baking sheet for 55 to 70 minutes, or until the cornbread is golden brown and the stew is thick and bubbly. Serve the pie hot or at room temperature with cheese, fresh limes, sour cream, and cilantro for garnish. Store it covered in the refrigerator for up to 5 days.

To reheat, place in 325°F oven for 12–15 minutes; until hot.

LAMB COBBLER

This pot pie has savory cheese scones cobbled on top of a lamb stew made rich with red wine and fresh herbs. It's a tasty spring dish while it's still chilly out. Use lamb shoulder meat because it has more fat and sinew to hold it together in the stew. Ask your butcher to cut it into large stew-sized chunks. The filling can be made the same day it is used because it doesn't need to cool before the scones are added; in fact, it should be hot. Alternatively, this filling could be made up as a shepherd's pie with mashed potatoes or as a pot pie with an Herbed Pastry Crust made with rosemary (page 43).

FILLING

2 pounds lamb shoulder meat, cut into 1½- to 2-inch chunks

1 tablespoon salt

1 teaspoon freshly ground black pepper

⅔ cup all-purpose flour, divided

8 tablespoons unsalted butter (1 stick), divided

1 tablespoon canola oil

3 cups chopped onions

2 cloves garlic, roughly sliced

2 to 3 tablespoons fresh thyme

1 tablespoon finely chopped fresh rosemary

1 cup full-bodied red wine

3 cups Chicken Stock (page 143)

1½ cups diced carrots

1½ cups diced parsnips

1 cup diced potatoes

½ cup sliced celery or fresh fennel bulb

¼ cup chopped fresh parsley

SAVORY CHEESE SCONES

3 cups all-purpose flour

1½ tablespoons baking powder

1½ tablespoons sugar

¼ teaspoon salt

¼ teaspoon cayenne (or ½ teaspoon black pepper)

½ cup grated sharp white Cheddar cheese

1½ cups heavy cream, plus extra for brushing on scones

Season the lamb with the salt and pepper and then toss it in ⅓ cup of the flour. In a large sauté pan, heat 4 tablespoons of the butter and the oil over medium-high heat. When it's hot and bubbly, carefully add the lamb. Stir and turn it occasionally, until it is really browned on all sides. Remove it from the pan to a platter to cool. Don't clean the pan.

Add the onions and garlic to the pan over medium heat. Sauté them until golden brown, stirring occasionally. Add the thyme and rosemary. To deglaze, turn the heat up to medium-high, pour in the wine, and scrape up the browned bits on the bottom of the pan. When the juices are thickened, transfer the pan contents to a heavy soup pot.

Add the stock, carrots, parsnips, potatoes, celery, and lamb to the pot. Simmer on low heat, uncovered, for about 1½ hours, until the liquid reduces by about one third.

MAKE A BLONDE ROUX: Melt the remaining 4 tablespoons butter in a small sauté pan over medium-high heat. Stir in the remaining flour with a wooden spoon, smashing up any lumps. Continue stirring for a few minutes, or until the roux has an even consistency and looks runny and bubbly. Remove it from the heat. (If the roux develops any color or scorches, start over.)

Add the roux to the lamb stew mixture, stirring as you add it. Simmer another 20 minutes. It should develop a thick, stew-like consistency. Taste and adjust the seasonings and remove the pot from the heat. Add the parsley. You can make the dish up to this point 24 hours in advance—it improves in flavor. Or you can make it for dinner the same day. If you are using stew that has been refrigerated, reheat it over medium heat to piping hot before topping with scones, or they will be soggy and dumpling-like on the bottom.

Preheat the oven to 375°F.

TO MAKE THE SCONE TOPPING: Sift together the flour, baking powder, sugar, salt, and cayenne, then stir in the cheese and add the cream. Stir until the ingredients are just combined.

Pour the hot stew into a 9 x 13-inch baking pan or 3-quart baking dish and top it with 2-tablespoon chunks of scone dough. Brush the top of the dough with extra cream. Bake the cobbler on a lipped baking sheet for 30 to 45 minutes, or until the biscuits are golden and the stew is bubbling.

Serve immediately. Store covered in the refrigerator for up to 5 days. Reheat in a moderate (325°F) oven for 12–15 minutes before serving.

Shepherd's Pie with Mashed Potato and Cheddar Crust

MAKES ONE 12-INCH PIE

A shepherd's pie is typically a ground meat stew—lamb or beef—topped with mashed potatoes, but we use chunks of lamb and chicken instead. In this recipe, chicken lightens up the gaminess of the lamb, but it's a flexible recipe, and meats, stocks, and vegetables can be substituted in and out according to your taste. Make the stew a day in advance so the flavors can marry.

STEW

3 tablespoons bacon fat, or vegetable oil, or unsalted butter

1 pound lamb shoulder stew meat, cut into 1½- to 2-inch chunks

1 pound boneless chicken breast, cut into 1½-inch chunks

1 teaspoon salt, plus extra to taste

Freshly ground black pepper

¼ cup all-purpose flour

2 cups diced yellow onions

1 tablespoon chopped garlic

½ cup full-bodied red wine

2 cups Chicken Stock (page 143)

2 cups finely diced carrots

1 cup frozen or fresh peas

1 cup finely sliced celery

1 cup diced fresh tomatoes

2 tablespoons fresh thyme

1 tablespoon minced fresh rosemary

½ cup heavy cream

MASHED POTATOES

2 pounds Idaho potatoes

¼ cup milk or buttermilk

3 tablespoons unsalted butter

2 cups grated sharp white Cheddar cheese

Heat the bacon fat in a large skillet over high heat. Season the lamb and chicken with the salt and pepper and toss it in the flour. When the oil is very hot, near smoking, carefully add the meat to the pan to sear it. Sauté, stirring, until the meat is crisp and browned. Add the onions and garlic and sauté until translucent. Add the wine to the skillet and scrape up the browned bits sticking to the bottom of the pan. Pour in the stock and add the carrots, peas, celery, tomatoes, thyme, and rosemary. Simmer, uncovered, for 45 minutes, stirring occasionally, then stir in the cream. Simmer for about 30 minutes more, until the sauce bubbles and gets blurpy.

Refrigerate the stew overnight in a covered dish to let the flavors marry.

Cover the potatoes with cold water in a large pot, lightly salt the water, and bring it to a rolling boil. Maintain the rolling boil until the potatoes are tender. Peel and mash the potatoes with the buttermilk and butter. Season with salt and pepper to taste.

Preheat the oven to 450°F.

Pour the stew into a 12-inch cast-iron skillet or ceramic pie plate. Cover it with the mashed potatoes and sprinkle the potatoes with the cheese. Bake the pie on a lipped baking sheet for 25 minutes, or until the filling is bubbly and the potatoes are browned.

Serve the pie hot. Store covered in the refrigerator for up to 5 days. Reheat, uncovered, in a moderate (325°F) oven for 12–15 minutes before serving.

SALMON TWEED KETTLE PIE

MAKES ONE 8-INCH PIE

A "tweed kettle" pie is a comforting and simple English dish of mashed potatoes on top of tender flaked salmon with a white sauce and baby peas. This is a good recipe for using up leftover poached or baked salmon, but you can also start from scratch.

MASHED POTATOES
1½ to 2 pounds Idaho potatoes
Salt
¼ cup milk
4 tablespoons cream cheese
3 tablespoons unsalted butter
¼ cup minced fresh chives or scallions

BÉCHAMEL SAUCE
6 tablespoons unsalted butter, divided
4 tablespoons all-purpose flour
1½ cups milk
Pinch salt
Pinch ground nutmeg

Pinch ground cloves
½ cup diced onion
1 cup fresh or frozen petite peas
2 tablespoons finely chopped fresh parsley

POACHED SALMON
1 teaspoon white vinegar
Salt
4 ounces fresh or cooked boneless salmon fillet

TOPPING
½ cup grated sharp white Cheddar cheese
Fresh chives, sliced in ½-inch sticks

Cover the potatoes with cold water in a large pot, lightly salt the water, and bring it to a rolling boil. Maintain the rolling boil until the potatoes are tender. Peel and mash the potatoes with the milk, cream cheese, and butter. Add the chives and season with salt to taste.

TO MAKE THE BÉCHAMEL: Heat 4 tablespoons of the butter in a heavy pan over low heat, add the flour, and stir to make a soft paste. Pour in the milk in a steady stream, whisking as you pour. Slowly bring the sauce to a simmer and cook for another 7 to 8 minutes, or until the sauce has thickened, whisking the entire time. Remove the sauce from the heat and add the salt, nutmeg, and cloves.

In a medium sauté pan, sauté the onions in the remaining 2 tablespoons of butter until soft and translucent. Add the onions and peas to the béchamel sauce. If you are using leftover salmon, flake and add it.

TO POACH SALMON: Heat 2 inches of water in a deep sauté pan and add a little salt and the vinegar. Bring the water to a simmer and add the salmon to the pan, skin side down. Simmer it for 6 to 8 minutes, or until it flakes but remains supple and dark pink inside. Drain, cool, and flake the salmon. Add it to the béchamel sauce with the parsley.

Preheat the oven to 450°F.

Fill an 8-inch ceramic or glass casserole with the salmon mixture. Top it evenly with the mashed potatoes. Scatter the cheese and chives over the mashed potatoes.

Bake the pie on a lipped baking sheet for 25 minutes, until the cheese is lightly browned.

Serve hot. Store covered in the refrigerator for up to 3 days. Reheat in the oven before serving.

Duck Confit Pie with Glazed Figs and Blackberry Glaze

MAKES ONE 12-INCH SINGLE-CRUST PIE

This pie originated as a "pie social" dish that Ron baked for the first annual Bubby's Brooklyn Bridge Park Pie Social in 2004. It was presented to friends in the spirit of offering something special. This pie takes a couple of days to make, disappears quickly, and lingers in memory for a long, long time.

DUCK CONFIT

6 duck legs

4 tablespoons kosher salt

2 tablespoons coarsely ground black pepper

4 shallots, peeled

4 dried figs

3 cloves garlic, peeled

2 sprigs fresh thyme

2 sprigs fresh rosemary

2 sprigs fresh tarragon

1 cinnamon stick

¼ teaspoon ground cloves

Pinch ground nutmeg

5 or 6 fennel seeds

½ cup ruby port

Pastry for a 12-inch single-crust pie, chilled, such as Lard Pastry Pie

Dough (page 28), Bubby's All-Butter Pastry Pie Dough (page 23), Basic Butter and Shortening Pastry Pie Dough (page 27), or duck fat variation (page 6)

GLAZED FIGS

10 fresh dark purple figs

2 tablespoons unsalted butter, plus extra as needed

Superfine sugar

GLAZE

1 cup blackberries, fresh or frozen

¼ cup sugar

Pinch salt

1 teaspoon ruby port

¼ teaspoon cornstarch

1 dozen fresh blackberries, to decorate the pie

Season the duck legs with the salt and pepper. Arrange them in the bottom of a heavy 6-quart saucepan with the shallots, figs, garlic, thyme, rosemary, tarragon, cinnamon, cloves, nutmeg, and fennel on top. Add the port. Cover the saucepan and place over very low heat to cook for about 5 hours. All the fat should be rendered and the duck very tender, falling off the bone.

Place a colander over a large bowl and pour the contents of the pot into the colander. With tongs, carefully remove the duck legs to a plate. Cover them with plastic and refrigerate overnight. Remove the shallots, garlic, and figs to a small covered container and refrigerate overnight. Pour the remaining liquid and fat from the saucepan into a container and refrigerate it overnight as well. Discard any leftover solid spices.

The next day, purée the figs, shallots, and garlic in a food processor. Set them aside. Remove the duck meat from the legs, discarding the skin and bones. Keep the meat in large pieces if possible. Remove the solid layer of duck fat from the top of the cooking liquid and set it aside. Pour the liquid into a medium saucepan with the fig/shallot purée. Simmer over medium heat until it is quite thick. Strain the hot liquid through a fine-mesh strainer and return it to the pan with the duck meat. Simmer over low heat for about 45 minutes, or until it is very thick, like a ragout. Taste and adjust the seasoning with salt and pepper if needed. Allow the mixture to cool down.

Roll out the pastry and line a 12-inch pie plate with the bottom crust. Rechill the pastry if necessary. Fully blind-bake the crust (see page 15) until it is golden brown; set aside to cool.

Preheat the oven to 450°F.

TO MAKE THE GLAZED FIGS: Cut the figs in half lengthwise. In a small saucepan, melt the butter. Toss the figs in the butter and then place them in a bowl of the superfine sugar. Toss the figs in the sugar until well coated. Bake the figs face up on a buttered baking sheet for 12 to 14 minutes, or until they are well caramelized. Watch them carefully so that they do not burn. Remove the figs from the oven and let them cool on a lightly buttered plate (so they don't stick to it).

TO MAKE THE GLAZE: In a small saucepan over medium heat, combine the blackberries, sugar, and salt. When the berries break down to mostly juice, strain the seeds out and return the strained juice back to the pan. Let it reduce over medium heat until it becomes a thick glaze. Stir together the port and cornstarch and then add them to the juice. Simmer for about 20 minutes more, until the juice coats the back of a spoon; set it aside to cool.

Spoon the duck confit mixture into the crust. Place the glazed figs around the perimeter of the pie. Place the whole blackberries, points up, in the center of the pie in a circle. Brush the figs and blackberries with the glaze.

Serve immediately. Store covered in the refrigerator for up to 6 days. Serve leftovers at room temperature or heat at 325°F for 12–15 minutes.

APPLE-ROQUEFORT-BACON PIE

MAKES ONE 12-INCH DOUBLE-CRUST PIE

This is another one of Ron's pie social recipes. The Roquefort makes the apples creamy and buttery; the bacon gives it a smoky edge. Tart, crisp apples (see page 104) and fresh thyme offset the richness of the cheese and bacon. A strong, dark honey, such as evergreen or buckwheat, would be good, but any kind will do.

Pastry for a 12-inch double-crust pie, chilled, such as Lard Pastry Pie Dough (page 28), Bubby's All-Butter Pastry Pie Dough (page 23), Basic Butter and Shortening Pastry Pie Dough (page 27), or bacon fat variation (page 6)

4 ounces thick-cut hickory-smoked bacon, diced

4 to 4½ cups (2 to 2¼ pounds) apples

2 tablespoons honey, plus extra for drizzling on the top crust

2 tablespoons all-purpose flour

2 teaspoons fresh-squeezed lemon juice

1 teaspoon fresh thyme

¼ teaspoon salt

¼ teaspoon freshly ground black pepper

2 ounces Roquefort cheese

Roll out the pastry and line a 12-inch pie plate with the bottom crust. Roll out the remaining dough for the top crust. Rechill the pastry until needed.

Preheat the oven to 450°F.

In a big skillet over medium heat, sauté the bacon until it's crispy. Drain the bacon on a paper towel and leave about 3 tablespoons worth of the fat in the pan. Peel, core, and slice the apples ¼ inch thick. In the same skillet, sauté the apples in the bacon fat over low heat for a few minutes, until the outer layer of apple softens a bit. Add the honey, flour, lemon juice, thyme, salt, and pepper and stir. Add back the bacon.

Scrape the filling into the bottom crust. Crumble the Roquefort on top and cover it with the second crust. Trim and crimp the crust; chill the pie for 10 minutes in the freezer. Cut vent slits in the top crust and drizzle the top with honey.

Bake for 15 minutes, until the crust is blistered and blonde. Turn the oven down to 350°F, and bake for at least 30 minutes more, or until the crust is golden brown and visible juices are thickened and bubble slowly through slits in the top crust. Be patient; it could take 1 hour more. Test apples for doneness by poking a wooden skewer down through the open vent slits of the top crust. Apples inside should yield to the skewer with slight resistance—cooked through but not mushy.

Cool the pie completely before cutting, at least a few hours.

Serve it warm or at room temperature. Store covered in the refrigerator for up to 5 days. Reheat the pie in a 325°F oven (12–15 minutes) before serving.

Spring Vegetable Risotto Pie

MAKES ONE 12-INCH PIE

This delicious risotto pie is light on the rice and ample on the vegetables and herbs, rendering a very green, flavorful pie. The rice binds the pie together and lends a creamy texture to it. Spring garlic is typically plentiful at farmer's markets; if you can't find it, you can substitute regular garlic. Fennel is the prominent flavor in the risotto. This recipe is easily adapted—vegetables, scallops, or shrimp can be substituted. As a rule of thumb, figure 5½ cups of cut-up vegetables or filling to 1 cup of dry rice. Sauté wet vegetables to extract water; cook very hard vegetables with the risotto; and add the delicate ones in at the end. Good substitutions for the fennel might include sautéed mushrooms or roasted eggplant. If you are using another risotto recipe, keep in mind that the ratios in ours lean well in favor of the vegetables. A standard risotto recipe—one heavier in rice—will be too heavy for this pie.

2 cups grated zucchini	1 cup fresh or frozen shelled peas
1 tablespoon salt	1 cup Arborio rice
1 bunch of asparagus	1½ cups sliced scallions
1½ cups diced baby or regular fennel	1 cup grated Parmesan
3½ to 4 cups Chicken Stock (page 143)	1 teaspoon salt
4 tablespoons (½ stick) unsalted butter	1 teaspoon freshly ground black pepper
2 cloves spring garlic, sliced very thinly	1 recipe Bread Crumb Crust for 12-inch single-crust pie (page 43), reserve 1 cup for topping

Salt the zucchini to draw out the liquid and set it in a colander with a bowl underneath to catch the liquid it releases. Drain it for 1 hour. Put the zucchini in a layer of cheesecloth and squeeze out any remaining liquid (most of the saltiness will go the way of the liquid). The zucchini should make 1 tightly packed cup.

Blanch the asparagus in rapidly boiling salted water. Remove it when the water returns to a boil and shock it in cold water. Blot dry. Cut the tips off the asparagus and set aside separately. Slice the stalks into ½-inch pieces. Soak the fennel in cold water to clean out any dirt. Drain.

In a medium pot, heat the stock to a simmer. Melt the butter in a 4-quart saucepan. Add the garlic and sauté it for 1 minute, until translucent. Add the fennel and peas to the pan. Sauté until the peas are bright green.

Add the rice and stir until it is coated with butter. Add a ladleful of hot stock. Stir the risotto constantly over medium-high heat. As the liquid gets absorbed, add a ladleful more broth. This little ladling and stirring dance goes on up to 25 minutes—don't do anything else, just stir and add a little, stir and add a little. Be judicious with the stock toward the end—better to add too little at a time than too much. Cook it for about 25 minutes, until the rice is tender but with an al dente tooth to it; turn the heat off. The rice should be sticky, not loose or runny. Add the zucchini, asparagus, scallions, and Parmesan and season with salt and pepper. Stir well and adjust the seasonings to taste.

Preheat the oven to 325°F.

Prepare and par-bake the crust, uncovered, for 12 to 15 minutes to develop the flavor. Add the hot risotto to the hot crust when it comes out of the oven. Fill the crust and sprinkle the reserved topping evenly over the filling. Bake on a lipped baking sheet for 8 to 10 minutes, until the top browns.

Cool the pie for 5 to 10 minutes before serving hot. You can also serve this pie at room temperature, and it can be made up to 4 hours in advance. This pie is best eaten the same day it's made.

Paella Pie

W ell, you could certainly argue the point that this is barely pie, save for the serving dish. Even so, skeptics will hush with concentrated pleasure when they taste the exquisite harmonies of shellfish, chorizo sausage, saffron rice, and manchego cheese. Leave the arguments to someone else!

This pie is best eaten the same day it is made.

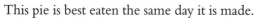

2 cups water

2 tablespoons salt

8 tiny cockles or littleneck clams

8 mussels

2 to 3 tablespoons olive oil

4 teaspoons minced garlic

1 cup diced red onion

1 cup chopped red, green, or yellow bell pepper

2½ cups chorizo sausage, cut into ½-inch slices

1½ cups diced fresh tomatoes

6 fresh jumbo shrimp

½ cup water

8 ounces boneless, skinless chicken breast, cut in strips crosswise

1½ cups Spanish rice (long-grain white rice)

½ teaspoon (about 6 to 8 strands) saffron

1½ cups Chicken Stock (page xx)

¼ cup chopped fresh parsley

1 cup grated Manchego cheese

TOPPING

4 tablespoons (½ stick) unsalted butter

2 cups Japanese bread crumbs (panko) or grated stale French bread

1 cup grated Manchego cheese

3 tablespoons chopped fresh parsley

1 teaspoon salt

½ teaspoon freshly ground black pepper

Anytime from 1 to 4 hours before cooking, make a brackish brine of 2 cups water and the salt to soak the cockles and mussels. Soaking them allows them to expel any grit inside them. Too much salt in the brine can kill the shellfish, so take care to measure. The shellfish should be kept alive until it's time to steam them or they won't open up.

Heat the oil in a large deep skillet over low heat. Add the garlic and sauté until translucent. Add the onion and peppers and sauté until tender. Add the chorizo and stir. When the sausage heats up, add the tomatoes. This mixture is called the *sofrito,* the flavor base of the paella. Stir it occasionally over low heat as you prepare the shellfish.

Drain the shellfish, and rinse well. Debeard the mussels. In a separate skillet, heat ½ cup water over medium-high heat until steaming. Add the cockles and mussels and cover. Check after 1 minute. When individual shells just begin to open up, pull them out of the liquid and cool in a bowl. Discard any shellfish that do not open. When all the shells are out, add the shrimp to the pan. Cook them a minute, until just pink. Remove to the plate of shellfish and cool. Reserve about ½ cup of the cooking liquid. Refrigerate the seafood and liquid.

Add the chicken to the sofrito and sauté it until it turns opaque. Then add the rice and stir briefly. Add the saffron and stock, stir, and then cover and simmer on low. Cook for about 20 minutes, or until rice is tender. Turn off the heat but leave the lid on.

Meanwhile, shuck the cockles and mussels and discard the shells. Peel the shrimp and devein by running a knife (about ⅛ inch deep) along the outside curve to expose the bluish-gray vein. Remove the vein and discard it. Do not rinse any of the seafood (rinsing would diminish the flavor). Refrigerate, covered, until needed.

Preheat the oven to 425°F.

Combine the ¼ cup of the parsley and 1 cup of the cheese with the rice mixture. Add the seafood and its cooking liquid to the rice. Stir. Pour the filling into a large 12-inch round ceramic or glass pie plate.

PREPARE THE TOPPING: In a small sauté pan, melt the butter and add the crumbs. Sauté briefly. Add the remaining 1 cup cheese and the 3 tablespoons parsley. Season to taste with salt and pepper. Sprinkle the mixture evenly on top of the paella.

Bake the pie on a lipped baking sheet for 20 minutes, or until the topping is melted and brown. Serve immediately.

Goat Cheese Pie with Pomegranate Molasses

MAKES ONE 9-INCH PIE

This delicious goat cheese custard is complemented with a drizzle of pungently sour pomegranate molasses and a crunchy pistachio nut crust. Pomegranate molasses is available in Middle Eastern grocery stores.

---

1 recipe Nut Pastry Pie Dough made with pistachios (page 30), par-baked and cooled

1 tablespoon unsalted butter

1 clove garlic, thinly sliced

1 cup plus 2 tablespoons heavy cream, divided

2 tablespoons dried cherries

1 tablespoon dried currants

1 tablespoon pomegranate molasses, plus more for garnish

½ cup buttermilk

3 large eggs, lightly beaten

1 teaspoon salt

Pinch cayenne

11 ounces soft goat cheese (chèvre)

2 tablespoons chopped pistachio nuts

Preheat oven to 350°F.

In a sauté pan over medium-low heat, melt the butter. Add the garlic and sauté until it is soft. Add 2 tablespoons of the cream, the dried fruit, and molasses. Stir well and reduce this mixture for 3 or 4 minutes, just until the bubbles get nice and big—about the size of your pinky tip. (Caution: During the reduction of the cream, the mixture can "break" or begin to separate if you reduce it too much. If this happens, add a little more cream to restore it.) Remove from the heat and pour the mixture into a large bowl.

Whisk the mixture with the remaining 1 cup of cream and the buttermilk. Add the eggs, salt, and cayenne, and whisk well. Adjust the seasoning to taste.

Place the pie shell on a lipped baking sheet. Pour in the filling. Using your fingers, pinch off and crumble big chunks of goat cheese (about 2 tablespoons in size) onto the pie. Direct them as they fall so they are distributed evenly throughout the filling. Sprinkle the pistachios on top.

Bake for about 35 minutes, or until just set. The filling should jiggle without sloshing in the center when the pie is given a little shake.

Cool on a cooling rack for at least 30 minutes before serving. Serve warm with a judicious drizzle (¼ teaspoon per slice) of pomegranate molasses. Store covered in the refrigerator for up to 4 days. Serve warm or at room temperature.

Let us go out early to the vine-gardens; let us see if the vine is in bud, if it has put out its young fruit, and the pomegranate is in flower. There I will give you my love.

—SONG OF SOLOMON 7:12

Fig and Prosciutto Pie

Whole figs, wrapped in prosciutto, resemble rosebuds as they peek out from the rosemary chèvre—a soft, tangy goat cheese—filling this pie. Any local honey and any variety of ripe fresh fig works well in this pie.

Pastry for a 9-inch single-crust pie, par-baked and cooled in tin, such as Nut Pastry Pie Dough (page 30), Bubby's All-Butter Pastry Pie Dough (page 23), Basic Butter and Shortening Pastry Pie Dough (page 27), or Lard Pastry Pie Dough (page 28)

11 ounces soft goat cheese (chèvre)

¾ cup heavy cream

⅓ cup high-quality honey

1 tablespoon minced fresh rosemary

Pinch salt

Freshly ground black pepper

2 large egg yolks

2 cups (1 pint) fresh ripe figs

4 ounces prosciutto, sliced paper-thin at butcher's

With an electric mixer, blend the cheese, cream, honey, rosemary, salt, and pepper until completely smooth. Add the yolks and blend until incorporated. Pour the mixture into the pie shell and chill.

Preheat the oven to 350°F.

Rinse the figs and gently pat them dry with paper towels or soft cloth. Trim the stem ends off. Cut the prosciutto slices into strips that will wrap around the figs easily. Wrap each fig in prosciutto and arrange them in the pie, stem ends up. Continue concentrically outward until you run out of room. If you have extra figs and prosciutto, they make great appetizers—bake them on a cookie sheet below your pie or eat them just as they are.

Bake the pie on a lipped baking sheet for about 30 minutes, or until the cheese filling puffs up and the center of the pie barely jiggles when the pie is given a little shake.

Cool the pie on a cooling rack for 30 minutes to 1 hour. This pie is best served warm or at room temperature. Store covered in the refrigerator for up to 4 days. Reheat at 325°F for 12–15 minutes.

Asparagus-Cheddar Quiche

MAKES ONE 9-INCH SINGLE-CRUST PIE

T his is a light luncheon quiche to showcase the pencil-thin new spring asparagus.

Pastry for a 9-inch single-crust pie, par-baked and cooled in pie tin, such as Bubby's All-Butter Pastry Pie Dough (page 23), Basic Butter and Shortening Pastry Pie Dough (page 27), or Bread Crumb Crust (page 43)

1½ pounds asparagus, root ends snapped off

1½ tablespoons unsalted butter

1½ cups finely diced yellow onions

1 cup heavy cream

2 large eggs, lightly beaten

1 teaspoon salt

½ teaspoon freshly ground black pepper

Pinch ground nutmeg

2 cups grated sharp white Cheddar cheese, divided

Blanch the asparagus in salted boiling water until tender. Drain it and shock it in cold water to stop the cooking process. Set aside to cool and dry off.

Melt the butter in a medium skillet and sauté the onions until golden; remove from the heat. Whisk together the cream, eggs, salt, pepper, and nutmeg in a medium bowl and add the onions.

Preheat the oven to 350°F.

Line up the asparagus by the tips and cut off the tips whole. Slice the rest of the stalks into ¼-inch pieces. Put the asparagus in the bowl with the eggs and 1½ cups of the cheese. Mix well and pour into the pie shell. Arrange the tips concentrically on top and sprinkle with the remaining ½ cup cheese.

Bake on a lipped baking sheet for about 30 minutes, or until the center is set and jiggles slightly when shaken gently. Do not overbake.

Cool the quiche on a cooling rack for at least 20 minutes before cutting. Serve warm or at room temperature. Store covered in the refrigerator for up to 2 days.

WILD RAMPS AND MOREL PIE

Ramps are wild leeks—they resemble a scallion with verdant, dagger-shaped greens—and are plentiful in the late spring at our local farmer's markets. Leeks may be substituted for ramps. Fresh morel mushrooms are harvested around the same time, in late May and early June. This light custard is the perfect showcase for these rare and special flavors.

Pastry for a 9-inch single-crust pie, par-baked and cooled in pie tin, such as Bubby's All-Butter Pastry Pie Dough (page 23), Basic Butter and Shortening Pastry Pie Dough (page 27), Herbed Pastry Crust (page 43), or garlic variation (page 28)

⅔ cup (5 ounces) ramps or leeks

1 cup (4 ounces) fresh morel mushrooms

4 tablespoons (½ stick) unsalted butter

1 tablespoon fresh thyme

1 teaspoon kosher salt

¼ teaspoon freshly ground black pepper

1 cup heavy cream

2 large eggs

Preheat the oven to 350°F.

Trim from the ramps the bottom ½ inch of the white parts and roots and discard. Fill a salad spinner with water and submerge the green ramps, or soak well in a cold water bath, then remove the floating ramps from the water. Drain and repeat at least three times, until the rinse water comes out clear. Drain and spin in a salad spinner or blot dry with paper towels. Chop ramps into 1- or 2-inch pieces.

Gently rinse the morels in a colander under running water just until clean. Do not soak or submerge them. Trim off the tip of the woody stem ends of the morels and quarter the morels lengthwise.

Melt the butter in a heavy sauté pan and sauté the morels until just soft. Add the ramps and thyme—these additions make a lot of liquidy sauce—and reduce the sauce over high heat, stirring with a wooden spoon, until the sauce thinly coats the back of the spoon. Remove from the heat and cool the mixture in a large bowl. Season it with salt and pepper to taste.

Whisk together the cream and eggs and add to the bowl. Stir to combine and pour the mixture into the pie shell.

Bake the pie on a lipped baking sheet for about 40 minutes, or until the center is set and jiggles slightly when shaken gently. Be careful not to over-bake.

Cool the pie for at least 20 minutes before cutting. Serve warm or at room temperature. Store covered in the refrigerator for up to 2 days.

WILD RAMPS AND STILTON PIE

MAKES ONE 9-INCH SINGLE-CRUST PIE

Stilton, a buttery, tangy, rich English blue cheese, makes this a robustly flavored custard pie.

Pastry for a 9-inch single-crust pie, par-baked and cooled in pie tin, such as Bubby's All-Butter Pastry Pie Dough (page 23), Basic Butter and Shortening Pastry Pie Dough (page 27), Herbed Pastry Crust (page 43), or garlic variation (page 28)

4 ounces ramps or leeks

1½ tablespoons unsalted butter

2 ounces Stilton cheese, crumbled

½ teaspoon salt

Freshly ground black pepper

Pinch ground nutmeg

1 cup heavy cream

2 large eggs

Preheat the oven to 350°F.

Trim from the ramps the bottom ½ inch of the white parts and roots; discard. Fill a salad spinner with water and submerge the green ramps, or soak well in a cold water bath, then remove the floating ramps from the water. Drain and repeat at least three times, until the rinse water comes out clear. Drain and spin or blot dry. Cut the ramps into 2-inch pieces.

Melt the butter in a medium skillet over very low heat and sauté the ramps just until wilted (they will look like spinach). Put them in a medium bowl with the Stilton. Season with the salt, pepper, and nutmeg to taste.

Whisk together the cream and eggs and add to the bowl of ramps. Stir to combine and pour into the pie shell.

Bake the pie on a lipped baking sheet for 40 minutes, or until the center is set and jiggles slightly when shaken gently. Do not overbake.

Cool the pie for at least 20 minutes before cutting. Serve warm or at room temperature. Store covered in the refrigerator for up to 2 days.

Tomato-Parmesan Custard Pie

MAKES ONE 9-INCH SINGLE-CRUST PIE

This pie is so simple, and yet, if the tomatoes are outstanding—such as the best heirloom tomatoes the season has to offer—nothing can compare with its understated splendor. Use a firm, flavorful, not-too-juicy tomato. Ripe plum tomatoes will work if there are no local varieties that fit the bill.

Pastry for a 9-inch single-crust pie, crimped and chilled in pie tin, such as Bubby's All-Butter Pastry Pie Dough (page 23), Basic Butter and Shortening Pastry Pie Dough (page 27), or Sharp Cheddar Cheese Pastry Crust (page 44)

¾ cup heavy cream

¼ cup buttermilk

2 large eggs

1 cup grated Parmesan cheese, divided

1 teaspoon salt

½ teaspoon freshly ground black pepper

Pinch ground nutmeg

2 pounds tomatoes

Par-bake the crust (see page 15) until it is blonde and blistered; set aside to cool.

Preheat the oven to 350°F.

In a medium bowl, whisk together the cream, buttermilk, and eggs. Add ¾ cup of the cheese and the salt, pepper, and nutmeg. Set aside.

Slice the tomatoes into ¼-inch rounds. Save a few of the prettiest slices to decorate the top. Layer the rest in the pie shell. Pour the custard over the top, evening out the cheese distribution if necessary. Place the reserved tomato slices on top. Sprinkle with the remaining ¼ cup cheese.

Bake the pie on a lipped baking sheet for about 40 minutes, until the filling jiggles but does not slosh. Do not overcook. Cool the pie on a cooling rack for at least 20 minutes before serving warm or at room temperature. It is best served on the day it is made, but may be stored, covered, in the refrigerator for up to 2 days. Allow the pie to come to room temperature before serving.

LEEK AND ONION PIE

A simple combination, this flavorful savory pie pairs well with a robust green salad. Sharp cheddar, Gruyère, Brie, or goat cheese—many cheeses will substitute well for the Parmesan.

Pastry for a 9-inch single-crust pie, par-baked and cooled in pie tin, such as Bubby's All-Butter Pastry Pie Dough (page 23), Basic Butter and Shortening Pastry Pie Dough (page 27), or garlic variation (page 28)

1 pound of leeks

1 cup heavy cream

2 large eggs

1 teaspoon salt

½ teaspoon freshly ground black pepper

Pinch ground nutmeg

3 tablespoons unsalted butter

2 large yellow onions, halved and thinly sliced

1 cup grated Parmesan cheese, divided

Preheat the oven to 350°F.

Chop off the green part of the leeks and the roots and discard them. Remove any old outer skins. Halve the leeks lengthwise and slice them in ½-inch segments. Fill a salad spinner with cold water and submerge and rinse the leeks. Drain and repeat until the rinse water comes out clear of grit. Drain and spin dry.

In a medium bowl, whisk together the cream, eggs, salt, pepper, and nutmeg.

Melt the butter in a medium skillet over medium heat. Add the onions and sauté until translucent. Add the leeks and sauté until tender. Cool to room temperature, then add to the bowl with the eggs and combine with ¾ cup of the cheese. Mix well. Pour into the pie shell and sprinkle the top with the remaining ¼ cup of cheese.

Bake the pie on a lipped baking sheet for about 40 minutes, until the filling jiggles but does not slosh. Do not overcook. Cool the pie on a cooling rack for at least 20 minutes before serving warm or at room temperature. It is best served on the day it is made but may be stored, covered, in the refrigerator for up to 2 days.

Lobster Empanadas

These little feather-light fried pies gently hold rich, buttery lobster and subtle roasted poblano chiles in a sauce that is indescribably beautiful. This is a good way to stretch a single lobster into thirty little pies. Poblanos are deep green, spade-shaped chiles with lots of flavor and very little heat to them. They are typically stocked in the produce department near other varieties of peppers and chiles. When selecting a fresh lobster, ask for a female because you will want to use the roe sac to flavor the sauce and lend it a rosy hue. Females have a broader lower abdomen and a shorter, wider fan to their tail. (If a female is not available, a male will do, but there will be no roe sac.) The stock cooks very quickly, so all of the vegetables should be chopped finely enough for their flavors to come out in that short time. These empanadas taste excellent fried but are also good baked. Either way, they are best cooked to order, so cook only as many as you plan to serve at one time. The uncooked empanadas keep well in the freezer for weeks if properly sealed. This is a rather long and somewhat complicated recipe, but yields an extraordinary result.

LOBSTER STEAMING LIQUID
¼ cup white vinegar
1 tablespoon salt
Pinch ground cloves
Pinch ground cinnamon
6 black peppercorns
One 2½- to 3-pound female lobster

FOR POACHING THE ROE
½ cup of white wine
½ cup water

LOBSTER STOCK
1 lobster body
2 small carrots, peeled and finely diced
1 cup white wine
½ large tomato, finely diced
3 tablespoons finely diced yellow onion
1 tablespoon extra-virgin olive oil
1 clove garlic, smashed
2 sprigs fresh thyme

1 whole bay leaf

1 sprig fresh tarragon (or ½ teaspoon dried)

1 sprig fresh parsley

½ teaspoon salt

½ teaspoon fennel seeds

¼ teaspoon ground cinnamon

3 black peppercorns

Pinch ground cloves

Pinch saffron (6 or 7 strands)

LOBSTER FILLING

1 fresh poblano chile

4 tablespoons unsalted butter

½ cup minced onion

2 cloves garlic, minced

⅓ cup rough-chopped fresh tomato

¼ cup all-purpose flour

1 teaspoon salt

Cayenne, as needed

EMPANADA DOUGH

4 cups all-purpose flour

1⅓ cups lard

1¼ teaspoon salt

1 large egg

2 tablespoons of water

Cornmeal, for baking

Canola oil, for frying

TO STEAM THE LOBSTER: Place a steamer basket inside a 12-quart stockpot with 1 cup water, the vinegar, salt, cloves, cinnamon, and peppercorns. Bring to a boil and then turn down to simmer for 5 minutes, covered. Place the lobster on the steamer basket inside the pot and cover. Cook for 13 minutes, until the lobster is bright red. Remove the lobster and let it cool intact. It will not be cooked all the way at this point.

TO DISMANTLE THE LOBSTER: Pull the par-cooked lobster apart over a large, wide bowl. Catch all the juice in the bowl to use for the stock, keep the heads but discard the empty shells—they have no flavor to lend to the stock. Save all of the lobster meat in separate bowl as you go.

Separate the upper torso from the lower torso by twisting it apart.

Twist off the tail and bend it back to crack it and then pull it apart from the other direction.

Squeeze the shell surrounding the tail meat to crack the shell.

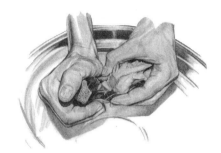

Pull it apart and extract the meat.

Break off the claws and arms where they attach to the body. Wrap the pincher claws in a soft cloth and whack them with the flat side of a cleaver to crack them open.

Extract the meat from the arms and claws. The claw meat has rigid white cartilage in it that should be separated out and discarded.

Pull the shell off of the body.

Find the soft pale green tomalley (liver) in the abdomen.

Just above it rests the roe sac. It is emerald green when raw and bright red when cooked. It may show signs of either or both colors at this point. Put the roe sac in a small dish and cover it with ½ cup of wine to keep it from drying out.

Cover and refrigerate the lobster meat that you have extracted for the filling. Take the exposed lobster torso, the pale green tomalley, the skinny legs, and the juice and transfer it to a medium-sized stockpot. Use the blunt, short end of a cleaver or a meat mallet to smash up the parts in the stock pot. (It's fine to include these last fragments of shell in the stock, since the remaining meat is difficult to extract.)

Add the carrots, wine, tomato, onion, oil, garlic, thyme, bay leaf, tarragon, parsley, salt, fennel, cinnamon, peppercorns, cloves, and saffron. The liquid will not cover the ingredients completely. Heat the stock over medium-low heat. Keep watch for bubbles near the edge and steam in the center. At the first sign of them, turn the stock down to very low and simmer it for 15 minutes more. Using a ladle, skim off any scum as it surfaces. Strain and cool.

Over very low heat in a small saucepan, cook the roe sac and the wine it has been soaking in with ½ cup water. Give it a little shake but be careful to keep the roe sac intact. Cook for about 3 minutes, or until the roe sac turns bright red all the way through and gets nice and firm. Strain the cooking liquid into the stock and dry the roe on a paper towel to get the excess liquid off of it. It will feel like a hard lump. Prior to this point, the roe must stay moist; now, the aim is to keep it dry. Take a big spoon and a dry sieve—not too fine—and line a wide soup bowl with paper towels. Break open the roe and coax the jewel-like, brilliant orange-red roe through the sieve with the back edge of a spoon, distributing it evenly as it falls to prevent it from clumping together. Add another layer of paper towels on top of the roe, wrap the bowl in plastic wrap, and refrigerate. Tap any roe bits remaining in the sieve into the stock juices.

Strain the stock through the same sieve over a saucepan. Press down on the solids in the sieve to release any extra juice. You should have about 2 cups of stock. Reduce the stock down to 1 cup over medium-high heat, to concentrate the flavor.

ROAST THE CHILE: Hold the chile with metal tongs over a gas fire, turning it as it sputters, crackles, and becomes evenly blistered and blackened. (If you don't have a gas stove, you can put it in a pan under the broiler in the oven or a toaster oven. Turn the chile a quarter turn each time its surface becomes evenly blistered and blackened.) It will smell great. Drop it into a small paper bag and seal it up to steam it for a few minutes. Peel under cold running water. Remove and discard the seeds, stems, and veins. Dice the pepper.

Melt the butter in a saucepan and add the onions and garlic. Sauté until they are translucent and then add the tomatoes. Add the flour and stir vigorously to break up the lumps, making a roux. Sauté the roux about 3 minutes, until it is pretty thick, in order to bind the filling. Whisk the stock into the roux and combine evenly. Simmer about 10 minutes over medium-low heat, stirring constantly, until the sauce is visibly thickened. Remove from the heat. Take out the lobster meat and chop it coarsely; combine it with the diced poblanos, salt, and cayenne. Add the thickened sauce to the lobster and poblanos and adjust the seasoning to taste. The filling can be made to this point and refrigerated, covered, until you are ready to assemble the empanadas.

Make the dough according to the Lard Pastry Pie Dough instructions (page 28), using the quantities in the recipe above. For this quantity of dough, the food processor method is recommended. Divide the dough into 30 golf ball–sized lumps. If you are working in a warm kitchen, chill most of the dough and take out only a few balls at a time. On a lightly floured surface, roll out each round until it is about the size of a tea saucer and about ⅟₁₆-inch thick. Stack up the rounds between parchment, and chill them, covered, for about 10 minutes.

In a small bowl, whisk together the egg and 2 tablespoons water to make an egg wash. Assemble only 3 or 4 empanadas at a time or they will dry out. Spoon 1 tablespoon of filling in the center of each round. Wet the edges with egg wash and fold the circle in half, stretching gently over the filling. Crimp to seal the edges with a lightly floured fork. Repeat with the re-

Frying

Oil improves with use, so if you have some previously used oil, add a couple of tablespoons of it to the new oil. The key to producing feather-light fried pastries is the temperature of the oil. It has to be very hot in order to work its wonders on the surface of the dough without soaking into it. Empanadas are best fried just once on each side; if you turn them multiple times, the crust gets heavy and saturated with oil. Always turn or flip food away from you when cooking with hot oil, so that if it sloshes, it sloshes away from you.

maining dough rounds and filling, then freeze the empanadas on a cookie sheet for at least 1 hour.

When the empanadas are fully frozen, they can be fried or baked. Uncooked empanadas will keep in a tightly sealed container or freezer bag in the freezer for up to 2 weeks.

TO BAKE: Heat the oven to 425°F.

Sprinkle a baking sheet with cornmeal and put the empanadas on it, with at least 1 inch of space between each one. Brush the top of each empanada with egg wash. Bake them for about 10 minutes, or until they show the first signs of browning. Then turn the oven down to 350°F and bake them for 10 to 13 minutes more, until the crust is golden brown. Serve warm.

TO FRY: Fill a large cast-iron skillet with canola oil until it is 1½ inches deep and clip a deep-frying thermometer to the side.

Monitor the heat of the oil and adjust the burner setting to keep the oil between 360° and 375°F. Wait until you hit the high end—375°F—before adding the empanadas, as they are cold and will cause the oil temperature to drop. Fry a couple of empanadas at a time, leaving a lot of space around them—don't overcrowd them. Cook them for a few minutes, until the first side is *completely* golden brown. Turn the empanadas and fry them for a few minutes more, until the second side is completely golden brown. Layer some paper towels on a plate. When the empanadas are fully fried, cool and drain them on the toweling. Hold them in a warm oven (225°F) until you have finished frying all the empanadas you intend to serve. Serve warm.

I will confess to what I know without constraint: if ye pinch me like a pasty, I can say no more.

—WILLIAM SHAKESPEARE,
All's Well That Ends Well

STEAK PASTIES

MAKES 8 PASTIES

These savory, hearty, and rich little meat pies hold tender pieces of steak and vegetables in a thick red wine sauce, baked in a half moon of flaky pastry. Pasties (pronounced *PASS-tees*) can be traced back to Cornwall, England, where they were pocketed by workers for sustenance down in the mines.

Pastry for a 9-inch double-crust pie, chilled, such as Lard Pastry Pie Dough (page 28), Bubby's All-Butter Pastry Pie Dough (page 23), or Basic Butter and Shortening Pastry Pie Dough (page 27)

FILLING

1 cup peeled, diced Idaho potatoes

⅔ cup finely diced carrots

3 tablespoons unsalted butter

¾ cup finely diced onion

1 teaspoon chopped fresh thyme

3 tablespoons all-purpose flour

1 teaspoon salt

½ teaspoon freshly ground black pepper

12 ounces beef stew meat (flank steak or top round), trimmed

1 tablespoon canola or vegetable oil

¼ cup red wine

3 tablespoons finely chopped fresh parsley

1 cup Chicken Stock (page 143) or water

1 large egg

Put the diced potatoes in a saucepan and cover them with cold water, lightly salted.

Put the diced carrots in another saucepan and cover them with cold water, lightly salted. Put both pots over high heat and cook until the vegetables are tender but still firm. (They are boiled separately because they cook at different rates.) Drain both in a colander and set aside.

Melt the butter in a medium skillet and sauté the onion until golden brown. Add the thyme and set aside, off the heat.

Combine the flour, salt, and pepper, and toss the steak in this mixture. Heat the oil in a heavy sauté pan or skillet over medium-high heat. Look for the first little wisp of smoke. The oil will smell hot. Brown the steak cubes in the oil until the outside edges are brown, and then add the wine, 1 cup of chicken stock (or water), and the onions and thyme. Simmer together briefly, then add the carrots and potatoes. Continue stirring until the liquid is as thick as gravy. Off the heat, add the parsley and adjust the seasonings to taste. Set aside to cool in a bowl.

Divide the pastry into 8 even balls. Roll out each little ball on a lightly floured surface until it is a round about 6 inches in diameter. Layer the pastry rounds between parchment and chill. Prepare an egg wash by whisking together the egg and 2 tablespoons of water.

Preheat the oven to 375°F.

To make up the pasties, lay out 2 rounds of dough at a time. Place ⅓ cup of the steak filling in the center of each round. Brush a thin layer of egg wash around the edges of the pastry and fold the pastry over the steak about ½ inch shy of the bottom edge, patting the filling down as you turn the dough over it. Fold the bottom lip of pastry up and over the top layer. Crimp to seal using a lightly floured fork. Place on a baking sheet lined with parchment and assemble the remaining pasties. Chill in the freezer 10 minutes. Dock them all with a fork a few times. Brush the top of each pasty with egg wash.

Bake them for 30 minutes, until the pastry is completely golden.

Serve warm. Refrigerate leftover pasties in foil in the refrigerator. Reheat them in a 325°F oven for 12–15 minutes before serving.

PORK PIE HATS

Ron's obsession with food has driven him to ramble all over the map, and one of those ramblings led him to the wonders of authentic barbecue. He competed twice in the whole hog division in the world championship in Memphis in May. Since Bubby's barbecue sauce is the only recipe that has been sworn to secrecy, we recommend using your favorite sauce for basting. This recipe is perfect for leftover smoky barbecued pork butt. Pulled pork should be cooked slowly over hickory or apple wood. But if you forgo cooking over a pit, it can also be tastily prepared in a very slow oven. The 6-pound pork butt is average to small. It makes a good dinner and enough for leftovers to use here. Enjoy your dinner, and save the leftovers for Pork Pie Hats.

DRY RUB

1 cup salt

1 cup packed dark brown sugar

2 tablespoons paprika

2 tablespoons ground cumin

2 tablespoons ground coriander

2 tablespoons garlic powder

2 tablespoons onion powder

1 tablespoon ground cinnamon

1 teaspoon cayenne

WASH

½ cup fresh-squeezed lemon juice

½ cup white vinegar

½ cup Worcestershire sauce

BARBECUED PORK BUTT

6 pound boneless Boston butt

4 cups tangy, good-quality, liquid-y

barbecue sauce for basting (To adjust a thicker sauce to suit, add a little white vinegar, water and spices like cumin, cayenne, cinnamon, cloves, coriander to taste.)

PORK PIE HATS

2⅔ cups pulled pork butt

⅔ cup thick barbecue sauce, such as Stubb's (or use your favorite)

1 large egg yolk mixed with 1 tablespoon of water

HOT WATER PASTRY CRUST

¾ cup plus 1 tablespoon (6 ounces) lard

½ cup water

2 cups all-purpose flour

2 teaspoons salt

TO MAKE THE RUB: In a medium bowl, mix all the ingredients together thoroughly so there are no lumps.

TO MAKE THE WASH: In a measuring cup, combine the lemon juice, vinegar, and Worcestershire. Pour it over the pork butt in a large casserole or nonreactive roasting pan. Generously coat the pork with the dry rub. Refrigerate the rubbed pork, covered, overnight.

TO SLOW COOK THE PORK: Use a grill that allows you to cook with indirect heat. A barbecue such as a Weber or a Brinkmann porch model, with a water bath between the fire and the grill, works fine. Preheat the grill with natural wood charcoal (available at gourmet and natural food stores) to a temperature of 225°F. Add wood pieces or chips such as apple, cherry, or hickory just before putting meat on the grill. If you are using an oven instead, preheat it to 225°F. Grill the pork, fat-side down, with indirect heat (or roast it in the oven in a covered pan) for about 4 hours. If you are grilling, keep the water pan between the fire and the meat filled with water. Turn the pork over, fat side up, and let it cook for another 2 hours, until it reaches 165°F on an instant-read meat thermometer. Baste with your favorite sauce every 15 minutes for another 1½ hours, until the internal temperature of the meat reaches 185°F and all the fat is rendered.

Alternatively, cook covered in foil in a 250°F oven for 4–5 hours until meat reaches 185°F.

TO MAKE THE PORK PIE HATS: Serve the pork immediately, saving leftovers for the pork pie hats. For the pork pie hat filling, let the pork cool completely, pull 2⅔ cups of it into bite-sized strips by hand, and proceed with the recipe.

Preheat the oven to 350°F.

In a medium bowl, mix together the pulled pork and sauce and set aside. If you want your pork pie hats creased like hats, make 8 foil ridges about 6 folds thick and cut them to fit the diameter of the bottom of a muffin tin.

TO MAKE THE CRUST: The dough must be moulded warm; do not make it in advance. Have the filling ready to go before you make this dough because you have to work pretty fast while the dough is still warm and pliable. Preheat the oven to 350°F. Heat the lard and water together in a saucepan until the lard is liquefied. Mix the flour and salt together in a bowl and make a well in the center. Pour the hot lard mixture into the well all at once and stir vigorously until combined. Knead the dough on a floured surface until it is soft and even.

Cut off about ⅓ of the dough. Seal it in a plastic bag and set aside in a warm place.

Divide the remaining ⅔ dough into 8 even parts and roll each out into a circle a little thicker than an ⅛ inch regular pastry crust and drape each inside a muffin tin prepared with a foil strip (see right), lifting the edges of the dough to help it settle in. There should be about ¼ inch of dough resting on the lip of the tin. Fill each pastry shell with ⅓ cup of the pork mixture.

Take the remaining dough out of the bag and divide it into 8 equal parts. Roll out each into a round a little thicker than ⅛-inch thick. Paint the tops of the dough lips resting on the tin with the egg. Center the pastry tops over each cup.

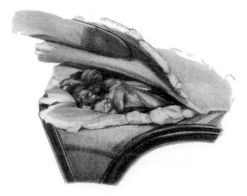

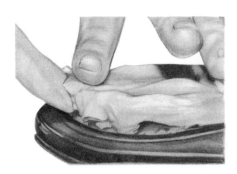 

Curl the edges under to form the rim of the hats. Press lightly to crimp. (The hats can be frozen uncooked at this stage, and baked later.)

Brush the tops with the mixture of egg yolk and water. Bake the hats for 40 minutes, or until they are light golden brown. Invert them onto a cookie sheet. Pull out the creased foil. Brush the hats with more egg and return them to the oven, brim sides down, for another 15 minutes, until golden brown.

Cool the hats for at least 20 minutes before eating. Serve warm. Store leftover hats wrapped in foil in the refrigerator. Reheat, uncovered, on a baking sheet in a 350°F oven for about 20 minutes, or until hot to the touch.

Joy's Potato Knishes

Joy Kaplan, a friend from Minneapolis, Minnesota, hooked us on these enticing little pies. The puff pastry is feather-light, and the filling of mashed potatoes with caramelized onions is heavenly. *Knish* (the *k* is pronounced) is a Yiddish word for "cake," but these tasty little appetizers are actually comforting, buttery, pastry-encased mashed potatoes. New York is famous for its knishes, especially those from the old Jewish delicatessens that line Houston on the Lower East Side. Knishes range in size—ours are bite-sized, whereas the larger versions in New York are as big as hamburger patties. Knishes take some patience to assemble, but they freeze beautifully and are wonderful baked to order. They are an addictive homemade snack or appetizer. We use frozen puff pastry because making puff pastry is fairly complicated and there's excellent frozen sheet puff pastry available. Read the ingredient list and choose a brand with very few additives, such as Pepperidge Farm. We use Dufour, a local brand in New York.

---

2 large sheets (17-ounce package) puff pastry, chilled

8 tablespoons (1 stick) unsalted butter, divided

1 large yellow onion, diced

1½ pounds boiling potatoes

1 tablespoon heavy cream

Salt

Freshly ground black pepper

All-purpose flour, as needed

Spicy mustard for dipping

Move frozen puff pastry to the refrigerator to thaw for 30 minutes while you prepare the remaining ingredients.

In a medium skillet over low heat, melt 4 tablespoons of the butter and add the onion. Slowly caramelize the onions for 30 minutes, until they are browned and soft.

Meanwhile, clean and peel the potatoes and put them in a medium pot. Cover the potatoes with cold salted water. Bring to a boil, then reduce the heat and simmer until a fork pierces the potatoes easily. Drain the potatoes in a colander and let them dry completely.

Mash the potatoes with a handheld masher or electric mixer, combining them with the remaining 4 tablespoons butter, the cream, and salt and pepper to taste. (Don't use a food mill or processor, or the starch will break and result in a gluey, unpleasant texture.) Stir the onions into the mashed potatoes. The potatoes should be stiff in consistency, and much drier than the mashed potatoes you'd make for dinner. Set them aside to cool.

Prepare a small bowl of water and a clean, dry rolling surface. Take the pastry sheets from the refrigerator 1 at a time. If the pastry warms up too much, it will get sticky and hard to work with; if this happens, pause to chill it, then resume. Use a minimum of flour on the rolling surface. Using a rolling pin, roll out the pastry into a long, narrow rectangle about 6 x 24 inches, finishing with the dough about ⅛ inch thick. Lift and turn the dough intermittently to prevent sticking.

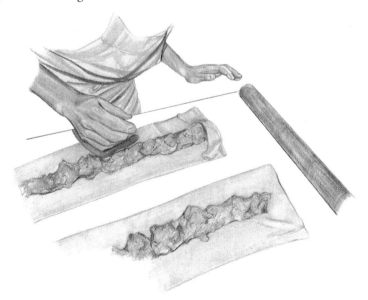

Align a long edge of the dough parallel with the edge of the counter. Spoon a long stripe of the mashed potato mixture (about ¾ to 1 inch in diameter) lengthwise along the center of the rectangle, with a wide margin on all sides. (Do not overfill, or the knishes won't seal up properly.) Curl the front edge of the dough up over the potatoes and snug up this edge of dough almost under the potatoes.

Fold in both ends of the dough and snug the folds up to the potatoes. Wet the lip of the remaining long edge with water and roll the dough-encased potatoes over it until the edge seals, and you have what looks like a very long egg roll about 1 inch in diameter.

Position your hand as if you plan to karate chop the knish log. Gently, using a slow sawing motion with the edge of your hand, divide the log into inch-wide knishes, one at a time. (You may be wondering: Why not cut it with a knife? The sawing motion with your hand simultaneously stretches the dough, moves the potato filling out of the way, and seals it.)

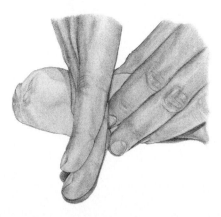

Take up each one as the knish breaks free and pinch the loose ends together if needed. Take the sealed, puckered ends of each knish and press them lightly with your thumb, "dimpling" the knish to seal it.

Place the formed knishes on a parchment-lined baking sheet in the freezer for at least 20 minutes. Clean the counter with a dough scraper and repeat the process with the next rectangle of puff pastry. The technique gets easier as you

repeat it. When the knishes are frozen through, they can be stored in a freezer bag until needed, for up to 2 weeks.

Preheat the oven to 400°F.

Bake frozen knishes on a baking sheet for 20 to 30 minutes, until golden brown.

Serve warm with spicy mustard. Store covered in the refrigerator. Reheat completely, uncovered, in a 350°F oven.

Chapter 6

DEEP-DISH DESSERTS:
CRUMBLES, CRISPS, COBBLERS,
BUCKLES, PANDOWDYS,
AND BROWN BETTYS

Humble deep-dish desserts are known for their flavor and charm; they easily avoid what Anthony Lane of the *New Yorker* calls "the fraught, perfectionist, slightly paranoid struggle that [cooking] has latterly become." They're delicious, quickly made, and unpretentious. They are, simply put, desserts of substance.

What's more, they have great names. So what is the difference between all of them, you might be wondering? Well, that might depend on whom you ask and where someone is from originally. There are regional differences between what people name the same dish, and you can easily find recipes to contradict every definition we give here. If you're lucky enough to have one in front of you, you have better things to do than argue. Our crumble might describe someone's crisp, while southern cobblers pretty much fit our description of a buckle. Even within the history of the words, it's easy to find contradicting definitions. Enjoy yourself and adopt what you like. Here are the basics.

Fruit Crumble

Crumble is an English dish made up with tart, juicy fruits like berries, rhubarb, plums, or apricots, without a bottom crust and offset by a fine, sweet, streusel-like crumb topping of flour, sugar, and butter. Little or no thickener is added to the fruits; fruit juices in a crumble should remain juicy and saucy. The crumble is spooned into a bowl; it is traditionally served with warm Vanilla Pouring Custard (a thin version of pudding; page 313) but is also wonderful with vanilla ice cream or cold heavy cream. If a crumble topping is used on an apple pie, its name is often shortened to "apple crumb pie."

CRUMBLE TOPPING

MAKES ABOUT 2 CUPS TOPPING; ENOUGH FOR ONE 9- TO 12-INCH PIE
OR 8-INCH FRUIT CRUMBLE

Crumble is fine, buttery, and sweet, like a streusel topping. British versions of crumble are often a little sweeter than American; you can adjust this one to your taste. If your filling is sweet, go light on the sugar in the topping; for a tart filling, you could bump up the sugar on top.

---

1 cup all-purpose flour

8 tablespoons (1 stick) cold unsalted butter, cubed

⅓ cup sugar

½ teaspoon ground cinnamon (optional)

Pinch salt

Pinch orange zest (optional)

Combine the flour, butter, sugar, cinnamon, salt, and zest (if using) in a food processor and pulse until the mixture resembles bread crumbs. Or, if you are working the crumble by hand, cut the butter into the flour with a pastry cutter and finish by rubbing in the butter with your fingertips until it resembles bread crumbs, then stir in the sugar and other ingredients. Refrigerate the crumble, covered, until the fruit filling is ready to top.

ALMOND CRUMBLE TOPPING

This variation on the standard Crumble Topping uses almond flour and ground ginger; the butter is minimized to compensate for the oil in the nuts. It's terrific on sour cherries, apricots, or juicy pears, and can be used to top a pie or a fruit crumble. Almond crumble browns easily, so keep oven temperatures low—around 300°F—when baking it. If you are adding it to a pie, you may need to extend the baking time (for an example, see Sour Cherry–Almond Crumble Pie on page 86). Almond flour is often available at Middle Eastern markets. Smell nut flour or nuts before you buy—the smell should be fresh, nutty, and sweet. It's very easy to grind your own almond flour in a food processor with blanched (peeled), raw, unsalted almonds—just be careful not to overprocess them, or you'll have almond butter.

2 cups almond flour (or 2½ to 3 cups whole blanched, raw, unsalted almonds)	2 tablespoons cold unsalted butter, cubed
½ cup sugar	1 teaspoon ground ginger
	¾ teaspoon salt

TO MAKE YOUR OWN ALMOND FLOUR: Pulse the nuts in a food processor or spice mill until they are a fine, fluffy flour. Tilt the machine back and forth, side to side, to disperse the nuts every few pulses. Don't switch the machine to ON (continuous) or you'll quickly wind up with almond butter. Sift out any larger pieces of nuts using a medium-mesh strainer or colander. Measure out 2 cups of almond flour.

TO MAKE THE CRUMBLE: Combine the flour, sugar, butter, ginger, and salt in a food processor and pulse until the mixture resembles bread crumbs. Or, if you are working the crumble by hand, cut the butter into the nut flour with a pastry cutter and finish by rubbing in the butter with your fingertips until it resembles bread crumbs, then stir in the sugar and other ingredients. Refrigerate the crumble, covered, until the fruit filling is ready to top.

PLUM CRUMBLE

A mixture of local plums is perfect for this dish; choose varied colors, shapes, and flavors for variety. The sweet crumble is a nice complement to the plums' texture and flavor.

2 pounds mixed plums

½ cup packed dark brown sugar

1 lemon, juiced

2 tablespoons all-purpose flour

1 teaspoon lemon zest

¼ teaspoon ground cinnamon

Pinch salt

1 recipe Crumble Topping (page 195) or Almond Crumble Topping (page 196)

Vanilla Pouring Custard (page 313), for topping (optional)

Preheat the oven to 350°F.

Clean, quarter, and pit the plums. (No need to peel them.) If they are underripe, cut them thinner. In a medium bowl, pile the sugar, lemon juice, flour, zest, cinnamon, and salt on top of the plums and mix them by tossing together just until they are combined. Pour the fruit into a 1½-quart baking dish or 9-inch ceramic or glass pie plate. Top it evenly with the Crumble Topping.

Bake the crumble on a lipped baking sheet for 1 hour, or until the fruit bubbles slowly and thickly and the Crumble Topping is golden brown.

Serve warm with Vanilla Pouring Custard or homemade ice cream. Store loosely covered at room temperature for up to 2 days. Reheat in a 350°F oven before serving.

APRICOT CRUMBLE

The delicate flavor of apricots is well-matched with this equally delicate topping.

2 pounds fresh apricots	½ teaspoon ground cinnamon
¾ cup packed light brown sugar	¼ teaspoon ground ginger
3 tablespoons unsalted butter, melted	Pinch salt
2 tablespoons all-purpose flour	1 recipe Crumble Topping (page 195) or Almond Crumble Topping (page 196)
½ lemon, juiced	
1 lemon, zested	
1 teaspoon almond extract	Vanilla Pouring Custard (page 313), for topping (optional)

Preheat the oven to 350°F.

Clean, quarter, and pit the apricots. (No need to peel them.) If they are underripe, cut them thinner. In a medium bowl, pile the sugar, butter, flour, lemon juice, zest, extract, cinnamon, ginger, and salt on top of the apricots and mix them by tossing together just until they are combined. Pour the fruit into a 1½-quart baking dish or 9-inch ceramic or glass pie plate. Top it evenly with the Crumble Topping.

Bake the crumble on a lipped baking sheet for 1 hour, until the fruit bubbles slowly and thickly and the crumb is pale gold. If the crumble browns too quickly, rest some tin foil loosely over it and turn the oven down to 300°F.

Serve warm with Vanilla Pouring Custard or homemade ice cream. Store loosely covered at room temperature for up to 3 days. Reheat in a 325°F oven before serving.

CRISP TOPPING

MAKES ABOUT 2 CUPS; ENOUGH FOR A 1½-QUART, 8-INCH,
OR 9-INCH CRISP

Fruit crisp is a hearty, more typically American rendition of the English crumble: It's a deep-dish fruit dessert with a topping of flour, nuts, oats, sugar, butter, and spices. Like it's name, it has a crisp, granola-like texture.

Sweet, mild fruits like pears and apples are complemented by this Crisp Topping of toasted oats, warm spices, and a buttery, brown sugar finish. Nuts are an optional but welcome addition.

1½ cups packed light brown sugar

¾ cup all-purpose flour

¾ cup rolled oats

½ cup chopped nuts (optional)

½ teaspoon salt

½ teaspoon ground cinnamon

⅛ teaspoon ground cloves

⅛ teaspoon ground nutmeg

12 tablespoons (1½ sticks) unsalted butter, melted

In a large bowl, combine the sugar, flour, oats, nuts (if using), salt, cinnamon, cloves, and nutmeg. Stir until evenly mixed. Add the butter and stir until the combination looks lumpy like gravel. Refrigerate the crumble, covered, until the fruit filling is ready to top.

Rhubarb Crisp

Tart, saucy rhubarb contrasted with sweet, sugary oat crisp is perfect served warm with Vanilla (page 272), Buttermilk (page 274), or Ginger Ice Cream (page 278).

3 pounds rhubarb, sliced in ½-inch pieces (6 cups)	2 tablespoons unsalted butter, melted
¾ cup sugar	1 tablespoon lemon zest
¼ cup all-purpose flour	Pinch salt
½ lemon, juiced	1 recipe Crisp Topping (page 199)

Preheat the oven to 425°F.

In a large bowl, layer the rhubarb, sugar, flour, lemon juice, butter, zest, and salt. Stir everything together just before scraping into a 1½-quart dish, 8-inch casserole, or 9-inch glass or ceramic casserole or pie plate (avoid reactive metal pans). Sprinkle the Crisp Topping over it, covering all the fruit.

Bake the crisp on a lipped baking sheet for 10 to 15 minutes, until the crisp begins to brown. Turn the oven down to 350°F and bake for about 25 minutes more, until the juice is bubbling rapidly and the crisp is nicely browned.

Serve warm. Rhubarb Crisp keeps well at room temperature, covered, for a few days. If the topping loses its crispness, refresh it in a 350°F oven for 5 to 10 minutes.

Pear-Ginger Crisp

This crisp features warm, sweet, buttery pears with a hint of cardamom, topped with rich crisp topping. Serve warm with Bubby's homemade Vanilla (page 272), Chocolate (page 286), or Ginger Ice Cream (page 278).

½ lemon, juiced	½ teaspoon ground ginger
2 pounds juicy ripe pears	½ teaspoon ground cinnamon
3 tablespoons sugar	½ teaspoon salt
2 tablespoons unsalted butter, melted	Pinch ground cardamom
2 tablespoons all-purpose flour	1 recipe Crisp Topping (page 199)

Preheat the oven to 450°F.

Pour the lemon juice in the bottom of a large bowl. Peel, halve, and core the pears with a melon baller, removing the stem and fiber, and slice them into the bowl, coating them with lemon as you go. Add the sugar, butter, flour, ginger, cinnamon, salt, and cardamom to the pears, mix gently, and then taste a pear slice. Add more sugar to taste, as needed. Pour the mixture into a 1½-quart dish, 8-inch casserole, or 9-inch glass or ceramic casserole or pie plate. Sprinkle the topping over the fruit.

Bake the crisp on a lipped baking sheet for 10 to 15 minutes, until the crisp begins to brown. Turn the oven down to 350°F and bake for about 30 minutes more, until the juice is bubbling rapidly and the crisp is nicely browned.

Serve warm. The crisp keeps well at room temperature, covered, for a few days. If the topping loses its crispness, refresh it in a 350°F oven for 5 to 10 minutes.

Autumn Apple Crisp

MAKES ONE 1½-QUART, 8-INCH, OR 9-INCH CRISP

Any autumn day—with any apple or combination—is sweetened by this dish. Serve with Vanilla (page 272), Caramel (page 282), Maple Syrup (page 293), or Ginger Ice Cream (page 278).

---

2 pounds tart, crisp apples	1 teaspoon ground cinnamon
½ cup packed light brown sugar	½ teaspoon salt
⅓ cup dried currants	Pinch ground cloves
2 tablespoons unsalted butter, melted	Pinch ground nutmeg
1 tablespoon all-purpose flour	1 recipe Crisp Topping (page 199)
½ lemon, juiced	

Preheat the oven to 450°F.

Peel, core, and slice the apples about ¼ inch thick. Mix them in a large bowl with the sugar, currants, butter, flour, lemon juice, cinnamon, salt, cloves, and nutmeg. Taste an apple slice. Add more sugar to taste, as needed. Pour the mixture into a 1½-quart dish, 8-inch casserole, or 9-inch glass or ceramic pie plate. Sprinkle the topping over the fruit.

Bake the crisp on a lipped baking sheet for 10 to 15 minutes, until the crisp begins to brown. Turn the oven down to 350°F and bake for about 30 minutes more, until the juice is bubbling rapidly and the crisp is nicely browned.

Serve warm. The crisp keeps well at room temperature, covered, for a few days. If the topping loses its crispness, refresh it in a 350°F oven for 5 to 10 minutes.

It has now been many months, at the present writing, since I have had a nourishing meal, but I shall soon have one, —a modest, private affair, all to myself. I have selected a few dishes, and made out a little bill of fare, which will go home in the steamer that precedes me, and be hot when I arrive—as follows:

Radishes. Baked apples, with cream.
Fried oysters; stewed oysters. Frogs.
American coffee, with real cream.
American butter.
Fried chicken, Southern style.
Porter-house steak.
Saratoga potatoes.
Broiled chicken, American style.
Hot biscuits, Southern style.
Hot wheat-bread, Southern style.
Hot buckwheat cakes.
American toast. Clear maple syrup.
Virginia bacon, broiled.
Blue points, on the half shell.
Cherry-stone clams.
San Francisco mussels, steamed.
Oyster soup. Clam Soup.
Philadelphia Terrapin soup.
Oysters roasted in shell—
    Northern style.
Soft-shell crabs. Connecticut shad.
Baltimore perch.
Brook trout, from Sierra Nevadas.
Lake trout, from Tahoe.
Sheephead and croakers from
    New Orleans.
Black bass from the Mississippi.

American roast beef.
Roast turkey, Thanksgiving style.
Cranberry sauce. Celery.
Roast wild turkey. Woodcock.
Canvasback-duck, from Baltimore.
Prairie hens, from Illinois.
Missouri partridges, broiled.
'Possum. Coon.
Boston bacon and beans.
Bacon and greens, Southern style.
Hominy. Boiled onions. Turnips.
Pumpkin. Squash. Asparagus.
Butter beans. Sweet potatoes.
Lettuce. Succotash. String beans.
Mashed potatoes. Catsup.
Boiled potatoes, in their skins.
New potatoes, minus the skins.
Early rose potatoes, roasted in the
    ashes, Southern style, served hot.
Sliced tomatoes, with sugar or vinegar.
    Stewed tomatoes.
Green corn, cut from the ear and served
    with butter and pepper.
Green corn, on the ear.
Hot corn-pone, with chitlings,
    Southern style.
Hot hoe-cake, Southern style.
Hot egg-bread, Southern style.
Hot light-bread, Southern style.
Buttermilk. Iced sweet milk.
Apple dumplings, with real cream.
Apple pie. Apple fritters.
Apple puffs, Southern style.
Peach cobbler, Southern style.
Peach pie. American mince pie.
Pumpkin pie. Squash pie.
All sorts of American pastry.

—MARK TWAIN, *Tramp Abroad*

Cobbler

The name for this dish probably comes from one version in which cobbles of biscuit dough are dropped onto the fruit, or it could be because it is "cobbled" together. This is one of the most widely varied regional categories of deep-dish recipes, and there are many different kinds of dishes that all bear this name. Cobblers are much easier to make in the heat of summer than pie because they are less sensitive to temperature.

We offer three that cobbler makers argue most passionately for: In the first definition, *cobbler* describes deep-dish fruit baked under rich biscuits.

A second variation, widely popular in the South, is made more like a buckle: A healthy quantity of butter is melted in the baking dish; a thin batter made with flour, sugar, baking powder, and milk and/or buttermilk follows; and then fruit is spooned onto the batter, sprinkled with brown sugar, and baked.

We prefer a third variation, like Mrs. Fisher's (see page 208), made with pastry dough.

Once Ron was chef for a catering company who catered a party at the Metropolitan Museum of Art for 800 people. It was an event for a very fancy bank, who wanted peach cobbler for dessert, (not so fancy). The morning of the party, Ron went into the bakery to taste the cobbler. Clearly, as he spat out his first bite, the baker who made the desserts mistakenly used salt instead of sugar. Dessert in the Met's Temple of Dendur that night was still warm from the oven.

Biscuit-style	Southern (batter)	Pastry-style
1½ cups all-purpose flour	1 cup all-purpose flour	Pastry pie dough, single- or double crust recipe
¼ cup sugar, plus extra for garnish	1 teaspoon baking powder	
2½ tablespoons baking powder	¼ cup sugar	
⅛ teaspoon salt	¼ cup light brown sugar	
1 cup heavy cream, plus extra for garnish	½ teaspoon salt	
	1 cup milk	
	4 tablespoons butter	
3 cups fruit	3 cups fruit	3 cups fruit

Blueberry-Nectarine Biscuit-Style Cobbler

MAKES ONE 1½-QUART DISH COBBLER

There must be as many cobbler recipes as there are shoes in the world. This one uses a bright combination of nectarines, dotted with blueberries and topped with a biscuit dough punched out in circles. The top of our biscuit cobbler looks like an old circle quilt. It's baked in two stages: First the fruit filling is baked alone until hot and juicy, then the biscuit dough is added to the hot fruit and the cobbler is returned to the oven. This ensures a light (not gummy) biscuit cobbler. The biscuits will have the flavor of the fruit on the bottom, but they won't be soggy with the juice.

FILLING
1½ pounds sliced nectarines (3 cups)
1½ cups blueberries
¾ cup packed dark brown sugar
3 tablespoons unsalted butter, melted
2 tablespoons flour
1 tablespoon fresh-squeezed lemon juice
½ teaspoon ground cinnamon
¼ teaspoon ground cloves
Pinch salt

BISCUIT DOUGH
1½ cups all-purpose flour
¼ cup sugar, plus extra for garnish
2½ teaspoons baking powder
⅛ teaspoon salt
1 cup heavy cream, plus extra for garnish

Preheat the oven to 450°F.

In a large bowl, mix together the nectarines, blueberries, sugar, butter, cornstarch, lemon juice, cinnamon, cloves, and salt. Scrape the mixture into a 3-quart sauce pan and cook it until the mixture is hot and bubbly. Meanwhile, make the biscuits.

FOR THE BISCUITS: In a medium bowl, combine the flour, sugar, baking powder, and salt and stir in the cream. Mix as little as possible, just until the ingredients are blended. Turn the dough onto a lightly floured counter and flatten it to about ½ inch thick. Use a 2-inch biscuit cutter to punch out circles. The scraps can be rerolled and cut just one time before getting over-worked. Chill the dough circles in the refrigerator until the fruit is hot and bubbly.

Take the casserole out of the oven and lay the biscuits on top so that the dough edges just barely touch each other. Brush the biscuits lightly with cream and sprinkle with sugar (the cream will turn a light caramel color and taste sweet). Bake the cobbler for 15 to 18 minutes more, until the biscuits are golden.

Serve the cobbler warm or at room temperature with homemade ice cream or fresh Whipped Cream (see page 302). Store the cobbler covered in the refrigerator for up to 3 days. Reheat in a 350°F oven before serving.

PASTRY-STYLE PEACH COBBLER

MAKES ONE 1½-QUART COBBLER

This cobbler is similar to Mrs. Abby Fisher's peach cobbler from 1881. Her book, *What Mrs. Fisher Knows About Southern Cooking,* was one of the first African-American cookbooks. Her cobbler with peaches, sugar, and cinnamon, had a pastry top and bottom. Our recipe for deep dish–cobbler has a lattice top crust and no bottom crust; fruit is predominant, with a light flaky pastry sprinkled with sugar. The better the peaches, the better the cobbler.

Pastry for a 9-inch single-crust pie, chilled, such as Bubby's All-Butter Pastry Pie Dough (page 23)	1 tablespoon fresh-squeezed lemon juice
6 cups (3 pounds)peaches	½ teaspoon ground cinnamon
¾ cup packed light brown sugar	Pinch ground cardamom
3 tablespoons unsalted butter, melted	Pinch ground cloves
2 tablespoons all-purpose flour	Pinch salt
	Sugar, for garnish

Blanch, peel (see page 97), and slice the peaches into a 1½-quart casserole. Sprinkle on the sugar, butter, flour, lemon juice, cinnamon, cardamom, cloves, and salt and toss them into the fruit gently.

Roll the pastry dough a little thicker than ⅛ inch and cut it in long ¾-inch-wide strips with a pizza cutter or a knife. Build the lattice crust on the diagonal, starting with a big X in the middle (read more about lattices on page 18). Sprinkle the pastry lightly with white sugar and freeze it for at least 10 minutes to chill the dough.

Preheat the oven to 375°F. Bake for about 1 hour, until the fruit juices are bubbly and thickened. Turn the oven up to 400°F and bake for another 10 minutes, until the lattice is browned.

Serve at room temperature, with homemade ice cream or fresh Whipped Cream (see page 302). Store the cobbler covered in the refrigerator for up to 3 days. Reheat in a 350°F oven before serving.

SOUTHERN BATTER-STYLE COBBLER

MAKES ONE 9 X 13-INCH COBBLER

S ome cobblers in the South, like this one, are made much like what we refer to as a buckle. Butter is melted in the baking pan, and a thin batter is poured on top. The fruit is spooned or dotted in and the whole thing is baked. It works well with berries and stone fruits like peaches, apricots, or plums; or with a mixture of the former and the latter.

3 cups sliced fresh peaches or nectarines, and/or berries	¼ cup packed light brown sugar
½ cup sugar, divided	1 cup all-purpose flour
1 teaspoon ground cinnamon	1 teaspoon baking powder
8 tablespoons (1 stick) unsalted butter, softened, divided	½ teaspoon salt
	1 cup milk

Grease a 9 x 13-inch baking pan with 2 tablespoons of the butter.

Preheat the oven to 350°F.

Add to the fruit ¼ cup of the white sugar and the cinnamon, mix briefly, and set it aside.

Cream the remaining 6 tablespoons butter, the remaining ¼ cup white sugar, and the brown sugar in an electric mixer until light and fluffy. In a small bowl, sift together the flour, baking powder, and salt. Add the dry ingredients and milk alternately to the butter mixture, beating to incorporate. Pour the batter into the prepared pan and scatter the fruit over the top.

Bake the cobbler for 30 minutes, until it is pale golden brown and a little crisp at the edges.

Serve the cobbler warm or at room temperature with homemade ice cream or fresh Whipped Cream (see page 302). Store covered in the refrigerator for up to 3 days. Reheat in a 350°F oven before serving.

Buckle

A buckle is a moist cake batter with fruit pressed down into it, topped with cinnamon and sugar. As it bakes, the topping buckles or crumples, engulfing the fruit in the process. You could call it a coffee cake crossed with a southern cobbler. We bake it in a skillet and call it breakfast.

Unlike pie recipes, buckle batter recipes are not very flexible. They are more like cakes—fixed, scientific, dependent on chemistry. Do not decrease the sugar in the given recipes. If you want your buckle to taste less sweet, use a little more tart fruit—not less sugar, or the whole thing loses its balance.

Buttermilk Buckle	*Chocolate Buckle*	*Ginger Buckle*
2 cups all-purpose flour	2 cups all-purpose flour	2 cups all-purpose flour
1 teaspoon baking soda	½ teaspoon baking soda	1 teaspoon baking soda
1½ cups packed light brown sugar	1 teaspoon baking powder	1 teaspoon ground cinnamon
8 tablespoons (1 stick) unsalted butter	½ cup cocoa powder	1½ teaspoons ground ginger
1 large egg	½ teaspoon salt	½ teaspoon ground nutmeg
½ teaspoon vanilla extract	1 cup packed light brown sugar	1 large egg, lightly beaten
1 cup buttermilk	10⅔ tablespoons unsalted butter, melted	½ cup vegetable oil
	2 large eggs	1 cup packed dark brown sugar
	1 teaspoon vanilla extract	½ cup molasses
	⅔ cup buttermilk	½ cup milk
		½ cup sour cream
3 cups tart fruit (berries, apples, pears, rhubarb)	2 cups berries or ripe pears	3 cups fresh freestone fruit (berries, sautéed apples, pears, rhubarb)
		1 teaspoon ground cinnamon
		¼ cup sugar
Topping	*Topping*	*Topping*
¼ cup sugar	1 cup packed light brown sugar	Optional fruit glaze (see Apricot Gingerbuckle, page 215)
1 tablespoon ground cinnamon	¼ cup all-purpose flour	
	2 teaspoons unsalted butter, melted	
	2 tablespoons shaved bittersweet chocolate	

Rhubarb Buckle

MAKES ONE 9-INCH BUCKLE

This is one of Jen's treasured family recipes from her mom. The moist, sweet, buttermilk cake is packed full of sour rhubarb and topped with a crust of cinnamon and sugar. Every bite vacillates between those three flavors in an exceedingly pleasant way. Bubby's makes it in the spring, when rhubarb is ample.

3 cups sliced rhubarb	1 cup buttermilk
2 cups all-purpose flour	1 large egg
1 teaspoon baking soda	½ teaspoon vanilla extract
1½ cups packed light brown sugar	¼ cup sugar
8 tablespoons (1 stick) unsalted butter, softened	1 tablespoon ground cinnamon

Preheat the oven to 350°F. Lightly butter a 9-inch square pan.

For a sweeter cake, cut the rhubarb sections in larger ½-inch slices; for a tart, moist cake, cut it in finer ¼-inch slices. You want about 3 cups total.

In a medium bowl, sift together the flour and baking soda and set aside. With an electric mixer, cream the brown sugar and butter until light and fluffy. Beat in the buttermilk, egg, and vanilla until smooth. Scrape down the sides. Add the flour mixture to the bowl and mix on low until smooth. Scrape down the bowl and mix briefly.

Stir in the rhubarb by hand and then pour the mixture into the pan. Smooth it all out—it will be very thick. Mix together the cinnamon and sugar and scatter all of it over the top.

Bake the buckle on a lipped baking sheet for 40 to 45 minutes, until a toothpick inserted in the center reveals a moist batter with no liquid remaining. Serve warm.

Store loosely covered at room temperature for up to 3 days.

PLUM BUCKLE

This is a wonderful buttermilk cake studded with a mix of summer plums. Use dark brown sugar for a sweet, homey effect and bake in an iron skillet: It gives the buckle an amazing texture at the edge.

2 cups all-purpose flour	1 large egg
1 teaspoon baking soda	½ teaspoon vanilla extract
1½ cups packed dark brown sugar	3 cups thickly sliced plums
8 tablespoons (1 stick) unsalted butter	¼ cup sugar
1 cup buttermilk	1 tablespoon ground cinnamon

Preheat the oven to 350°F. Lightly butter a 9-inch cast-iron skillet.

In a medium bowl, sift together flour and baking soda and set it aside. In an electric mixer, cream the brown sugar and butter until light and fluffy. Beat in the buttermilk, egg, and vanilla until smooth. Scrape down the sides. Add the flour mixture to the bowl while the beater is running. Scrape down and mix briefly, just until combined.

Pour the batter into the skillet. Smooth it out—it will be very thick. Pour the plums over the batter and lightly press them down so they are partially submerged in the batter. Mix together the cinnamon and sugar and scatter it over the top.

Bake the buckle on a lipped baking sheet for 40 to 45 minutes, until a toothpick inserted in the center reveals a moist crumb with no liquid remaining. Serve warm.

Store loosely covered at room temperature for up to 3 days.

BLACKBERRY BUCKLE

This chocolate-blackberry buckle is a coffeecake-like buckle, a delicious midsummer treat with Buttermilk Ice Cream.

¾ cup butter, melted, divided

TOPPING
1 cup packed light brown sugar
¼ cup all-purpose flour
2 tablespoons shaved bittersweet chocolate

FILLING
2 cups all-purpose flour
½ cup Dutch-processed cocoa powder

1 teaspoon baking powder
½ teaspoon baking soda
½ teaspoon salt
1 cup packed light brown sugar
⅔ cup buttermilk
2 large eggs
1 teaspoon vanilla extract
2 teaspoons butter, melted
2 cups blackberries

Preheat the oven to 375°F.

Melt ¾ cup butter in a 9-inch cast-iron skillet. Use some for the batter, some for the topping, and the rest to grease the skillet it was melted in.

MAKE THE TOPPING: In a small bowl, mix together the sugar, flour, chocolate, and 2 teaspoons of the melted butter. Set aside.

In a medium bowl, sift together the flour, cocoa, baking powder, baking soda, and salt. Combine the sugar with the buttermilk, 2 tablespoons melted butter, eggs, and vanilla and stir well. Mix the dry ingredients into the wet.

Spread the batter (it will be quite thick) into the skillet. Sprinkle the berries over the batter and press them down gently, so they're partially submerged. Sprinkle the reserved topping evenly over the top.

Bake the buckle on a lipped baking sheet for about 50 minutes, or until a toothpick inserted in the buckle comes out free of batter (berry juice is to be expected). Cool it for 30 minutes, then serve warm or at room temperature.

Store loosely covered at room temperature for up to 3 days.

Apricot Gingerbuckle

Moist, spicy gingerbread coupled with tender, flavorful apricots make this one of our favorite buckles. The hot skillet gives the edges of the buckle a wonderful texture.

Butter to grease the skillet

3 cups fresh apricots (or 2 cups dried apricots)

¼ to ½ cup sugar

1 teaspoon ground cinnamon

¼ cup brandy, for dried fruit only (optional)

1 cup packed dark brown sugar

½ cup molasses

½ cup vegetable oil

1 large egg

2 cups all-purpose flour

1½ teaspoons ground ginger

1 teaspoon baking soda

1 teaspoon ground cinnamon

½ teaspoon ground nutmeg

½ cup milk

½ cup sour cream

Fresh Whipped Cream (page 302)

Preheat the oven to 350°F. Grease a 10½-inch cast-iron skillet with butter.

If using fresh apricots, slice them in quarters, or thinner if they're very large. Toss them with ¼ cup white sugar and the cinnamon and set aside while you prepare the buckle batter.

Alternatively, poach dried apricots in a mixture of 3 cups water, ½ cup sugar, the cinnamon, and the brandy over medium heat, covered, for 20 minutes. Strain the fruit from the liquid and save both. Cool the fruit. Reduce the poaching liquid over medium heat until it coats the back of a spoon. Use the apricots in the buckle and use the syrup to drizzle over the warm buckle.

In an electric mixer, cream the brown sugar, molasses, oil, and egg on low speed until just combined. In a medium bowl, sift together the flour, ginger, baking soda, cinnamon, and nutmeg. Add them to the sugar mixture ½ cup at a time and mix just until blended. Stir together the milk and sour cream, add them to the batter, and mix just until blended.

Pour the batter into the skillet. Drop in the apricots and poke them down slightly so that they're partially submerged.

Bake the buckle on a lipped baking sheet for 1 hour, or until a toothpick inserted in the center comes out clean.

Serve warm or at room temperature with a drizzle of the poaching syrup (if available) and a dollop of fresh Whipped Cream. Store covered at room temperature for up to 3 days.

Pandowdy

Maybe the jumbled mix of crust and filling called a *pandowdy* was invented by accident when someone's pie fell from the windowsill. Wonderful things can come out of the occasional unexpected turn of events. To "dowdy" any pie, bake it fully, let it cool, and then chop it up in the dish, and bake it again. Or, take a leftover pie and do the same.

The most traditional pandowdy is typically made with apple and molasses. We top ours with a sprinkle of cinnamon and sugar. It's a really good way to take an excellent pie on the verge of staleness and turn it (just like you would stale bread in a bread pudding) into something magical and deliciously transformed. If you are making a dowdy out of a different kind of pie than the recipe here, you might want to forgo the molasses on top.

Shoo-fly Pie and Apple Pandowdy. Makes your eyes light up and your stomach say howdy!

—UNKNOWN

Molasses-Apple Pandowdy

These flavors behave like gingerbread, apple pie, and bread pudding in love with each other. The apples turn a deep molasses brown and glaze like they do in an upside-down apple pie. Serve with Vanilla Ice Cream (page 272).

Pastry for a 9-inch double-crust pie, chilled, such as Bubby's All-Butter Pastry Pie Dough (page 23) or Basic Butter and Shortening Pastry Pie Dough (page 27)

6 cups (3 pounds) tart, crisp apples

½ cup packed dark brown sugar

⅓ cup plus 3 tablespoons molasses, divided

2 tablespoons fresh-squeezed lemon juice

2 tablespoons flour

2 teaspoons ground cinnamon, divided

Pinch salt

¼ cup sugar

Vanilla Ice Cream (page 272)

Preheat the oven to 450°F.

Roll out the pastry and line a 9-inch pie tin with the bottom crust. Roll out the remaining dough for the top crust. Rechill the pastry if necessary.

Peel, core, and slice the apples. In a large bowl, combine the apples with the brown sugar, ⅓ cup of the molasses, the lemon juice, flour, 1 teaspoon of the cinnamon, and the salt.

Scrape the filling into the bottom crust and cover it with the second crust. Trim and crimp the crust; chill the pie for 10 minutes in the freezer. Cut vent slits in the top crust and sprinkle it lightly with sugar.

Bake the pie on a lipped baking sheet for 7 to 10 minutes, or until the crust is blistered and dry looking. Turn the oven down to 375°F and bake the pie until it is fully cooked, bubbly, and nicely browned. Cool it completely before dowdying.

To dowdy it, use a metal spatula to chop up the pie and overturn portions of it so that the crust mixes with the filling. Drizzle the mixture with the remaining 3 tablespoons molasses. Stir together the remaining 1 teaspoon cinnamon and the white sugar and sprinkle it over the top of the pandowdy.

Bake at 350°F for another hour.

Serve warm with Vanilla Ice Cream. Store lightly covered at room temperature for up to 3 days. Reheat in a 350°F oven before serving.

> Apple Dowdy is not a dumpling, a pudding or a pie—deep dish or otherwise, it is just a dowdy—sort of common, homely, gingham-like, but it has character. . . .
>
> —DELLA LUTES, *The Country Kitchen*

Brown Betty

A brown betty is any deep-dish fruit layered with buttery bread crumbs, spices, and brown sugar. Brown bettys may have evolved from English steamed puddings. According to *The American History Cookbook,* these economical American desserts date back to the late nineteenth century and are documented in an essay by Mrs. Mary Hinman Abel on how to feed a family on thirteen cents a day. However, there are earlier references to thickening pies with bread or cake crumbs. Different varieties of crumbs will lend different flavors to the betty. This is a flexible, economical dessert, so use what you have on hand (avoid savory breads, though).

Peachy Brown Betty

The topping for this betty is so dark and deep a brown that the color of the peach seems like a little revelation. Peel or don't peel the peaches—as you like them. If you don't peel the peaches, rub off the fuzz. You could also use an equal quantity of apples, apricots, plums, or pears in a betty.

FILLING

4 cups sliced peaches

¾ cup packed dark brown sugar

3 tablespoons unsalted butter, melted

2 tablespoons all-purpose flour

½ teaspoon ground cinnamon

Pinch ground cloves

Pinch salt

TOPPING

1½ cups dry bread crumbs

⅔ cup packed dark brown sugar

½ cup rolled oats

5 tablespoons unsalted butter, melted

1 teaspoon ground cinnamon

Pinch salt

Preheat the oven to 375°F.

In a large bowl, toss together the peaches, sugar, butter, flour, cinnamon, cloves, and salt and set the fruit aside to macerate.

In a medium bowl, stir together the bread crumbs, sugar, oats, butter, cinnamon, and salt. Sprinkle about ½ cup of the mixture in the bottom of a 1½-quart baking dish, spoon the fruit on top, and sprinkle the remaining topping over the surface.

Bake the betty on a lipped baking sheet for about 1 hour, until the juices are thick and bubbly and the fruit is tender.

Store loosely covered at room temperature up to 3 days. Serve at room temperature or reheated in a 350°F oven.

Grunts and Slumps

A grunt is a New England dish of sweetened stewed fruit with steamed doughy dumplings on top that "grunts" when cooked on the stovetop. A slump is basically the same dish baked tightly covered in the oven. In both recipes, pieces of biscuit dough are dropped on top when the fruit is hot and steamy. Some recipes call for a more batter-like mixture that is poured over the fruit. In all versions, the dough is on top and the fruit is steamed, covered. They are often served with whipped cream, and sometimes with nutmeg sauce.

Louisa May Alcott nicknamed her family home "Apple Slump," after one of her family's favorite desserts. The Alcott family home in Concord, Massachusetts—also known as the Orchard House—was surrounded by the family's apple orchards. We came across a tempting old New England recipe in a newsletter for an "apple slumper" made with apples, molasses, and small cubes of salted fatback, topped with a rich crust and then baked nice and slow. It sounds tempting because it's not really a slump, but rather a pie in slump's clothing.

Both grunts and slumps appeal in name only to us, but there's a good incentive to keep the names alive.

DUMPLINGS, FRIED PIES, AND PASTRIES

T he pastries in this chapter are all individual, self-enclosed desserts made to be eaten by one person.

Baked Dumplings

Fruit dumplings are intimate, pleasing affairs. They are tailor-made for one piece of fruit, and are intended as a single serving. Dumpling dough is wrapped around fruit to cover it completely—sometimes the pitted or cored fruit encloses an additional pocket of hidden flavors like cinnamon, raisins, candied ginger, or nuts. Baked dumplings are typically made with a hard fruit like an apple, a Bosc pear, or a quince.

Baked Apple Dumplings

Food writer M. F. K. Fisher was a big fan of naked, buttery, cream-filled, spiced, baked apples and would tuck them into any available corner of a hot oven. We surround our baked apple dumplings with a pastry crust. The result is an apple-shaped pie for one, with a little reservoir of hot cream and wonderful flavors in its hollowed-out core. It makes a very pleasing breakfast.

This is a really flexible recipe—meant to give you a suggestive, rough idea. You can use what you have on hand for the filling—a handful of blanched almonds, honey, and sweet butter; or candied grapefruit peel, a sprinkling of currants, sugar, and heavy cream. You'll just need about 2 tablespoons of filling per apple. You don't even have to mix up the filling in advance; you can just sprinkle things inside the cored apple and fill it up with cream, sour cream, or butter before wrapping the fruit in dough. Any tart, crisp, firm-fleshed apple will do (see page 104). (Choose some that sit squarely on their bases.)

If you want to prepare the dough in advance, you can; keep it wrapped and refrigerated, and make only as many dumplings as you will serve in one sitting.

Pastry for a 9-inch double-crust pie, chilled, such as Bubby's All-Butter Pastry Pie Dough (page 23) or Basic Butter and Shortening Pastry Pie Dough (page 27)

FILLING
¼ cup currants

3 tablespoons sour cream or heavy cream

2 tablespoons sugar

1 teaspoon minced candied ginger

Pinch salt

4 firm, flavorful, large apples

Preheat the oven to 450°F.

In a small bowl, stir together the currants, sour cream, sugar, ginger, and salt. Set aside.

Peel the apples. Entering from the top stem indentation, core the apple with a paring knife but don't go all the way through to the bottom. Keep the flower-end or base of the apple intact so the filling doesn't leak out. Use the smaller end of a melon baller to scrape out any remaining core parts. If you like, roll the peeled apple in cinnamon and sugar.

Divide the pastry into 4 parts. Roll out each part to a round 12 inches in diameter ⅛ inch thick, and place an apple in the center. Fill each apple's center with ¼ of the filling mixture, stopping about ½ inch shy of the top of the apple. Drape the sides of the pastry up over the top of the apple, creating folds as you go. Wet the top inside edge of the last piece with a drop of water and press gently to seal it. Make a little vent on top. Chill all of the dumplings for 10 minutes in the freezer before baking (but not longer—you want the dough to chill without freezing the apple).

Bake the apples on a parchment-lined baking sheet for 10 minutes, until the pastry is blonde and blistered. Turn down the temperature to 350°F and bake for about 45 minutes more, until the crust is golden and the apple is tender when pierced with a toothpick.

Cool the dumplings slightly before serving. Dumplings may also be served and stored at room temperature, unless they have cream inside. In that case, cover cooled dumplings loosely and store them in the refrigerator for up to 4 days.

Boiled or Steamed Fruit Dumplings

Boiled dumplings differ considerably from the baked variety: a soft, pliable, and tender potato-based dough surrounds a juicy freestone fruit such as a plum or apricot. In old recipes like the ones in *The National Cookbook* (1932), dumpling cloths or nets were tied around the dumplings to help keep the dough and fruit intact while they boiled. A piece of cheesecloth tied with butcher's twine could be used for this purpose.

BOILED PLUM DUMPLINGS

This soft, delicious dough is compatible with apricots or other stone fruits as well as plums. Don't try substituting standard pastry dough; it won't hold up to the boiling water. This recipe is adapted from *The Settlement Cookbook* (1941), a wonderful resource for dumplings of all kinds. These are an Eastern European boiled variety of dumpling, served with butter and a sprinkle of cinnamon and sugar or breadcrumbs.

---

1 pound Idaho potatoes

½ cup all-purpose flour

1 large egg

¾ teaspoon salt

Pinch ground nutmeg

8 to 12 firm blue freestone, Damson, or Italian prune plums

½ teaspoon ground cinnamon, for filling

2 tablespoons sugar, for filling

Unsalted butter, melted, for garnish

Cover the potatoes in cold, salted water and boil them in their jackets until they are tender. Peel the potatoes, then mash them while they are still warm.

Mix the mashed potatoes with the flour, egg, salt, and nutmeg and mix the dough until smooth, stirring it either by hand or in a food processor.

Fill a large stockpot with water. Salt it and bring it to a boil. Clean the plums and pit them by making a slit from stem end to flower end along the indented seam and extract the stones, leaving the plums intact. (Do not peel them.) Fill the center of each plum with a pinch of cinnamon and sugar.

At this point, make 1 or 2 dumplings from start to finish to see how they hold up before assembling a big batch. The dumplings will teach you how they hold up best when you test them. As the woman who coached us on plum dumplings at the farmer's market said, "You have to play with it."

Flour your hands and the work surface. The dough will be very soft and sticky. Take a piece of dough about the same size as a plum and pat it out about ⅛ inch thick in the palm of your hand, until it's about the size of a teacup saucer. Wrap the dough around a plum and pinch it closed. Roll the wrapped dumpling around lightly in your hands to smooth the seams.

To cook them, lower the dumplings gently into the boiling water with a slotted spoon. Don't crowd them; it's better to cook them in two or three batches. Boil the dumplings for about 10 minutes, until they float on the surface and look puffy and tender. Lift them out with a slotted spoon. Serve them with melted butter, and cinnamon and sugar. These are best eaten hot or at room temperature in one sitting. They don't make good leftovers.

The whole secret of good frying comes from the surprise; for such is called the action of the boiling liquid which chars or browns, at the very instant of immersion, the outside surface of whatever is being fried.

By means of this surprise, a kind of a glove is formed, which contains the body of food, keeps the grease from penetrating, and concentrates the inner juices, which themselves undergo an interior cooking which gives to the food all the flavor it is capable of producing.

—JEAN ANTHELME BRILLAT-SAVARIN,
The Physiology of Taste, 1825

Fried Pies

Fried pies are a delicacy in the southern United States where, if you're lucky, you can chance upon some homemade on the counter of an old-fashioned general store. Fried pies are often made with reconstituted dried fruit because its moisture content is discreet and manageable inside the pie. Typical fillings include peach, apple, cherry, and sweet potato, and they are all delicious.

Fried pies are best made with Basic Butter and Shortening Pastry Pie Dough (page 27) and then frozen raw so that they hold up well when they hit the hot oil. We recommnd canola oil because it has a high smoking point and a mild flavor. Reuse oil for frying three or four times, strain and refrigerate it up to two weeks. Used oil fries better than new oil (see page 181 for more detail). The key to producing feather-light fried pastries is the temperature of the oil. It has to be very hot in order to work its wonders on the surface of the dough without soaking into it. Wait until you hit 375°F before adding the frozen pies, as they are cold and will cause the oil temperature to drop. Monitor the heat of the oil with a clip-on deep-frying thermometer and adjust the burner setting to keep the oil between 360° and 375°F at all times during the frying process.

Always turn frying food away from yourself so that if the oil splashes, it splashes away from you. Take precautions when you are working with hot oil, as burns from it are severe and painful. Keep baking soda nearby—water will not put out an oil fire; the smallest drop of water in the oil will cause it to splatter and pop madly.

Fried Cherry Pies

This filling has the pungent, concentrated flavors of dried cherries (they are soft and hot in the filling) and warm spices (a hint of clove), with a buttery pastry finish.

---

1 double-crust recipe Basic Butter and Shortening Pastry Pie Dough (page 27)	2 tablespoons sugar
	½ teaspoon ground cinnamon
8 ounces dried cherries	Pinch ground cloves
4 tablespoons (½ stick) unsalted butter, melted	Pinch salt
	Canola or peanut oil, for frying

In a medium saucepan, combine the cherries, butter, sugar, cinnamon, cloves, salt, and water. Simmer the mixture, covered, over low heat for 25 minutes, until the cherries are softened, plump, and flavorful. Stir occasionally. Pour the filling into a bowl and cool it in the refrigerator for at least 2 hours before filling the pies.

Divide the dough into 6 balls. Roll out each ball to a 6-inch square and fill it with 3 tablespoons of the filling. Fold it over into a half moon and seal the edge with a little water. Fold the edges up and crimp them down with a fork. Put the pies on a parchment-lined baking sheet and continue with the remaining dough and filling. Freeze the pies completely (they keep this way, well covered, up to 2 weeks) before deep-frying.

TO FRY: Fill a large 12- to 14-inch cast-iron skillet with oil until it is 1½ inches deep and clip a deep-frying thermometer to the side of the pan. Wait until the oil reaches 375°F. Fry the pies a few at a time until the first side is a deep golden brown. Monitor the oil temperature; it should be at least 360°F. Carefully turn over each pie (away from you) and fry until the second side browns a deep gold. When the pies are fully fried, rest them on a sheet pan lined with paper towels to drain off any excess oil.

Serve warm and make only the number of pies you plan to serve in one sitting. Strain the oil and store it covered in the refrigerator if you plan to make another batch soon. Used oil works a lot better than new. It's best if it's used 3 to 4 times.

Fried Peach Pies

Dried apricots or nectarines are also good in these pies.

1 double-crust recipe Basic Butter and Shortening Pastry Pie Dough (page 27)	¼ cup sugar
	1 teaspoon lemon zest
	1 cup water
8 ounces dried peaches, chopped	Pinch salt

Combine the peaches, sugar, zest, salt, and water in a medium saucepan. Simmer, covered, over low heat for 25 minutes, until the peaches are softened, plump, and flavorful. Stir occasionally. Puree the peaches if you want a wetter, juicier filling. Cool the filling in the refrigerator for at least 2 hours before filling the pies.

Divide the dough into 6 balls. Roll out each ball to a 6-inch square and fill it with 3 tablespoons of the filling. Fold it over into a half moon and seal the edge with a little water. Fold the edges up and crimp them down with a fork. Put the pies on a parchment-lined baking sheet and continue with the remaining dough and filling. Freeze the pies completely (they keep this way, well covered, up to 2 weeks) before deep-frying.

TO FRY: Fill a large 12- to 14-inch cast-iron skillet with oil until it is 1½ inches deep and clip a deep-frying thermometer to the side of the pan. Wait until the oil reaches 375°F. Fry the pies a few at a time until the first side is a deep golden brown. Monitor the oil temperature; it should be at least 360°F. Carefully turn over each pie (away from you) and fry until the second side browns a deep gold. When the pies are fully fried, rest them on a sheet pan lined with paper towels to drain off any excess oil.

Serve warm and make only the number of pies you plan to serve in one sitting. Strain the oil and store it covered in the refrigerator if you plan to make another batch soon.

FRIED APPLE-WHISKEY PIES

The filling is applesaucy and tart. (For apple recommendations, see page 104).

1 double-crust recipe Basic Butter and Shortening Pastry Pie Dough (page 27)	2 tablespoons whiskey (optional)
	½ lemon, juiced
2 tart, firm apples	¼ teaspoon ground cinnamon
2 tablespoons unsalted butter	Pinch ground cloves
2 tablespoons light brown sugar	Pinch salt

Peel the apples, core them, and cut them into ½-inch chunks.

Melt the butter in a small saucepan. Add the apple chunks and coat them with butter. Add the sugar, whiskey (if using), lemon juice, cinnamon, cloves, and salt and stir until combined. Cover and simmer over low heat for 25 minutes, until the apples are soft and broken down like chunky applesauce. Then stir the mixture briskly and roughly, smashing up the apples with a wooden spoon. Cool the filling in the refrigerator for at least 2 hours before filling pies.

Divide the dough into 6 balls. Roll out each ball to a 6-inch square and fill it with 3 tablespoons of the filling. Fold it over into a half moon and seal the edge with a little water. Fold the edges up and crimp them down with a fork. Put the pie on a parchment-lined baking sheet and continue with the remaining dough and filling. Freeze the pies completely (they keep this way, well covered, up to 2 weeks) before deep-frying.

TO FRY: Fill a large 12- to 14-inch cast-iron skillet with oil until it is 1½ inches deep and clip a deep-frying thermometer to the side of the pan. Wait until the oil reaches 375°F. Fry the pies a few at a time until the first side is a deep golden brown. Monitor the oil temperature; it should be at least 360°F. Carefully turn over each pie (away from you) and fry until the second side browns a deep gold. When the pies are fully fried, rest them on a sheet pan lined with paper towels to drain off any excess oil.

Serve warm and make only the number of pies you plan to serve in one sitting. Strain the oil and store it covered in the refrigerator if you plan to make another batch soon. Used oil works a lot better than new. It's best if it's used 3 to 4 times.

FRIED SWEET POTATO PIES

MAKES 6 INDIVIDUAL PIES

Leftover mashed sweet potatoes won't go to waste in these pies. They're the perfect snack or finish to a big Southern meal.

---

1 double-crust recipe Basic Butter and Shortening Pastry Pie Dough (page 27)

1 cup cooked mashed sweet potato

2 tablespoons light brown sugar or maple syrup

1 tablespoon unsalted butter, melted

1 teaspoon fresh-squeezed lemon juice

½ to 1 teaspoon Cointreau or Grand Marnier (optional)

¼ teaspoon ground cinnamon

Pinch ground cloves

Pinch cayenne pepper

Pinch salt

With an electric mixer, whip together the mashed sweet potato, sugar, butter, lemon juice, Cointreau (if using), cinnamon, cloves, cayenne, and salt until smooth. Cool the mixture completely in the refrigerator, if necessary, before filling the pies.

Divide the dough into 6 balls. Roll out each ball to a 6-inch square and fill it with 3 tablespoons of the filling. Fold it over into a half moon and seal the edge with a little water. Fold the edges up and crimp them down with a fork. Put the pie on a parchment-lined baking sheet and continue with the remaining dough and filling. Freeze the pies completely (they keep this way, well covered, up to 2 weeks) before deep-frying.

TO FRY: Fill a large 12- to 14-inch cast-iron skillet with oil until it is 1½ inches deep and clip a deep-frying thermometer to the side of the pan. Wait until the oil reaches 375°F. Fry the pies a few at a time until the first side is a deep golden brown. Monitor the oil temperature; it should be at least 360°F. Carefully turn over each pie (away from you) and fry until the second side browns a deep gold. When the pies are fully fried, rest them on a sheet pan lined with paper towels to drain off any excess oil.

Serve warm and make only the number of pies you plan to serve in one sitting. Strain the oil and store it covered in the refrigerator if you plan to make another batch soon. Used oil works a lot better than new. It's best if it's used 3 to 4 times.

Homemade Pop-Tarts™

Bubby's has always made as much from scratch as possible. However, certain store-bought snack foods bring back sweet memories of childhood. These are the items we especially like to make from scratch, and they are better tasting than the packaged versions. These recipes are fun for everyone—kids and grown-ups alike.

Pastry for a 9-inch double-crust pie, chilled, such as Bubby's All-Butter Pastry Pie Dough (page 23) or Basic Butter and Shortening Pastry Pie Dough (page 27)

¼ cup water

1 large egg, lightly beaten

½ cup homemade or high-quality jam (your favorite flavor)

Sugar, for topping

PREPARE AN EGG WASH: Whisk together the egg and ¼ cup water and set aside.

Roll out one of the balls of dough to make a big rectangle measuring about 11 x 16 inches and about 1⁄16 inch thick, thinner than for pie. Use a ruler and a knife to cut 8 rectangles from it, each one measuring about 3 x 5 inches. On a large baking sheet lined with parchment, lay out the rectangles of dough with a ½-inch between them. Cover them with cloth or parchment to keep them from drying out.

Repeat the process with the second ball of dough, but cut the 8 rectangles about ½ inch smaller in both directions (each one measuring about 2½ x 4½ inches). Dock these smaller rectangles with the tines of a fork.

Uncover the pastry on the baking sheet. Spoon 1 tablespoon of jam in the center of each rectangle. Lightly brush the edges of the lower rectangle with egg wash and top each one with a smaller rectangle, docked side up. Fold the bottom lip of dough over the top rectangle all the way around. Seal with the flat tines of a fork. Repeat until all of the pop-tarts are finished. Put the baking sheet full of pop-tarts in the freezer for at least 30 minutes before baking.

Pop-tarts will hold well in the freezer, tightly covered, for 2 to 3 weeks and can be baked to order later.

Preheat the oven to 425°F.

Sprinkle the pop-tarts with sugar and bake them for 10 minutes, or until the pastry is golden brown. Cool before serving—the jam gets very hot inside the pop-tart.

Store leftovers at room temperature, loosely covered, for up to 3 days. Reheat in a 350°F oven to serve.

Quince Turnovers

The quince is sometimes called a "honey apple"; it's aromatic, almost flowery, and practically flavors itself. Quinces were traditionally given to couples celebrating a union. They are barely sweet but they are intoxicating nonetheless—lending credence to the claims that they are an aphrodisiac. This ratio of fruit to crust suits the quince extremely well, perhaps even better than a standard pie.

Pastry for a 9-inch double-crust pie, chilled, such as Bubby's All-Butter Pastry Pie Dough (page 23)

1 pound quinces

3 tablespoons unsalted butter

¼ cup honey

Pinch ground cloves

Pinch salt

Sugar, for garnish

Peel, core, and thinly slice the quinces. Melt the butter in a skillet and simmer the quinces, covered, until soft, stirring occasionally; the consistency should be that of a rough applesauce. Stir in the honey, cloves, and salt. Chill completely before using.

Divide the dough into 8 balls. Roll out each ball to a 6-inch square and fill it with 3 tablespoons of the quince filling. Fold it over into a half moon and seal the edge with a little water. Fold the edges up and crimp them down with a fork, then poke them gently in the center a few times with the tines of the fork. Line a baking sheet with parchment and dust it with sugar (the sugar will caramelize on the bottom of the turnovers as they bake). Lay the turnovers down on the tray and chill in refrigerator.

Preheat the oven to 450°F. Bake the turnovers for 10 minutes, until blonde and blistered, then turn down the oven to 350°F and bake them for 10 minutes more, or until the pastry is golden brown.

Store leftovers at room temperature, loosely covered, for up to 3 days. Reheat in a 350°F oven to serve.

Chapter 8

CREAM AND CUSTARD PIES: PUDDING PIES, CHIFFON PIES, CUSTARD PIES, AND MERINGUE PIES

O ften the people who love cream pies prefer them to fruit pies. When they say they love pie, they mean *these* pies. Lucky for the cream-pie lover, these recipes can be made year-round and are less dependent on seasonal ingredients.

Pudding pies are made from a rich stovetop custard of eggs, milk, and sugar; chiffon pies are essentially the same base with lofty whipped cream or meringue folded in, often with a stabilizer like gelatin to keep it aloft. Custard pies are essentially egg and milk–based pies baked in a slow oven (and typically served cold). Meringue pies are usually custard or pudding pies topped with a cloud-like layer of sweet, light meringue that has been browned on top.

Crusts for cream pies are par-baked or fully blind-baked in advance because the filling is either cooked entirely on the stovetop or baked at a low temperature for a short time (insufficient to make a crisp bottom crust). Crumb crusts are quite compatible with the pies in this chapter because they cling to the creamy filling and have a delicious flavor and texture, even when cold.

Vanilla Pudding Pie

Pudding for pies is best made a day in advance so that it has plenty of time to chill and set. Creamy pudding pies go perfectly with crumb crusts and are quite amenable to a layer of fresh fruit, particularly berries. Puddings take a bit of practice to make with ease. Read through the directions completely before beginning. This recipe needs to be followed precisely. Yes (in case you're wondering if it's correct), there *is* sugar added separately to the two parts before they are combined. Heed the advance preparation and process notes and have all the tools and equipment you'll need in front of you before you begin cooking, and you'll have little trouble. Puddings can curdle, turning into scrambled-eggs if they get too hot. This basic recipe is the foundation for almost all of the pudding pies in this chapter, so make a big batch and try a second pudding pie recipe after the first pie is completely devoured.

Pastry for a 9-inch single-crust pie, blind-baked, such as Bubby's All-Butter Pastry Pie Dough (page 23), Basic Butter and Shortening Pastry Pie Dough (page 27), Nut Pastry Pie Dough (page 30), Sour Cream Pastry Pie Dough (page 29), Graham Cracker Crust (page 36), or Chocolate Crumb Crust (page 41)	4 cups whole milk 1 cup sugar, divided 1 vanilla bean, split in half lengthwise Pinch salt 1 cup egg yolks (about 12 yolks) ½ cup cornstarch 8 tablespoons (1 stick) cold unsalted butter, cubed

In a large, heavy, nonreactive saucepan (aluminum reacts and will cause a pudding to turn dingy gray), combine the milk, ½ cup of the sugar, the vanilla bean, and salt. In a medium bowl, whisk together the yolks, remaining ½ cup sugar, and cornstarch until smooth.

Have the whisk, a ladle, and a large glass or ceramic dish handy. Heat the milk mixture in the saucepan over medium heat until it *just* comes to a simmering slow boil, whisking it a bit as it gets steamy. When you see the first bubbles boiling up, take the pan off the heat and place it on a potholder next to the egg mixture. (To make life a little easier on yourself, put the egg bowl on the right if you're right-handed, or on the left if you're left-handed. Use your stronger arm to whisk; use your weaker arm to ladle the hot milk.)

During the next steps, stir constantly or the eggs will coagulate and you'll have scrambled eggs. This is quick work. Take a ladleful of hot milk and pour it in a thin stream into the eggs, whisking constantly. Continue stirring, and add one or two more ladlefuls of hot milk to the eggs in the same way. The tempered eggs are now ready to add back into the hot milk.

To do this, whisk the hot milk constantly and slowly pour the tempered eggs in. When fully combined, put this mixture back on the stovetop over medium heat and continue to whisk constantly. The mixture should be ready to come back to a simmer very quickly. When the custard nears the consistency of pudding, take very short pauses in stirring to look for signs of a bubble surfacing (it is more like a single volcanic blurp). Don't look too closely, or you'll risk getting spattered with hot pudding. Just stir, pause briefly, stir, and so on.

When you see the first blurp, remove the pan from the heat immediately and whisk in the cubes of butter. Whisk until fully combined and immediately pour the pudding into a large glass or ceramic dish to cool it down. While the pudding is still very hot, stretch plastic wrap directly on the surface of the pudding. Smooth out any air pockets to make the pudding airtight. This will prevent a skin or condensation from forming on top of the pudding. Refrigerate the pudding until completely cold—at least 4 hours.

Stir the cold pudding and retrieve the vanilla bean. Squeeze out the excess seeds (those little black specks) in the interior of the pod with your thumb and forefinger—pinch and slide your fingers down the length of the bean, freeing the

Half Batch Ratios for Vanilla Pudding

Useful for fruit and pudding pies

MAKES 3 CUPS

2 cups whole milk

½ vanilla bean, split in half lengthwise

½ cup sugar, divided

Tiny pinch salt

½ cup egg yolks (about 6 yolks)

¼ cup cornstarch

4 tablespoons (½ stick) cold unsalted butter, cubed

black seeds as you go. Do this with each half of the bean, returning as many seeds as possible to the pudding. Stir the pudding again and pour it into the crust. Smooth the top with a spatula.

Chill the pie, covered with plastic wrap, in the refrigerator for at least 4 hours before serving. It holds for up to 4 days.

This pudding holds very well before it is made up in a pie, so we recommend making 6 cups even if only 3 are needed.

CRÈME FRAÎCHE PUDDING VARIATION

Make the recipe above for half batch of Vanilla Pudding but substitute Crème Fraîche for the milk. Serve with fresh berries.

STRAWBERRIES AND CREAM PIE

Homemade vanilla pudding should be made in advance so that it has plenty of time to chill. It's layered here with fresh, flavorful, glazed strawberries in a flaky pastry crust. This is equally good made with fresh raspberries, blackberries, or blueberries and any variety of cookie crumb crust.

Pastry for a 9-inch single-crust pie, blind-baked, such as Bubby's All-Butter Pastry Pie Dough (page 23), Basic Butter and Shortening Pastry Pie Dough (page 27), Nut Pastry Pie Dough (page 30), Sour Cream Pastry Pie Dough (page 29), Graham Cracker Crust (page 36), or Chocolate Crumb Crust (page 41)

4 cups strawberries, divided

1½ tablespoons fresh-squeezed orange juice

1 teaspoon orange zest

2½ tablespoons sugar

1½ tablespoons cornstarch

Pinch salt

3 cups Vanilla Pudding (page 240)

Clean and trim the strawberries. Reserve ½ cup of your best-looking whole strawberries to decorate the top of the pie. Slice 2 cups of the strawberries in half or quarters and set aside.

To make strawberry sauce, roughly chop the remaining strawberries and combine with the orange juice and zest in a covered saucepan over low heat. Simmer for 5 minutes, until the berries are broken down and juicy. Take the lid off and smash up the berries a little. Simmer for 15 minutes more, until completely liquid, with thick bubbles showing.

Combine the sugar, cornstarch, and salt in a bowl and mix well. Whisk this mixture into the strawberry reduction and cook over medium heat until it is just at a boil—the opacity goes out of the sauce and it looks shiny and steamy. Cool the sauce for 10 minutes, then fold the sliced berries into the sauce. Chill the sauce completely.

To assemble the pie, you can choose which layer you want on top—pudding or berries. Spread the cold strawberry mixture in the pie shell, then layer on the Vanilla Pudding, smoothing the top with a spatula. Chill the pie, covered with plastic wrap, in the refrigerator for at least 4 hours before serving. Serve it cold, garnished with the reserved ½ cup of whole or halved strawberries.

Store loosely covered in the refrigerator for up to 2 days.

Put-Up Peaches and Vanilla Cream Pie

MAKES ONE 9-INCH SINGLE-CRUST PIE

This is comfort food *par excellence*! The recipe is intended for "put-up" or canned peaches—those preserved in light syrup and canned in mason jars at home. If you use store-bought, choose some preserved in light syrup. You can also use fresh, fully ripe local peaches if you're making this in the summer. The vanilla pudding should be made in advance so that it has plenty of time to chill. All of the ingredients can be prepared in advance, but the pie should be assembled shortly before serving. This can also be made well with fresh or put-up apricots.

Pastry for a 9-inch single-crust pie, blind-baked, such as Bubby's All-Butter Pastry Pie Dough (page 23), Basic Butter and Shortening Pastry Pie Dough (page 27), Nut Pastry Pie Dough (page 30), Sour Cream Pastry Pie Dough (page 29), Graham Cracker Crust (page 36),

Chocolate Crumb Crust (page 41), or Gingersnap Crumb Crust (page 39)

2 cups quartered "put-up" or canned peaches

3 cups Vanilla Pudding (page 240)

Strain the quartered peaches over a bowl for 30 minutes in the refrigerator. If you are using fresh peaches, wait to skin them (see page 97) and cut them just before you assemble the pie.

Fold the pudding and peaches together and pour the mixture into the pie shell. Smooth the top with a spatula. Serve immediately. This pie is delicious but fragile—it is best eaten right after it is made.

Banana Cream Pie with Candied Pecans

MAKES ONE 9-INCH SINGLE-CRUST PIE

This pie has been on the Bubby's menu since we opened. Lots of bananas tossed lightly in sour cream are topped with a vanilla pudding and pecan pralines. This is the best banana cream pie we've ever tried. Select ripe bananas without any sign of spots or green near the stem.

Pastry for a 9-inch single-crust pie, blind-baked, such as Bubby's All-Butter Pastry Pie Dough (page 23), Basic Butter and Shortening Pastry Pie Dough (page 27), Nut Pastry Pie Dough (page 30), Sour Cream Pastry Pie Dough (page 29), or Chocolate Crumb Crust (page 41)

4 to 5 medium-sized ripe bananas

1½ tablespoons fresh-squeezed lemon juice

¼ teaspoon vanilla extract

¼ cup sour cream

3 cups Vanilla Pudding (page 240)

Candied Pecans or Walnuts (page 314)

Slice the bananas ¼ inch thick to get about 4 cups and immediately toss them in the lemon juice to prevent them from browning. Stir the vanilla extract into the sour cream, then gently fold in with the bananas. Layer the coated bananas in the pie crust, and flatten them gently. Layer the pudding on top and smooth it with a spatula.

Refrigerate the pie, covered with plastic wrap, for at least 2 hours before cutting.

Serve wedges of pie cold with Candied Pecans; their salty accent is quite nice next to the custard and bananas. Store loosely covered in the refrigerator for up to 3 days.

Banana-Mocha Pudding Pie

M ake chocolate pudding according to the directions on page 248, but increase the espresso powder measure by two teaspoons for a stronger coffee flavor.

Pastry for a 9-inch single-crust pie, blind-baked, such as Bubby's All-Butter Pastry Pie Dough (page 23), Basic Butter and Shortening Pastry Pie Dough (page 27), Nut Pastry Pie Dough (page 30), Sour Cream Pastry Pie Dough (page 29), or Chocolate Crumb Crust (page 41)

3 cups Chocolate Pudding (page 248)

3 teaspoons instant espresso powder, divided

4 to 5 medium bananas

⅓ cup sour cream

Make the Chocolate Pudding according to the directions, but add an extra 2 teaspoons of espresso powder (2½ teaspoons total in pudding). Refrigerate it.

When the pudding is completely cold, slice the bananas ½ inch thick to make about 4 cups. Mix 1 teaspoon hot water with the ¾ teaspoon espresso powder in a large bowl. Add the sour cream and stir until smooth. Add the bananas and fold them gently into the sour cream mixture. Pour the banana mixture into the pie shell and even it out with a spatula, compressing it lightly. Stir the pudding and layer it evenly over the bananas.

Refrigerate the pie, covered with plastic wrap, for at least 4 hours before serving.

Serve wedges of pie cold. Store loosely covered in the refrigerator for up to 3 days.

CHOCOLATE PUDDING PIE

MAKES 6 CUPS PUDDING; ONE 9-INCH SINGLE-CRUST PIE

Delicious variations on this pie include Chocolate Pudding Pie in hazelnut pastry crust topped with Candied Hazelnuts (page 315), Chocolate Pudding Pie in Chocolate Crumb Crust topped with Espresso Meringue (page 306), and Chocolate Pudding Pie in an almond pastry crust topped with fresh sweet cherries.

Pastry for a 9-inch single-crust pie, crimped and chilled in pie tin, such as Nut Pastry Pie Dough (page 30), Bubby's All-Butter Pastry Pie Dough (page 23), Chocolate Crumb Crust (page 41), Chocolate-Peppermint Crumb Crust (page 41), or Graham Cracker Crust (page 36)

4 cups whole milk

¾ cup sugar, divided

1 vanilla bean, split in half lengthwise

¼ teaspoon salt

1 cup egg yolks (about 12 yolks)

½ cup cornstarch

8 tablespoons (1 stick) cold unsalted butter, cubed

6 ounces bittersweet chocolate

2 tablespoons unsweetened cocoa powder

½ teaspoon instant espresso powder

Whipped Cream (page 302), Espresso Meringue (page 306), or other toppings, as desired

---

In a large, heavy, nonreactive saucepan (aluminum reacts and will cause a pudding to turn dingy gray), combine the milk, ½ cup of the sugar, the vanilla bean, and salt. In a medium bowl, whisk together the yolks, remaining ½ cup sugar, and cornstarch until smooth.

Have the whisk, a ladle, and a large glass or ceramic dish handy. Heat the milk mixture in the saucepan until it *just* comes to a boil, whisking it a bit as it gets steamy. When you see the first bubbles boiling up, take the pan off the heat and place it on a potholder next to the egg mixture. (To make life a little easier on yourself, put the egg bowl on the right if you're right-handed, or on the left if you're left-handed. Use your stronger arm to whisk; use your weaker arm to ladle the hot milk.)

During the next steps, stir constantly or the eggs will coagulate and you'll have scrambled eggs. This is quick work. Take a ladleful of hot milk and pour it in a thin stream into the eggs, whisking constantly. Continue stirring and add a few more ladlefuls of hot milk to the eggs in the same way. The tempered eggs are now ready to add back into the hot milk.

To do this, whisk the hot milk constantly and pour the tempered eggs in slowly. When fully combined, put this mixture back on the stovetop over medium heat and continue to whisk constantly. The mixture should be ready to come back to a simmer very quickly. When the custard nears the consistency of pudding, take very short pauses in stirring to look for signs of a bubble surfacing (it is more like a single volcanic blurp). Don't look too closely, or you'll risk getting spattered with hot pudding. Just stir, pause briefly, stir, etc.

When you see the first blurp, remove the pan from the heat immediately and whisk in the cubes of butter. Whisk until fully combined and immediately pour the pudding into a large glass or ceramic dish to cool it down.

Half Batch Ratios for 3 Cups Pudding

Useful for fruit and pudding pies

MAKES 3 CUPS

2 cups whole milk

½ vanilla bean, split in half lengthwise

¼ cup plus 2 tablespoons sugar, divided

⅛ teaspoon salt

½ cup egg yolks (about 6 yolks)

¼ cup cornstarch

4 tablespoons (½ stick) cold unsalted butter, cubed

3 ounces bittersweet chocolate

1 tablespoon Dutch-process cocoa powder

¼ teaspoon instant espresso powder

In the top of a double boiler over low heat, melt the chocolate. Stir in the cocoa and espresso powder until the espresso crystals have dissolved and the chocolate is uniformly smooth. Stir the mixture into the hot pudding. While it is still very hot, stretch plastic wrap directly on the surface of the pudding. Smooth out any air pockets to make the pudding airtight. This will prevent a skin or condensation from forming on top of the pudding. Refrigerate the pudding until completely cold—at least 4 hours.

Stir the cold pudding and retrieve the vanilla bean. Squeeze out the excess seeds (those little black specks) in the interior of the pod with your thumb and forefinger—pinch and slide your fingers down the length of the bean, freeing the black seeds as you go. Do this with each half of the bean, returning as many seeds as possible to the pudding. Stir the pudding again and pour it into the prepared crust of your choice. Smooth the top with a spatula. Top with fresh Whipped Cream, Espresso Meringue, or another topping of your choice.

Chill the pie, covered with plastic wrap, in the refrigerator for at least 4 hours before serving. It holds for up to 4 days.

This pudding holds very well before it is made up in a pie, so we recommend making 6 cups even if only 3 are needed.

BLOOD ORANGE–CHOCOLATE PUDDING TART

MAKES ONE 10-INCH SINGLE-CRUST TART

B lood oranges and chocolate pair well in this decadent tart. Make candied blood orange slices 24 hours in advance. Blood oranges are available from early December to the end of January.

Pastry for a 10-inch single-crust tart, such as Graham Cracker Crust (page 36), Bubby's All-Butter Pastry Pie Dough (page 23), Basic Butter and Shortening Pastry Pie Dough (page 27), Short Dough for Tarts (page 32), or Sour Cream Pastry Pie Dough (page 29)

4 blood oranges, juiced

Zest of 1 blood orange, finely chopped

3 cups Chocolate Pudding (page 248), hot

Candied blood orange slices (page 317), for serving with pie

Shaved chocolate, for serving with pie

In a small non-reactive pan over high heat, reduce the juice for about 5 to 7 minutes, until it measures 2 tablespoons. Set aside.

While the pudding is still hot, whisk the reduced juice into it vigorously to incorporate it. Use a rubber spatula to get every last bit from the pan and stir it into the pudding. Stir in the zest.

To cool the pudding, pour it into a large glass or ceramic dish. While it is still very hot, stretch plastic wrap directly on the surface of the pudding so that a skin doesn't form on top. Refrigerate the pudding until completely cold—at least 4 hours.

Roll out the pastry and line a 10-inch tart pan with the bottom crust. Rechill the pastry if necessary. If using a pastry dough, fully blind-bake the crust (see page 15) until it is golden brown; set aside to cool completely before filling it with pudding. For a crumb or cracker crust, do not prebake it.

Stir the pudding and pour it into the tart shell. Let it chill for at least 30 minutes before serving. Top with chocolate shavings and candied blood oranges to serve.

Store the pie, covered with plastic wrap, in the refrigerator for up to 4 days.

Bubby's Original Peanut Butter–Chocolate Pie

MAKES ONE 9-INCH SINGLE-CRUST PIE

Our peanut butter pie is a permanent feature on our menu, and has been since we opened. A light peanut butter mousse is piled into a Graham Cracker Crust lined with a layer of chocolate ganache (a rich spread of cream and chocolate) and chocolate shavings on top. This would also be good with a Chocolate Crumb Crust. If you're going to make this decadent pie, go all the way and definitely use sweet, store-bought peanut butter.

1 recipe Graham Cracker Crust (page 36) or Chocolate Crumb Crust (page 41)	1 teaspoon vanilla extract
	1½ cups heavy cream
	GANACHE
PEANUT BUTTER MOUSSE	6 ounces bittersweet chocolate
1 cup confectioners' sugar	¾ cup heavy cream
1 cup creamy peanut butter	
3 ounces cream cheese, at room temperature	2 tablespoons shaved chocolate, to decorate the top

Use the paddle attachment of an electric mixer at medium, then high speed, to beat together the sugar, peanut butter, cream cheese, and vanilla until they are light and fluffy. In a separate bowl, whip the cream until it holds good, stiff peaks. Place a few spoonfuls of whipped cream in the peanut butter mixture and mix on medium speed to combine evenly. Add the remaining whipped cream and fold it into the mousse on the slowest setting, until all the chunks are gone. Cover and refrigerate.

TO MAKE THE GANACHE: Melt the chocolate in the top of a double boiler over low heat and stir until smooth. Add the cream, stirring continuously, until completely combined. Spread a thick layer of ganache in the pie shell, covering the bottom and the sides of the crust as evenly as possible, using an offset spatula, spreading from the center outward and up the sides with arcing strokes. Chill the crust in the freezer until the ganache is set.

Set aside about ½ cup of mousse. Fill the pie with the remaining mousse, smoothing the top with a spatula. Use a pastry bag with a plain tip to pipe the reserved mousse into peanut butter kisses around the edge of the pie for decoration. Sprinkle the top of the pie with the shaved chocolate.

Refrigerate the pie for at least 2 hours before serving. Store it in the refrigerator loosely covered for up to 4 days.

KEY LIME PIE

M ade with real Key limes or Key lime juice and baked in our home-made Graham Cracker Crust, this creamy and tangy pie is a year-round favorite at Bubby's. We buy real Key lime juice from Jeanette Richards, who gets her lime juice from Florida and freezes it. There's no comparison between Key lime juice and regular lime juice. This pie is great with fresh raspberries.

---

1 recipe Graham Cracker Crust (page 36), blind-baked

3 large eggs

1 cups sweetened condensed milk

½ teaspoon cream of tartar

⅓ cup fresh-squeezed or bottled Key lime juice

Whipped Cream (page 302), for garnish

Preheat the oven to 300°F.

Use the whisk attachment of an electric mixer to beat the eggs until frothy. Add the condensed milk and cream of tartar and mix well. With the mixer on low speed, pour in the lime juice in a thin stream. Increase the speed to medium-high and whisk for 5 minutes. There's no danger of over-whipping this pie—just of overbaking. Pour the filling into the crust just to the lip of the shell.

Bake the pie on a lipped baking sheet for 15 to 20 minutes, or just until it is set. The top should jiggle and have a sheen but no sign of browning. It will set as it cools.

Put the pie on a cooling rack for 20 minutes. Refrigerate the pie for at least 4 hours before serving. Serve it cold, with whipped cream.

Store the pie loosely covered in the refrigerator for up to 4 days.

Double Lemon Chess Pie

MAKES ONE 9-INCH SINGLE-CRUST PIE

Southerners go misty when this pie gets mentioned. The filling ingredients that distinguish it are buttermilk and cornmeal. So why is it called chess pie? There are a few possible answers: It's kept cold, so back in the days of ice chests it was known as "chest" pie. It's also a pretty humble pie, and some people say the name comes from the expression "Aw, it's jest pie." Ours is a little different from most old recipes we've found—somewhere between a lemon bar and lemon meringue pie filling—the lemon curd gives it an extra pucker, and the traditional chess pie base gives it a creamy consistency.

Pastry for a 9-inch single crust, blind-baked, such as Sour Cream Pastry Pie Dough (page 29), Bubby's All-Butter Pastry Pie Dough (page 23), or Basic Butter and Shortening Pastry Pie Dough (page 27)

2 cups sugar

8 tablespoons (1 stick) unsalted butter, softened

5 large eggs

½ cup plus 2 tablespoons buttermilk

⅓ cup heavy cream

1 tablespoon all-purpose flour

1 tablespoon cornmeal

½ teaspoon salt

¼ cup fresh-squeezed lemon juice

2 lemons, zested

½ cup Lemon Curd (page 307)

Preheat the oven to 350°F.

With an electric mixer, cream the sugar and butter together until light and fluffy. Add the eggs, buttermilk, and cream; beat well.

In a small bowl, combine the flour, cornmeal, and salt, add them to the butter mixture, and mix just until incorporated. Add the lemon juice and zest and mix briefly. Pour the filling into the pie shell.

Bake the pie on a lipped baking sheet for 40 to 45 minutes, until the top is a pale golden brown and the center is only a wee bit loose.

Cool the pie on a cooling rack for 20 minutes before refrigerating. Chill

completely before topping the filling with Lemon Curd. Use an offset pastry spatula to distribute it evenly, stopping just shy of the pastry crust. Chill for at least 4 hours and serve cold and plain. This pie cuts like a pudding pie—a little yielding.

Store the pie loosely covered in the refrigerator for up to 3 days.

Buttermilk Pie with Fresh Berries

MAKES ONE 9-INCH SINGLE-CRUST PIE

L ike the Italian custard *pane cotta,* this buttermilk pie delivers the pure unadulterated texture of cream. It is delicious with any cookie crumb crust and any kind of fresh berry—particularly strawberries and raspberries. The gelatin called for is approximately one packet; however, double-check the measure, because they are often somewhat off and this filling depends on an exact measure.

Pastry for a 9-inch single-crust pie, crimped and chilled in pie tin, such as Gingersnap Crumb Crust (page 39), Graham Cracker Crust (page 36), Nut Pastry Pie Dough (page 30), Bubby's All-Butter Pastry Pie Dough (page 23), or Basic Butter and Shortening Pastry Pie Dough (page 27)

2 cups buttermilk, divided

2¾ teaspoons unflavored powdered gelatin

2 cups sour cream

1 small vanilla bean

6 tablespoons sugar, plus extra as needed

2 cups fresh raspberries

If using a pastry dough, fully blind-bake the crust (see page 15) until it is golden brown; set aside to cool. For a crumb or cracker crust, do not prebake it.

Put 1 cup of the buttermilk in a small saucepan. Sprinkle the gelatin evenly over the surface and let it sit undisturbed for 10 minutes to soften. Then warm the mixture over medium-low heat, whisking constantly, until the buttermilk emits its first steam and the gelatin dissolves completely. Take care not to cook this mixture past this point; if the buttermilk comes to a boil, it will curdle. Remove the pan from the heat and set aside.

Prepare an ice water bath in a bowl large enough to surround the mixing bowl with ice. Use lots of ice cubes and about 1 quart of water.

Whisk the remaining 1 cup buttermilk and the sour cream until smooth. Split the vanilla bean lengthwise and scrape out seeds with the back of a chef knife. Add them to the buttermilk along with the sugar. Mix briefly, just to combine. With the mixer on low speed, pour the hot buttermilk into the bowl in a thin stream. When it is completely incorporated, remove the entire bowl to nest in the ice water bath. Whisk occasionally for about 10 minutes, until the mixture gets quite cold (50°F).

Pour the cooled mixture into the crust and refrigerate it for at least 4 hours before serving. If you have more filling than will fit in the crust, pour it into individual ramekins and chill them alongside the pie for a snack.

Serve the pie cold with fresh, lightly sugared berries. Refrigerate, loosely covered, for up to 2 days.

NESSELRODE PIE

MAKES ONE 9-INCH SINGLE-CRUST PIE

This once very popular pie is a decadent Christmas pie—a wonderful blend of creamy vanilla custard, honey-roasted chestnuts, and candied orange, topped with toasted coconut and shavings of dark chocolate. Like many holiday pies, it likely became so because one of its ingredients—chestnuts—is in season at Christmastime. Our recipe is based on that of Count Nesselrode's chef, M. Mouy. It was once considered a New York specialty.

It took us a couple of tries to make a pie we love, but what we arrived at is truly a magnificent, decadent pie and well worth the labor it takes to make it. You'll taste every bit of love you put into it. We've tried it with chestnuts we've prepared ourselves and with the variety that come vacuum-packed or loose in glass jars, and we can say with confidence that they are both good. As a result, we go the easier route and save the fresh chestnuts for roasting over a fire. Both the chestnuts and the puree can be purchased at gourmet specialty food shops.

Pastry for a 9-inch single-crust pie, blind-baked, such as Bubby's All-Butter Pastry Pie Dough (page 23), Basic Butter and Shortening Pastry Pie Dough (page 27), Graham Cracker Crust (page 36), or Chocolate Crumb Crust (page 41)

ROASTED CHESTNUTS

8 ounces chestnut pieces

¼ cup honey

1 tablespoon Cointreau or other orange-flavored liqueur (optional)

Pinch salt

Pinch ground nutmeg

ORANGE PASTE

¼ cup sugar

2 oranges, zested

1 teaspoon Cointreau or other orange-flavored liqueur (optional)

CHESTNUT CREAM

One 15½-ounce can high-quality chestnut puree

2 cups heavy cream

½ cup honey

1 tablespoon cornstarch

1 teaspoon ground nutmeg

6 cups Vanilla Pudding (page 240)

½ cup toasted sweetened coconut

2 tablespoons dark chocolate shavings, for garnish

Preheat the oven to 300°F.

In a medium bowl, mix together the chestnuts, honey, Cointreau (if using), salt, and nutmeg until combined. Roast the mixture on a parchment-lined baking sheet for 30 minutes, stirring occasionally. The chestnuts will not brown but they should be hot with a drier look. Set aside to cool.

TO MAKE THE ORANGE PASTE: Mix the sugar with the zest and Cointreau (if using). Add to the cooled chestnuts and set aside.

Prepare an ice water bath in a bowl large enough to surround the top half of the double boiler with ice. Use lots of ice cubes and about 1 quart of water. In a heavy enamel or steel pan, whisk together the chestnut puree, cream, honey, cornstarch, and nutmeg. Cook over medium-low heat, stirring constantly, until thickened and creamy. Stir in 1 cup of the roasted chestnuts. Rest the pot in the ice bath until the mixture is very cold to the touch. Fold in the Vanilla Pudding gently.

Sprinkle the remaining roasted chestnuts in the bottom of the crust. Layer it with the chestnut cream, smoothing it with a spatula, and then top it with the toasted coconut and chocolate shavings.

Refrigerate for at least 4 hours before serving. Store loosely covered in the refrigerator for up to 4 days.

SOUR CREAM–RAISIN PIE

The sour cream-raisin pie recipes we came across resembled dense library paste with raisins. Sometimes raisin pie is called funeral pie; maybe that's what inspired them. Our idea of how good the pie could taste appealed to us, so we set out to make homemade sour cream custard atop a warm spicy layer of raisins. It's tasty.

Pastry for a 9-inch single-crust pie, blind-baked, such as Bubby's All-Butter Pastry Pie Dough (page 23) or Basic Butter and Shortening Pastry Pie Dough (page 27)

RAISINS

2 cups raisins

¼ cup sugar

2 tablespoons all-purpose flour

2 teaspoons white vinegar

1 teaspoon orange zest

½ teaspoon ground cinnamon

¼ teaspoon ground nutmeg

Pinch ground cloves

Pinch salt

CUSTARD

2 cups sour cream

1 cup milk

5 large egg yolks

½ cup sugar

¼ cup cornstarch

3 tablespoons dark brown sugar

Tiny pinch salt

4 tablespoons (½ stick) unsalted butter, cubed

Measure the raisins, sugar, flour, vinegar, zest, cinnamon, nutmeg, cloves, and salt into a heavy nonreactive pot. Stir. Bring the mixture to a boil, then cover it and turn it down to a low simmer. Stir occasionally until the raisins get plump and the sauce coats the back of a spoon. Remove it from the heat and set aside.

In the top of a double boiler, whisk together the sour cream, milk, yolks, sugar, cornstarch, brown sugar, and salt. Heat the mixture over simmering water and stir constantly until it thickly coats the back of a wooden spoon. Off the heat, add the butter and stir until incorporated. Transfer the pudding to a bowl and cover the surface with plastic wrap. Refrigerate to cool completely.

When everything is cold, scrape the raisin mixture into the crust and spread it out evenly. Layer the sour cream pudding on top, smoothing it with a spatula. Chill for at least 4 hours, loosely covered, before serving.

Serve cold and store loosely covered in the refrigerator for up to 4 days.

> I'm admittin' tastes are diff'runt, I'm not settin' up myself
> As the judge an' final critic of the good things on the shelf.
> I'm sort o' payin' tribute to a simple joy on earth,
> Sort o' feebly testifyin' to its lasting charm an' worth,
> An' I'll hold to this conclusion till it comes my time to die,
> That there's no dessert that's finer than a chunk o' raisin pie.
>
> —EDGAR GUEST,
> *"Raisin Pie"*

MILE-HIGH LEMON MERINGUE PIE

MAKES ONE 9-INCH SINGLE-CRUST PIE

Start early (at least six hours in advance, preferably twenty-four) to allow adequate chilling time for the pie to set up properly. The intense lemon custard of this pie is topped with a flavorful Italian meringue that is light, creamy and has a hint of brown sugar. Italian meringue holds up better than any other meringue we've tried. To keep the meringue from weeping, observe all notes about the temperature and chilling times. Also, spread the meringue to completely cover the edge of the lemon filling or moisture will accumulate there. Chill the whole pie thoroughly before transporting it anywhere. We use a propane kitchen torch on the meringue, and recommend the torch as the best option for this pie.

Pastry for a 9-inch single-crust pie, par-baked, such as Bubby's All-Butter Pastry Pie Dough (page 23) or Basic Butter and Shortening Pastry Pie Dough (page 27)

6 large eggs

1½ cups sugar

¾ cup fresh-squeezed lemon juice

1 cup heavy cream

1 tablespoon lemon zest

Italian Meringue (page 305)

Preheat the oven to 300°F.

In a medium bowl, whisk together the eggs and sugar until combined. Add the lemon juice and whisk until smooth. Mix in the cream and strain the mixture into a bowl. Add the zest to the strained mixture.

Place the pie shell on a lipped baking sheet and put them on a rack in the oven with the shelf pulled out slightly. Carefully pour the filling mixture directly into the crust and slide the rack into the oven gently. The pie will be very full, so be careful not to slosh it.

Bake the pie for about 1 hour, or until the filling barely jiggles when the pie is given a little shake. Let the pie cool on a rack for 20 minutes, then refrigerate it uncovered for several hours or overnight (covered) before making and adding the meringue to it.

Scrape the warm meringue onto the chilled lemon pie and use a spatula to shape it into a smooth dome, pushing gently. Make sure the meringue covers the filling completely, touching all the edges of the crust and sealing the top of the pie.

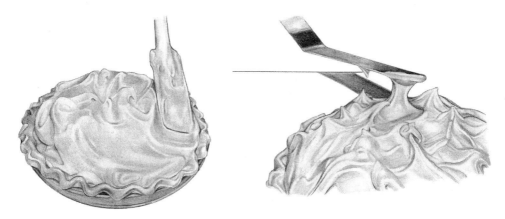

With the back of a spatula or wooden spoon, touch and pull the meringue to make decorative peaks in it. Work quickly, before the meringue cools and sets.

Use a propane kitchen torch to evenly brown the meringue. Point the flame slightly above the peaks to avoid flare-ups. If you don't have a torch, place the pie on the lower rack of a 475°F oven for 5 to 10 minutes, until the peaks brown nicely.

Cut and serve the pie immediately or chill it until needed. If storing it overnight or longer in the refrigerator, use toothpicks to prop up plastic wrap to cover the pie. The meringue will definitely get weepy once the pie has been cut and stored, but it is fine. It will last up to 3 days refrigerated.

LOFTY COCONUT CLOUD PIE

MAKES ONE 9-INCH SINGLE-CRUST PIE

J en coveted an extraordinary coconut cream pie from a pie place in Palominas, Arizona. Because her diplomatic attempts to attain the recipe were unsuccessful, we worked long and hard to figure out how to recreate this high, silky, ethereal, and creamy pie. This would be great with freshly shaved coconut too.

Pastry for a 9-inch single-crust pie, blind-baked and chilled, such as Bubby's All-Butter Pastry Pie Dough (page 23) or Basic Butter and Shortening Pastry Pie Dough (page 27)

2 cups milk, divided

2 tablespoons unflavored gelatin

6 large eggs

1 cup unsweetened toasted coconut, plus extra for topping the pie

1 cup sugar

1 tablespoon vanilla extract

Pinch salt

1½ cups heavy cream

Fully blind-bake the crust (see page 15) until it is golden brown; set aside to cool completely before filling it with pudding.

Measure ⅔ cup of the milk into a wide bowl. Sprinkle the gelatin over it and let it soften for 5 minutes, whisk together, and set the bowl aside.

Separate the eggs—put the yolks into the bowl of an electric mixer and put the whites into a separate bowl until later.

In a medium saucepan over medium heat, combine the remaining 1⅓ cups milk and the coconut. When the milk forms small bubbles at the edge and gets steamy, remove the pan from the heat.

With the electric mixer, whip the yolks and sugar until light in color and a smooth and ribbony design is left by the whisk. With the mixer on low speed, pour in 1 cup of the hot milk in a slow steady stream to temper the eggs. Whisking constantly, pour the egg mixture into the milk and return the pan to the heat. Stir constantly with a whisk over medium heat until slightly thickened. Remove the pan from the heat and whisk in the milky gelatin.

Add the vanilla and salt. (If you want even more coconut, you can stir a cup more into the filling.) Pour the mixture into a bowl and refrigerate it, covered, for 2 hours or until it is cold and thickened up.

With an electric mixer, whip the cold pudding until it is really smooth (it will be pretty dense and gelatinous at first). There should be no lumps. Separately, whip the cream until stiff. Fold the whipped pudding and cream together gently with a rubber spatula. Separately, whip the egg whites until stiff. Fold the whipped egg whites into the creamy pudding. Mound the mixture into the crust and smooth it with an offset spatula. Top it with additional toasted coconut.

Chill the pie for a couple of hours before cutting and store it in the refrigerator. Use toothpicks to prop up plastic wrap to cover the pie. It will last up to 3 days refrigerated.

COCONUT CUSTARD PIE

The coconut settles to the bottom of the pie as it bakes, offering a nice contrast in textures between the toothy coconut and the smooth custard. Serve it still warm from the oven.

Pastry for a 9-inch single-crust pie, par-baked and cooled, such as Bubby's All-Butter Pastry Pie Dough (page 23) or Basic Butter and Shortening Pastry Pie Dough (page 27)

1¼ cups milk

½ cup sweetened shredded coconut

1¼ cups regular (full-fat) coconut milk

5 large egg yolks

½ cup sugar

1 teaspoon vanilla extract

⅛ teaspoon salt

In a medium saucepan over medium heat, combine the milk, coconut, and coconut milk. When it forms small bubbles at the edge and steams slightly, remove it from the heat. Do not boil it or it will scorch.

Separate the eggs. With an electric mixer, whip the yolks, sugar, vanilla, and salt until frothy. Temper the egg mixture by adding the hot milk in a thin stream while the mixer is running on low. Add all the milk this way.

Preheat the oven to 350°F.

Pull the oven rack out a little and place the crust on a lipped baking sheet on the oven rack. Carefully pour the filling into the crust and push the rack gently back in. Bake the pie for 35 to 40 minutes, until the filling jiggles but doesn't slosh when nudged.

Cool the pie at room temperature for at least 20 minutes before serving it warm or at room temperature. Store in the refrigerator for up to 4 days. Once it has been chilled, it's best served cold.

Chapter 9

HOMEMADE ICE CREAM AND ICE CREAM PIES

Pie à la mode is a natural pairing and an exciting contrast in flavors and temperatures. Vanilla Ice Cream (page 272) goes well with pies year-round. In the heat of summer, we opt for refreshing and flavorful Buttermilk Ice Cream (page 274) or homemade Peach Ice Cream (page 276) to serve with plentiful summer berry pies. When autumn arrives, we start offering Ginger Ice Cream (page 278) or Caramel Ice Cream (page 282) with Bubby's autumn fruit pies, crisps, and bettys.

Bubby's homemade ice cream is especially popular during the hot, sticky New York City summers. Our ice cream pies indulge our nostalgic, decadent side. At Bubby's, we aim to make high-quality renditions of childhood favorites from scratch. Our ice cream pies celebrate our fabulous homemade cookie crumb crusts under childhood favorites like Strawberry Ice Cream (page 280) or Rocky Road Ice Cream (page 288; Chocolate Ice Cream with dark chocolate shavings, toasted almonds, and Homemade Marshmallows). The possibilities are endless: Cappuccino Meringue Pie (page 299)—a variation on a baked Alaska—Espresso Ice Cream in a homemade cookie crumb crust topped with Espresso Meringue.

Soon after our ice cream pie obsession took hold, we were on to Eskimo Pies—homemade cookie crumb crusts with a layer of bittersweet chocolate ganache, topped with a layer of homemade Banana–Chocolate Chip Ice Cream (page 291) or any other kind that struck our fancy. The Grasshopper Eskimo Pie (page 297) made with Mint Chip Ice Cream in a Chocolate Peppermint Crumb Crust served with a layer of rich chocolate ganache definitely satisfied a nostalgia for childhood favorites. In honor of kids and their love of making their own ice cream sundaes, we came up with the Sweetie Pie (page 298): two different kinds of ice cream layered in a homemade cookie crumb crust, with whatever toppings you want to make available—whipped cream, fruit, nuts, sprinkles, and so on.

We have a dozen ice cream recipes to try here, but encourage you to invent your own flavors after you've become familiar and confident with the basic process. We've offered recipes that are great complements to pie and a couple that make exceptional ice cream pies. The Vanilla Ice Cream is easily adapted to fruits, nuts, and additions of many kinds—use your imagination! However, some advance consideration should be given to the frozen texture of the ingredients you add. For example, a fruit purée will blend harmoniously, whereas overly large chunks of fruit will become rock-hard. Swirl in chopped ingredients after the ice cream has been removed from the machine. Follow the manufacturer's instructions for your model regarding stir-ins.

When choosing a crust for an ice cream pie, opt for one that has an appealing texture straight from the freezer; any cookie crumb crust will do.

It is well worth it to take your freezer's temperature before you make your first batch of ice cream. If it is not cold enough, even the most lovingly crafted ice cream will not freeze. The ideal temperature for ice cream is −18°C/0°F. Home freezers don't go this low so it's best to serve a day or two after it's made. Make sure the freezer is uncluttered (it will freeze more efficiently), with plenty of room to easily fit the container of ice cream. When preparing ice cream, care should be taken to keep everything you use scrupulously clean. Heed the directions and follow them carefully to avoid error or waste. The ingredients are expensive and sensitive; they curdle if overheated or not cooled quickly enough, and form flecks of butter if over-churned.

Ice cream makers come in many different models and varieties. For home use, we recommend the electric motor-driven version of the old-fashioned hand-cranked machine that uses rock salt and ice, or the good old-fashioned hand-cranked machine itself. The reason why we like these best: They offer the best control over the temperature; you can keep adding ice and salt to chill down the mixture. We don't recommend using ice cream machines that employ the canister prechilled by freezing because they don't stay cold long enough to get the job done well (and once the canister becomes too warm, there's no way to correct the problem). More-over, they often are designed to make a very small quantity, and our ice cream pies call for up to 8 cups of ice cream (4 rounds of mixing in a pint-sized machine)!

Vanilla Ice Cream

MAKES 6½ CUPS ICE CREAM

This recipe is the base for most of the ice cream recipes in this chapter. It is rich, creamy, and flecked with flavorful real vanilla. It is particularly excellent made with vanilla sugar. To make vanilla sugar, put whole vanilla beans in granulated sugar for at least a week to impart the flavors of the beans to the sugar—2 to 3 beans will flavor 8 cups of sugar. Store the mixture in an airtight container in a cool place. Regular sugar works just fine, too.

3 cups whole milk	¾ cup plus 2 tablespoons vanilla sugar
1½ vanilla beans, split lengthwise	
¾ cup large egg yolks (about 10 yolks)	1½ cups heavy cream
	Pinch salt

Freeze the empty container in which you plan to store the finished ice cream.

Heat the milk and vanilla beans in a heavy, nonreactive saucepan over medium heat, until the mixture is steamy and hot, with tiny bubbles forming at the pan's edge. Don't let it boil. Remove the pan from the heat and cover.

With an electric mixer, whip the yolks and sugar until they are pale yellow and silky looking. The mixture should stiffen up enough to hold its shape. With the mixer running, or whisking briskly by hand, add the hot milk slowly, in a thin stream, mixing the whole time. Add all of the milk (vanilla beans included).

Prepare an ice water bath in a bowl large enough to surround the top half of a double boiler. Use lots of ice cubes and about 1 quart of water.

Prepare a double boiler and cook the milk mixture in the top of it over medium heat, stirring constantly until the mixture thickens. To test it, remove the pan from the heat and coat the back of a wooden spoon with the mixture; if a line drawn through the coating holds its shape, the custard is thick enough (185°F on an instant-read thermometer). Do not cook it beyond this point or the custard will curdle. Move the top of the double boiler over to rest in the ice water bath, stirring the custard to cool it down as quickly as possible. When the mixture is very cold, it can be refrigerated in a tightly sealed container to further develop the flavors overnight, or it can be made up immediately as follows.

Before pouring the ice cream custard into the machine, remove the vanilla beans and scrape the seeds into the custard. Add the cream and salt and mix well. Pour the ice cream custard into the ice cream machine and mix it for 15 to 20 minutes, until it's the consistency of soft-serve ice cream. (Be careful: Overmixing can churn your cream into butter—there will be little flecks of it everywhere if this happens.)

Quickly fill the prechilled container with the ice cream, using a spatula to compress it. Cover the container and thwack it down on the counter a few times to get the air bubbles out. Place a layer of waxed paper directly on top of the surface of the ice cream and cover it tightly with the lid of the container. Allow the ice cream to set up in the freezer for at least 4 hours before serving.

Homemade ice cream is best served within a couple of days. For optimal flavors, ice cream is ideally served softened a bit. To achieve the proper consistency, take hard ice cream from the freezer and temper it in the refrigerator for 20 to 30 minutes before serving.

Buttermilk Ice Cream

Tangy and refreshing, this special ice cream makes a welcome accompaniment to summer berry pies, peach pies, apple pies, and Rhubarb Crisp (page 200). The base for this ice cream needs to be made a day before freezing it, to allow the flavors to develop.

1¼ cups heavy cream	1½ cups sugar
1 vanilla bean, split lengthwise	4 cups buttermilk
4 large egg yolks	

Freeze the empty container in which you plan to store the finished ice cream.

Heat the cream and vanilla bean in a heavy, nonreactive saucepan over medium heat, until the mixture is steamy and hot, with tiny bubbles forming at the pan's edge. Don't let it boil. Remove the pan from the heat and cover.

With an electric mixer, whip the yolks and sugar until they are pale yellow and silky looking. The mixture should stiffen up enough to hold its shape. With the mixer running, or whisking briskly by hand, add the hot milk slowly, in a thin stream, mixing the whole time. Add all of the milk (vanilla beans included).

Prepare an ice water bath in a bowl large enough to surround the top half of a double boiler. Use lots of ice cubes and about 1 quart of water.

Prepare a double boiler and cook the milk and egg mixture in the top of it over medium heat, stirring constantly until the mixture thickens. To test it, remove the pan from the heat and coat the back of a wooden spoon with the mixture; if a line drawn through the coating holds its shape, the custard is thick enough (185°F on an instant-read thermometer). Do not cook it beyond this point or the custard will curdle. Move the top of the double boiler over to rest in the ice water bath, stirring the custard to cool it down as quickly as possible.

When the mixture is very cold, it should be refrigerated in a tightly sealed container to further develop the flavors overnight.

Remove the vanilla bean and scrape the seeds into the mixture. Dispose of the vanilla pod. Stir in the buttermilk right before mixing the ice cream in the ice cream maker. This custard may separate if allowed to sit after adding the buttermilk, but it'll still be fine. Churn the mixture in the ice cream machine for 15 to 20 minutes, or until it resembles thick cream. This ice cream easily turns to butter (there will be little flecks of it everywhere if this happens), so take care not to overmix it.

Quickly fill the chilled container with the ice cream, using a spatula to compress it. Cover the container and thwack it down on the counter a few times to get the air bubbles out. Place a layer of waxed paper directly on top of the surface of the ice cream and cover it tightly with the lid of the container. Allow the ice cream to set up in the freezer for at least 4 hours before serving.

Homemade ice cream is best served within a couple of days. For optimal flavors, ice cream is ideally served softened a bit. To achieve the proper consistency, take hard ice cream from the freezer and temper it in the refrigerator for 20 to 30 minutes before serving.

PEACH ICE CREAM

Use ripe, sweet, flavorful peaches at the height of their seasonal perfection for this ice cream—get the maximum amount of flavor out of your fruit in the fruit purée. You may wish to add sugar or a touch of lemon juice to the peaches to get the perfect flavor balance. If your peaches are anything short of impressively ripe, consult page 93 for roast-ripening techniques. This ice cream pairs well with Peach–Vanilla Bean Pie (page 94), Blackberry Pie (page 75), Blueberry-Peach Pie (page 98), or Baked Blueberry Pie (page 72).

3 cups whole milk	2 cups peaches
1 vanilla bean, split lengthwise	1½ cups heavy cream
¾ cup large egg yolks (about 10 yolks)	Pinch salt
¾ cup plus 2 tablespoons sugar, plus extra as needed	

Freeze the empty container in which you plan to store the finished ice cream.

Heat the milk and vanilla bean in a heavy, nonreactive saucepan over medium heat, until the mixture is steamy and hot, with tiny bubbles forming at the pan's edge. Don't let it boil. Remove the pan from the heat and cover.

With an electric mixer, whip the yolks and sugar until they are pale yellow and silky looking. The mixture should stiffen up enough to hold its shape. With the mixer running, or whisking briskly by hand, add the hot milk slowly, in a thin stream, mixing the whole time. Add all of the milk (vanilla bean included).

Prepare an ice water bath in a bowl large enough to surround the top half of a double boiler. Use lots of ice cubes and about 1 quart of water.

Prepare a double boiler and cook the milk mixture in the top of it over medium heat, stirring constantly until the mixture thickens. To test it, remove the pan from the heat and coat the back of a wooden spoon with the mixture; if a line drawn through the coating holds its shape, the custard is thick enough (185°F on an instant-read thermometer). Do not cook it beyond this point or the custard will curdle. Move the top of the double boiler over to rest in the ice water bath, stirring the custard to cool it down as quickly as possible. When the mixture is very cold, it can be refrigerated in a tightly sealed container to further develop the flavors overnight, or it can be made up immediately as follows.

Peel the peaches (see page 97), cut them open, and remove the stones. Purée 1 cup of the peaches and dice 1 more cup of fresh peaches quite small. Refrigerate until needed.

Before pouring the ice cream custard into the machine, remove the vanilla bean and scrape the seeds into the custard. Add the cream, salt, and the peach purée and mix well. Pour the ice cream custard into the ice cream machine and mix it for 15 to 20 minutes, until it's the consistency of soft-serve ice cream. (Be careful: Overmixing can churn your cream into butter—there will be little flecks of it everywhere if this happens.)

Swirl the chopped peaches into the partially frozen ice cream and quickly fill the prechilled container with the ice cream, using a spatula to compress it. Cover the container and thwack it down on the counter a few times to get the air bubbles out. Place a layer of waxed paper directly on top of the surface of the ice cream and cover it tightly with the lid of the container. Allow the ice cream to set up in the freezer for at least 4 hours before serving.

Ice cream is best served within a couple of days. For the best-tasting ice cream flavors, ice cream is ideally served softened a bit. To achieve the proper consistency, take hard ice cream from the freezer and temper it in the refrigerator for 20 to 30 minutes before serving.

GINGER ICE CREAM

MAKES 7 CUPS ICE CREAM

This is delicious served with autumn pies like Ginger-Honey Apple Pie (page 114) or Quince-Pear Pie (page 125), or with hearty cool weather desserts like Peachy Brown Betty (page 219), Autumn Apple Crisp (page 202), or Pear-Ginger Crisp (page 201).

4 ounces fresh ginger	3 cups whole milk
2 ¾ cups plus 2 tablespoons sugar, divided	1 vanilla bean, split lengthwise
1 cup water	¾ cup large egg yolks (about 10 yolks)
4 tablespoons finely chopped candied ginger	1½ cups heavy cream
	Pinch salt

Freeze the empty container in which you plan to store the finished ice cream.

Peel and then grate the fresh ginger by hand or in food processor to make about 1 cup of shredded ginger.

In a small, heavy saucepan, combine 2 cups of the sugar, 1 cup water, and the ginger. Bring to a slow boil and simmer it over low heat for 12 to 15 minutes to make a ginger syrup. Pour the syrup through a strainer; save the syrup and discard the grated ginger. Add the candied ginger to the hot syrup to soften it.

Heat the milk and vanilla bean in a heavy, nonreactive saucepan over medium heat, until the mixture is steamy and hot, with tiny bubbles forming at the pan's edge. Don't let it boil. Remove the pan from the heat and cover.

With an electric mixer, whip the yolks and remaining sugar until they are pale yellow and silky looking. The mixture should stiffen up enough to hold its shape. With the mixer running, or whisking briskly by hand, add the hot milk slowly, in a thin stream, mixing the whole time. Add all of the milk (vanilla bean included).

Prepare an ice water bath in a bowl large enough to surround the top half of a double boiler. Use lots of ice cubes and about 1 quart of water.

Prepare a double boiler and cook the milk mixture in the top of it over medium heat, stirring constantly until the mixture thickens. To test it, remove the pan from the heat and coat the back of a wooden spoon with the mixture; if a line drawn through the coating holds its shape, the custard is thick enough (185°F on an instant-read thermometer). Do not cook it beyond this point or the custard will curdle. Move the top of the double boiler over to rest in the ice water bath, stirring the custard to cool it down as quickly as possible. When the mixture is very cold, it can be refrigerated in a tightly sealed container to further develop the flavors overnight, or it can be made up immediately as follows.

Before pouring the ice cream custard into the machine, remove the vanilla beans and scrape the seeds into the custard. Add the ginger syrup, cream and salt and mix well. Pour the ice cream custard into the ice cream machine and mix it for 15 to 20 minutes, until it's the consistency of soft-serve ice cream. (Be careful: Overmixing can churn your cream into butter—there will be little flecks of it everywhere if this happens.)

Quickly fill the prechilled container with the ice cream, using a spatula to compress it. Cover the container and thwack it down on the counter a few times to get the air bubbles out. Place a layer of waxed paper directly on top of the surface of the ice cream and cover it tightly with the lid of the container. Allow the ice cream to set up in the freezer for at least 4 hours before serving.

Ice cream is best served within a couple of days. For the best-tasting ice cream flavors, ice cream is ideally served softened a bit. To achieve the proper consistency, take hard ice cream from the freezer and temper it in the refrigerator for 20 to 30 minutes before serving.

Strawberry Ice Cream

MAKES 8 CUPS ICE CREAM

M ake this in the late spring when local strawberries are at their sweetest, ripest, and most outstanding. In our area, there is a second and third strawberry harvest that extends well into summer, but none as good as those first ones. This could also be made with other fresh berry purées like raspberry. Sure, you could use frozen berries, but the whole point of making your own is to achieve a really remarkable flavor you couldn't find in store-bought ice cream. We prefer to serve this in ice cream pies topped with macerated strawberries (fresh berries with sugar) or with a rich layer of chocolate ganache in an Eskimo Pie (page 296).

3 cups fresh strawberries	¾ cup plus 2 tablespoons sugar
3 cups whole milk	1½ cups heavy cream
1 vanilla bean, split lengthwise	Pinch salt
¾ cup large egg yolks (about 10 yolks)	Confectioners' sugar

Freeze the empty container in which you plan to store the finished ice cream.

Wash and stem the strawberries. With a food processor, purée about 2 cups strawberries to make 1 cup of fresh strawberry purée and roughly chop another 1 cup into a small dice. Refrigerate until needed.

Heat the milk and vanilla bean in a heavy, nonreactive saucepan over medium heat, until the mixture is steamy and hot, with tiny bubbles forming at the pan's edge. Don't let it boil. Remove the pan from the heat and cover.

With an electric mixer, whip the yolks and sugar until they are pale yellow and silky looking. The mixture should stiffen up enough to hold its shape. With the mixer running, or whisking briskly by hand, add the hot milk slowly, in a thin stream, mixing the whole time. Add all of the milk (vanilla bean included).

Prepare an ice water bath in a bowl large enough to surround the top half of a double boiler. Use lots of ice cubes and about 1 quart of water.

Prepare a double boiler and cook the milk mixture in the top of it over medium heat, stirring constantly until the mixture thickens. To test it, remove the pan from the heat and coat the back of a wooden spoon with the mixture; if a line drawn through the coating holds its shape, the custard is thick enough (185°F on an instant-read thermometer). Do not cook it beyond this point or the custard will curdle. Move the top of the double boiler over to rest in the ice water bath, stirring the custard to cool it down as quickly as possible. When the mixture is very cold, it can be refrigerated in a tightly sealed container to further develop the flavors overnight, or it can be made up immediately as follows.

Before pouring the ice cream custard into the machine, remove the vanilla bean and scrape the seeds into the custard. Add the cream and salt and mix well. Pour the ice cream custard into the ice cream machine and mix it for 15 to 20 minutes, until it's the consistency of soft-serve ice cream. (Be careful: Overmixing can churn your cream into butter—there will be little flecks of it everywhere if this happens.)

Toss the chopped strawberries with confectioners' sugar (just enough to lightly coat them) and swirl them into the ice cream. The confectioner's sugar prevents the berries from getting icy. Quickly fill the prechilled container with the ice cream, using a spatula to compress it. Cover the container and thwack it down on the counter a few times to get the air bubbles out. Place a layer of waxed paper directly on top of the surface of the ice cream and cover it tightly with the lid of the container. Allow the ice cream to set up in the freezer for at least 4 hours before serving.

Ice cream is best served within a couple of days. For the best-tasting ice cream flavors, ice cream is ideally served softened a bit. To achieve the proper consistency, take hard ice cream from the freezer and temper it in the refrigerator for 20 to 30 minutes before serving.

Caramel Ice Cream

MAKES 8 CUPS ICE CREAM

This goes well with fall fruit pies—pears in particular, Pecan Pie, Autumn Apple Crisp, Apple Pandowdy, and apple brown betty. It's delicious made into an ice cream pie served with extra Caramel Sauce and Candied Pecans (page 314).

3 cups whole milk	1 recipe Caramel Sauce, at room temperature (page 309)
1 vanilla bean, split lengthwise	
¾ cup large egg yolks (about 10 yolks)	1½ cups heavy cream
	Pinch salt
¾ cup plus 2 tablespoons sugar	

Freeze the empty container in which you plan to store the finished ice cream.

Heat the milk and vanilla bean in a heavy, nonreactive saucepan over medium heat, until the mixture is steamy and hot, with tiny bubbles forming at the pan's edge. Don't let it boil. Remove the pan from the heat and cover.

With an electric mixer, whip the yolks and sugar until they are pale yellow and silky looking. The mixture should stiffen up enough to hold its shape. With the mixer running, or whisking briskly by hand, add the hot milk slowly, in a thin stream, mixing the whole time. Add all of the milk (vanilla beans included).

Prepare an ice water bath in a bowl large enough to surround the top half of a double boiler. Use lots of ice cubes and about 1 quart of water.

Prepare a double boiler and cook the milk mixture in the top of it over medium heat, stirring constantly until the mixture thickens. To test it, remove the pan from the heat and coat the back of a wooden spoon with the mixture; if a line drawn through the coating holds its shape, the custard is thick enough (185°F on an instant-read thermometer). Do not cook it beyond this point or the custard will curdle. Move the top of the double boiler over to rest in the ice water bath, stirring the custard to cool it down as quickly as possible. When the mixture is very cold, it can be refrigerated in a tightly sealed container to further develop the flavors overnight, or it can be made up immediately as follows.

Before pouring the ice cream custard into the machine, remove the vanilla beans and scrape the seeds into the custard. Add 1 cup of Caramel Sauce, cream, and salt and mix well. Pour the ice cream custard into the ice cream machine and mix it for 15 to 20 minutes, until it's the consistency of soft-serve ice cream. (Be careful: Overmixing can churn your cream into butter—there will be little flecks of it everywhere if this happens.)

Quickly fill the prechilled container with the ice cream and swirl in the remaining Caramel Sauce, using a spatula to compress the ice cream. Cover the container and thwack it down on the counter a few times to get the air bubbles out. Place a layer of waxed paper directly on top of the surface of the ice cream and cover it tightly with the lid of the container. Allow the ice cream to set up in the freezer for at least 4 hours before serving.

Ice cream is best served within a couple of days. For the best-tasting ice cream flavors, ice cream is ideally served softened a bit. To achieve the proper consistency, take hard ice cream from the freezer and temper it in the refrigerator for 20 to 30 minutes before serving.

Espresso Ice Cream

MAKES 8 CUPS ICE CREAM

We use this rich, intense ice cream for our Cappuccino Meringue Pie (page 299), but you might also enjoy it paired with Mocha-Pecan Pie (page 131), Baked Apple Dumplings (page 222), or an Eskimo Pie (page 296) with a Chocolate Crumb Crust (page 41).

1½ cups good-quality espresso beans	2¼ cups sugar
4½ cups whole milk	3 cups heavy cream
1 cup egg yolks, plus 1 more yolk (about 15 yolks)	Pinch salt

---

Freeze the empty container in which you plan to store the finished ice cream.

Grind the espresso beans a little coarser than those you'd use for drip coffee.

In a large nonreactive saucepan, combine the espresso, milk, and cream. Heat gently until the mixture is steamy and hot, with tiny bubbles forming at the pan's edge. Don't let it boil. Turn off the heat and let the mixture sit for at least 10 minutes to allow the espresso to brew. Strain the ground espresso beans from the milk using a fine sieve. Discard the beans and return the milk to the pan.

With an electric mixer, whip the yolks and sugar until they are pale yellow and silky looking. The mixture should stiffen up enough to hold its shape. With the mixer running, or whisking briskly by hand, add the hot milk slowly, in a thin stream, mixing the whole time. Add all of the milk.

Prepare an ice water bath in a bowl large enough to surround the top half of a double boiler. Use lots of ice cubes and about 1 quart of water.

Prepare a double boiler and cook the milk mixture in the top of it over medium heat, stirring constantly until the mixture thickens. To test it, remove the pan from the heat and coat the back of a wooden spoon with the mixture; if a line drawn through the coating holds its shape, the custard is thick enough (185°F on an instant-read thermometer). Do not cook it beyond this point or the custard will curdle. Move the top of the double boiler over to rest in the ice water bath, stirring the custard to cool it down as quickly as possible. When the mixture is very cold, it can be refrigerated in a tightly sealed container to further develop the flavors overnight, or it can be made up immediately as follows.

Add the cream and salt and mix well. Pour the ice cream custard into the ice cream machine and mix it for 15 to 20 minutes, until it's the consistency of soft-serve ice cream. (Be careful: Overmixing can churn your cream into butter—there will be little flecks of it everywhere if this happens.)

Quickly fill the prechilled container with the ice cream, using a spatula to compress it. Cover the container and thwack it down on the counter a few times to get the air bubbles out. Place a layer of waxed paper directly on top of the surface of the ice cream and cover it tightly with the lid of the container. Allow the ice cream to set up in the freezer for at least 4 hours before serving.

Ice cream is best served within a couple of days. For the best-tasting ice cream flavors, ice cream is ideally served softened a bit. To achieve the proper consistency, take hard ice cream from the freezer and temper it in the refrigerator for 20 to 30 minutes before serving.

Chocolate Ice Cream

Use a good-quality chocolate with at least 70% cocoa content.

---

2 cups plus 2 tablespoons whole milk	1⅓ cups Dutch-process powdered cocoa
1 vanilla bean, split lengthwise	
½ cup large egg yolks plus 1 more yolk (about 7 yolks)	¾ cup hot water
	⅓ cup sugar
½ cup plus 1 tablespoon sugar	1 cup plus 1 tablespoon heavy cream
3 ounces bittersweet chocolate	Pinch salt

Freeze the empty container in which you plan to store the finished ice cream.

Heat the milk and vanilla bean in a heavy, nonreactive saucepan over medium heat, until the mixture is steamy and hot, with tiny bubbles forming at the pan's edge. Don't let it boil. Remove the pan from the heat and cover.

With an electric mixer, whip the yolks and sugar until they are pale yellow and silky looking. The mixture should stiffen up enough to hold its shape. With the mixer running, or whisking briskly by hand, add the hot milk slowly, in a thin stream, mixing the whole time. Add all of the milk (vanilla bean included).

Prepare an ice water bath in a bowl large enough to surround the top half of a double boiler. Use lots of ice cubes and about 1 quart of water.

Prepare a double boiler and cook the milk mixture in the top of it over medium heat, stirring constantly until the mixture thickens. To test it, remove the pan from the heat and coat the back of a wooden spoon with the mixture; if a line drawn through the coating holds its shape, the custard is thick enough (185°F on an instant-read thermometer). Do not cook it beyond this point or the custard will curdle. Move the top of the double boiler over to rest in the ice water bath, stirring the custard to cool it down as quickly as possible. When the mixture is very cold, it can be refrigerated in a tightly sealed container to further develop the flavors overnight, or it can be made up as follows.

In the top of a double boiler over low heat, melt the chocolate. Sift the cocoa to remove any lumps and mix it with the hot water and sugar until the mixture is smooth. Combine the cocoa mixture with the melted chocolate and whisk well. Whisk in the cream and salt. Chill it in the refrigerator until cool.

Before pouring the ice cream custard into the machine, remove the vanilla bean and scrape the seeds into the custard. Add the chocolate mixture to the custard and stir. Pour the ice cream custard into the ice cream machine and mix it for 15 to 20 minutes, until it's the consistency of soft-serve ice cream. (Be careful: Overmixing can churn your cream into butter—there will be little flecks of it everywhere if this happens.)

Quickly fill the prechilled container with the ice cream, using a spatula to compress it. Cover the container and thwack it down on the counter a few times to get the air bubbles out. Place a layer of waxed paper directly on top of the surface of the ice cream and cover it tightly with the lid of the container. Allow the ice cream to set up in the freezer for at least 4 hours before serving.

Ice cream is best served within a couple of days. For the best-tasting ice cream flavors, ice cream is ideally served softened a bit. To achieve the proper consistency, take hard ice cream from the freezer and temper it in the refrigerator for 20 to 30 minutes before serving.

ROCKY ROAD ICE CREAM

MAKES 9 CUPS ICE CREAM

Rocky Road is a nostalgic, blissful combination of tastes: Chocolate Ice Cream with bittersweet chocolate shavings, toasted almonds, and wonderful Homemade Marshmallows. We only serve this one plain or in an ice cream pie; it's too rich to serve with other pies.

1 heaping cup blanched raw almonds, roughly chopped	1 cup Homemade Marshmallows (page 319)
8 ounces bittersweet chocolate, roughly chopped	1 recipe Chocolate Ice Cream (page 286)

Preheat the oven to 325°F.

Toast the almonds on a lipped baking sheet for 15 minutes , or until lightly toasted and fragrant. Cool them before proceeding.

Freeze the empty container in which you plan to store the finished ice cream. Combine the chocolate, marshmallows, and almonds and freeze them on a baking sheet for at least 1 hour. When they are frozen, break the mixture up into small (¼–½-inch) pieces.

Prepare Chocolate Ice Cream as instructed. When the ice cream churning is finished, stir in the frozen chocolate, marshmallow, and almond mix by handfuls.

Quickly fill the prechilled container with the ice cream, using a spatula to compress it. Cover the container and thwack it down on the counter a few times to get the air bubbles out. Place a layer of waxed paper directly on top of the surface of the ice cream and cover it tightly with the lid of the container. Allow the ice cream to set up in the freezer for at least 2 hours before serving.

Ice cream is best served within a couple of days. For optimal flavors, ice cream is ideally served softened a bit. To achieve the proper consistency, take hard ice cream from the freezer and temper it in the refrigerator for 20 to 30 minutes before serving.

MINT CHIP ICE CREAM

This ice cream for our Grasshopper Eskimo Pie (page 297), but it would also be great in an Eskimo Pie with a layer of chocolate ganache in a Chocolate-Peppermint Crumb Crust (page 41).

SIMPLE SYRUP

½ cup water

½ cup sugar

1 cup clean fresh peppermint leaves or ½ teaspoon peppermint extract

¾ cup plus 2 tablespoons sugar

3 cups whole milk

1 vanilla bean, split lengthwise

¾ cup large egg yolks (about 10 yolks)

1½ cups heavy cream

Pinch salt

2 cups bittersweet chocolate shavings (grated by hand or in a food processor)

Freeze the empty container in which you plan to store the finished ice cream.

In a medium pot over low heat, make the simple syrup by combining the sugar and water. When the sugar is fully dissolved, stir in the fresh mint to the syrup. Stir and heat for 30 minutes, until flavorful. Strain the syrup from the mint leaves and discard the leaves. If using extract, bring syrup to a boil, then add the extract.

Heat the milk and vanilla bean in a heavy, nonreactive saucepan over medium heat, until the mixture is steamy and hot, with tiny bubbles forming at the pan's edge. Don't let it boil. Remove the pan from the heat and cover.

With an electric mixer, whip the yolks and sugar until they are pale yellow and silky looking. The mixture should stiffen up enough to hold its shape. With the mixer running, or whisking briskly by hand, add the hot milk slowly, in a thin stream, mixing the whole time. Add all of the milk (vanilla bean included).

Prepare an ice water bath in a bowl large enough to surround the top half of a double boiler. Use lots of ice cubes and about 1 quart of water.

Prepare a double boiler and cook the milk mixture in the top of it over medium heat, stirring constantly until the mixture thickens. To test it, remove the pan from the heat and coat the back of a wooden spoon with the mixture; if a line drawn through the coating holds its shape, the custard is thick enough (185°F on an instant-read thermometer). Do not cook it beyond this point or the custard will curdle. Move the top of the double boiler over to rest in the ice water bath, stirring the custard to cool it down as quickly as possible. When the mixture is very cold, it can be refrigerated in a tightly sealed container to further develop the flavors overnight, or it can be made up immediately as follows.

Before pouring the ice cream batter into the machine, remove the vanilla bean and scrape the seeds into the custard. Stir in the cream, mint syrup, and salt. Pour the ice cream custard into the ice cream machine and mix it for 15 to 20 minutes, until it's the consistency of soft-serve ice cream. (Be careful: Overmixing can churn your cream into butter—there will be little flecks of it everywhere if this happens.) When the ice cream churning is finished, stir in the bittersweet chocolate shavings.

Quickly fill the prechilled container with the ice cream, using a spatula to compress it. Cover the container and thwack it down on the counter a few times to get the air bubbles out. Place a layer of waxed paper directly on top of the surface of the ice cream and cover it tightly with the lid of the container. Allow the ice cream to set up in the freezer for at least 4 hours before serving.

Ice cream is best served within a couple of days. For the best-tasting ice cream flavors, ice cream is ideally served softened a bit. To achieve the proper consistency, take hard ice cream from the freezer and temper it in the refrigerator for 20 to 30 minutes before serving.

Banana–Chocolate Chip Ice Cream

This ice cream is great in an Eskimo Pie with Chocolate Ganache and a Chocolate Crumb Crust (see page 41). Choose bananas freckled with some black spots for good banana flavor.

3 cups whole milk	2 tablespoons fresh-squeezed lemon juice
1 vanilla bean, split lengthwise	
¾ cup large egg yolks (about 10 yolks)	2 tablespoons banana liqueur
	2 cups bittersweet chocolate shavings
¾ cup plus 2 tablespoons sugar	1½ cups heavy cream
6 cups ripe banana purée	Pinch salt

Freeze the empty container in which you plan to store the finished ice cream.

Heat the milk and vanilla bean in a heavy, nonreactive saucepan over medium heat, until the mixture is steamy and hot, with tiny bubbles forming at the pan's edge. Don't let it boil. Remove the pan from the heat and cover.

With an electric mixer, whip the yolks and sugar until they are pale yellow and silky looking. The mixture should stiffen up enough to hold its shape. With the mixer running, or whisking briskly by hand, add the hot milk slowly, in a thin stream, mixing the whole time. Add all of the milk (vanilla bean included).

Prepare an ice water bath in a bowl large enough to surround the top half of a double boiler. Use lots of ice cubes and about 1 quart of water.

Prepare a double boiler and cook the milk mixture in the top of it over medium heat, stirring constantly until the mixture thickens. To test it, remove the pan from the heat and coat the back of a wooden spoon with the mixture; if a line drawn through the coating holds its shape, the custard is thick enough (185°F on an instant-read thermometer). Do not cook it beyond this point or the custard will curdle. Move the top of the double boiler over to rest in the ice water bath, stirring the custard to cool it down as quickly as possible. When the mixture is very cold, it can be refrigerated in a tightly sealed container to further develop the flavors overnight, or it can be made up immediately as follows.

Remove the vanilla bean from the custard and scrape the seeds into it. Add the cream, bananas, and salt and mix well. In a food processor, mix the bananas, lemon juice, and banana liqueur until smooth. Stir it into the cold custard. Pour the ice cream custard into the ice cream machine and mix it for 15 to 20 minutes, until it's the consistency of soft-serve ice cream. (Be careful: Overmixing can churn your cream into butter—there will be little flecks of it everywhere if this happens.)

Stir the chocolate shavings into the ice cream and quickly fill the prechilled container, using a spatula to compress it. Cover the container and thwack it down on the counter a few times to get the air bubbles out. Place a layer of waxed paper directly on top of the surface of the ice cream and cover it tightly with the lid of the container. Allow the ice cream to set up in the freezer for at least 4 hours before serving.

Ice cream is best served within a couple of days. For the best-tasting ice cream flavors, ice cream is ideally served softened a bit. To achieve the proper consistency, take hard ice cream from the freezer and temper it in the refrigerator for 20 to 30 minutes before serving.

Maple Syrup Ice Cream

MAKES 8 CUPS ICE CREAM

This ice cream is prepared a little bit differently. The custard isn't fully cooked and the cream is added sooner. It is delicious with Pecan Pie (page 129), waffles, or any autumn fruit pie. When collected, maple syrup is boiled down from sap. It takes over 6 gallons of raw sap to make the syrup used in this ice cream.

4 cups maple syrup	½ cup packed light brown sugar
4½ cups milk	2¼ cups heavy cream
1 cup egg yolks plus 1 more yolk (about 15 yolks)	

Cook the syrup, uncovered, over medium-high heat for about 20 minutes, until it reduces to 2 cups. Cool completely.

Heat the milk in a heavy, nonreactive saucepan over medium heat, until the mixture is steamy and hot, with tiny bubbles forming at the pan's edge. Don't let it boil. Remove the pan from the heat and cover.

With an electric mixer, whip the egg yolks and sugar until they are pale yellow and silky looking. The mixture should stiffen up enough to hold its shape. With the mixer running slowly, or whisking briskly by hand, add the hot milk slowly, in a thin stream, mixing the whole time. Keep whisking and add the heavy cream, and then gradually add the reduced maple syrup in a thin stream.

Prepare an ice water bath in a bowl large enough to surround the top half of a pan. Use lots of ice cubes and about 1 quart of water.

Move the bowl of milk mixture to rest in the ice water bath, stirring the custard to cool it down as quickly as possible. When the mixture is very cold, it can be refrigerated in a tightly sealed container to further develop the flavors overnight, or it can be made up immediately as follows.

Freeze the empty container in which you plan to store the finished ice cream. Pour the ice cream custard into the ice cream machine and mix it for

15 to 20 minutes, until it's the consistency of soft-serve ice cream. (Be careful: Overmixing can churn your cream into butter—there will be little flecks of it everywhere if this happens.)

Quickly fill the prechilled container with the ice cream, using a spatula to compress it. Cover the container and thwack it down on the counter a few times to get the air bubbles out. Place a layer of waxed paper directly on top of the surface of the ice cream and cover it tightly with the lid of the container. Allow the ice cream to set up in the freezer for at least 4 hours before serving.

Ice cream is best served within a couple of days. For the best-tasting ice cream flavors, ice cream is ideally served softened a bit. To achieve the proper consistency, take hard ice cream from the freezer and temper it in the refrigerator for 20 to 30 minutes before serving.

K ids and parents love these pies for summer birthdays.

---

1 recipe any type of cookie crumb crust (page 34 to 42), frozen	Sauces or toppings (optional)
6 cups homemade or good quality ice cream, frozen	

Fill the crumb crust of your choice with the ice cream of your choice, smoothing out the ice cream with an offset pastry spatula. Refreeze immediately, uncovered.

Freeze the pie for at least 1 hour more before serving. When the pie is fully frozen, cover it loosely with plastic wrap until served. Prepare any desired sauces or toppings.

To serve, cut pieces with a knife warmed in hot water. If the ice cream starts to stick to the knife, dip it in hot water and dry it with a paper towel before resuming cutting the pie. Serve immediately, alone, or with desired sauces or toppings.

Eskimo Pie

Almost any excellent ice cream will taste great inside Bubby's home-made Chocolate Crumb Crust. Spread a thick layer of rich dark Chocolate Ganache on top of the ice cream and you've got a seriously delicious mix of flavors and textures. You can use any kind of sweet crumb crust for this pie, any kind of ice cream that pairs well with Chocolate Ganache, and top it all with whatever you like—fresh strawberries or candied nuts, for example. Use your imagination.

1 recipe Chocolate Crumb Crust (page 41), frozen

4 cups (2 pints) homemade or good-quality ice cream

2 cups Chocolate Ganache (page 308), room temperature

Soften the ice cream in the refrigerator for 20 to 30 minutes, until it's the consistency of soft-serve ice cream. Spread the ice cream in the crust using a cake spatula, working it from the center outward.

Freeze the pie for at least 2 hours, uncovered, until the ice cream is solid (times will vary according to ice cream and freezer). Spread the ganache evenly over the top of the ice cream, covering up the ice cream but stopping just shy of the crumb crust. Refreeze immediately, uncovered.

Freeze the pie for at least 1 hour more before serving. When the pie is fully frozen, cover it loosely with plastic wrap until served.

To serve, cut pieces with a knife warmed in hot water. If the ice cream starts to stick to the knife, dip it in hot water and dry it with a paper towel before resuming cutting the pie. Serve immediately.

Banana-Chocolate Eskimo Pie

1 recipe Chocolate Crumb Crust (page 41), frozen
4 cups Banana–Chocolate Chip Ice Cream (page 291)
2 cups Chocolate Ganache (page 308), room temperature

Grasshopper Eskimo Pie

1 recipe Chocolate Crumb Crust (page 41), frozen
4 cups Mint Chocolate Chip Ice Cream (page 289)
2 cups Chocolate Ganache (page 308), room temperature

Sweetie Pie

MAKES ONE 9-INCH SINGLE-CRUST PIE

Put out lots of fun toppings and let kids build individual creations on their own slice of this layered Strawberry and Chocolate Ice Cream Pie. It's a great one for a messy birthday party. Or make tiny individual pies, and little ones can eat their unique creations.

1 recipe Chocolate Crumb Crust, frozen (page 41)	Hot Fudge Sauce (page 311)
2 cups Chocolate Ice Cream (page 286)	Whipped Cream (page 302)
2 cups Strawberry Ice Cream (page 280)	Fresh sweet cherries or strawberries
	Candy sprinkles
	Chopped nuts

Spread Chocolate Ice Cream in the Chocolate Crumb Crust, smoothing it out with an offset pastry spatula. If the ice cream is soft, freeze uncovered until solid. Layer Strawberry Ice Cream on top, smoothing it out with an offset pastry spatula. Refreeze immediately.

Freeze the pie for at least 1 hour more before serving. When the pie is fully frozen, cover it loosely with plastic wrap until served. Prepare any desired sauces or toppings.

To serve, cut pieces with a knife warmed in hot water. If the ice cream starts to stick to the knife, dip it in hot water and dry it with a paper towel before resuming cutting the pie. Serve immediately.

CAPPUCCINO MERINGUE PIE

MAKES ONE 9-INCH SINGLE-CRUST PIE

This one is a favorite for coffee ice cream lovers. Frozen meringue imitates foam on a cappuccino, and its texture and caramel flavor is a delicious complement. You can also substitute Espresso Meringue (page 306).

1 recipe Chocolate Crumb Crust (page 41), frozen

4 cups Espresso Ice Cream (page 284)

2 cups Italian Meringue (page 305), cooled

Soften the ice cream in the refrigerator for about 30 minutes, until it's the consistency of soft-serve ice cream. Spread the ice cream in the crust using a cake spatula, working it from the center outward.

Freeze the pie for at least 2 hours, uncovered, until the ice cream is solid (times will vary according to ice cream and freezer).

Top the ice cream pie with the meringue. Be thorough when spreading the meringue, and make sure you form a seal with the meringue and crust all the way around. Otherwise, if there is any exposed filling, the meringue will "weep," or release moisture, creating a watery mess. Use the back of a wooden spoon or spatula to pull the meringue up into peaks. Style away until the meringue topping is curvaceous.

Clear the area of flammable materials, tuck back any loose hair or clothing and proceed to light a propane kitchen torch according to the torch's instructions. Hold it about 6 inches away from the meringue and move it continuously to prevent flare-ups. The flame should not touch the pie directly. Work with the heat just beyond the flame to singe the peaks of the meringue curls caramel brown. If the meringue catches fire, blow out the flare up immediately and continue working. When you've finished, most of the curls should be caramel colored. Freeze the pie, uncovered, for at least 3 hours for the pie to set and chill before serving or transporting it. When the pie is fully frozen, cover it loosely with plastic wrap until needed.

To serve, cut pieces with a knife warmed in hot water. If the ice cream starts to stick to the knife, dip it in hot water and dry it with a paper towel before resuming cutting the pie. Serve immediately.

Chapter 10

SAUCES, TOPPINGS,
AND CANDIES

The recipes in this chapter form the building blocks and components of some of our favorite pies, like the Chocolate Ganache in the Eskimo Pies, Italian Meringue in the Mile-High Lemon Meringue Pie, Lemon Curd for tarts or our Double Lemon Chess Pie, Vanilla Pouring Custard for fruit crumbles, and Candied Pecans or Walnuts for the Banana Cream Pie or Pumpkin Pie. Conceiving of them as building blocks will help you compose your own new pies, too. Beyond that, there some wonderful optional sauces and decorative and delicious flourishes like Candied Citrus Slices and Homemade Marshmallows.

WHIPPED CREAM

MAKES 2 CUPS

Use cold, heavy whipping cream in a chilled bowl to make the best whipped cream. Whipped cream should be made shortly before serving and used immediately.

---

1 pint heavy cream, very cold

Chill the bowl, whisk, and cream well before making whipped cream.

Whip the cream either by hand with a whisk or with an electric mixer. If you want to use it to dollop on the side, whip it to soft peaks; for spreading on top of a pie or cake, whip it to medium peaks; if you want to pipe the whipped cream, whip it to medium-stiff peaks. Add any flavor you desire, such as a pinch of sugar, a splash of vanilla extract, or a drop of brandy, after the cream forms soft peaks. It does not hold particularly well once it has been whipped but it will hold for a half an hour or so covered in the refrigerator (for second helpings).

CRÈME FRAÎCHE

MAKES 2 CUPS

Crème fraîche is thickened cultured cream about the consistency of sour cream or thick yogurt. It's simple to make and less expensive than store-bought, though it must be started at least twelve hours in advance (you can also make Quick Crème Fraîche, page 304). It lasts longer than plain heavy cream—up to 3 weeks! Crème fraîche is terrific on Fresh Blueberry Pie (page 71) or Concord Grape Pie (page 101). This recipe is easily halved if you only want 1 cup.

2 cups pasteurized heavy cream (ultra-pasteurized won't work)	2 tablespoons buttermilk
	2 tablespoons sugar

Combine the cream and buttermilk (but not the sugar) in a jar with a tight-fitting lid and place it in a warm (70° to 80°F) spot, such as the top of the refrigerator. Allow it to sit, undisturbed overnight or until thickened but still pourable. Chill it and it will become the consistency of sour cream.

To use, add 1 tablespoon sugar for each cup of crème fraîche needed and whisk lightly by hand. Sweeten only the portion you plan to serve immediately.

Crème Fraîche lasts for 3 weeks, tightly covered in the refrigerator.

Quick Crème Fraîche

MAKES 1¾ CUPS

In a pinch, this quick version can be substituted for Crème Fraîche. It is a bit less tangy than the real thing and it only lasts for one day.

¾ cup heavy cream
¼ cup sour cream

1 tablespoon sugar

Combine the cream, sour cream, and sugar in a small bowl and refrigerate them, covered, for at least 15 minutes to chill them down. Using a whisk or electric mixer, beat the mixture just until soft peaks form when the beater is raised or until it mounds when dropped from a spoon.

Serve immediately or refrigerate in an airtight container up to 24 hours only. Beat again, lightly, before using.

Clotted Cream

Clotted or "clouted" cream is a rich (about 60 percent fat content) congealed form of thick cooked cream of English origin. It's used similarly to whipped cream or crème fraîche and is excellent with mince pies (essential, we might argue).

We buy it in the dairy section of gourmet groceries around the fall and winter holidays; we find it is only available seasonally in New York. The product sold as "brandy clotted cream" is overbearingly strong with brandy flavor. A much more desirable balance can be made by mixing your own from plain clotted cream.

To mix up brandy clotted cream, stir a drop or two of good-quality Calvados (apple brandy) or cognac into a jar (about a ½ cup) of plain clotted cream. Clotted cream, plain or with brandy added, keeps for a few days, once opened.

MAKES 4 CUPS MERINGUE; ENOUGH FOR ONE 9-INCH PIE

Many meringue fillings impress the eye but are kind of boring to the palate. Bubby's meringue has a distinctively caramel flavor from the caramelized brown sugar that assures not a morsel goes uneaten. It also holds up much better than any other meringue we've tried. It doesn't weep or get watery. We use it on our Mile-High Lemon Meringue Pie (page 263) and our Cappuccino Meringue Pie (page 299). Meringue topping works best in sharp contrast to a filling that is either tart or bittersweet. It's helpful to have a small propane kitchen torch to singe the meringue. Separate eggs carefully. If the whites have any yolk in them—even the smallest bit—they won't whip up properly.

4 large egg whites	⅔ cup sugar
3 tablespoons water	⅛ teaspoon cream of tartar
1 cup packed light brown sugar	

Place the egg whites in the bowl of an electric mixer but do not mix them yet.

Pour the water into a heavy saucepan and add both sugars; do not stir. Attach a candy thermometer to the saucepan and bring to a boil over high heat. When the sugar syrup reaches the hard-ball stage, approximately 253°F, remove from the heat.

Whisk the egg whites on low speed briefly, then on medium speed, until they are frothy and have increased in volume. Add the cream of tartar. Pour in a little of the sugar mixture with the mixer off and then quickly turn it on medium-high to combine the syrup. Continue in batches this way. When all the sugar syrup is added, turn the mixer to high and continue mixing until the whites develop a stiff peak (demonstrated by a peak that when pulled with the back of a spoon, takes a strong shape and does not slump back down afterwards). The meringue will cool as it gets there but will still be slightly warm.

Scrape the warm meringue onto the chilled pie and use a spatula to shape it into a smooth dome, pushing gently. Be thorough when spreading meringue on a pie and make sure you form a seal between the meringue and crust all the way around. Otherwise, if there is any exposed filling the meringue will "weep," or release moisture, creating a watery mess. Use the back of a wooden spoon or spatula to pull the meringue up into peaks. Style away until the meringue topping is covered with curvy, pointed peaks. Work quickly, before the meringue cools and sets.

Use a propane kitchen torch to evenly brown the meringue. Point the flame slightly above the peaks to avoid flare-ups. If you don't have a torch, place the pie in a 400°F oven for 5 to 10 minutes, until the peaks brown nicely.

Cut and serve the pie immediately or chill it until needed. If storing it overnight or longer in the refrigerator, use toothpicks to prop up plastic wrap to cover the pie. It will last up to 3 days refrigerated.

Espresso Meringue

This variation is delicious for Cappucino Meringue Pie; it would also be excellent on a Chocolate Pudding Pie. The espresso complements the caramelly flavors in the meringue and cuts its sweetness.

1 tablespoon espresso powder
1 teaspoon hot water

Stir together the espresso powder and hot water until thick and perfectly smooth; set aside. Add to the meringue after all of the sugar syrup has been added, but before the mixer is turned to high speed.

Lemon Curd

This recipe is based on Rose Levy Beranbaum's Classic Lemon Curd—so sour, it makes you shiver. It makes our Double Lemon Chess Pie exceptional, and is adapted to all sorts of tarts where it forms a bright field for fresh summer berries. It can be adapted for other citrus fruits; we use a variation of it—tangerine curd—in the Raspberry Tangerine Tart (page 139).

1½ cups sugar

½ cup egg yolks (about 8 yolks)

8 tablespoons (1 stick) unsalted butter

¾ cup fresh-squeezed lemon juice

⅛ teaspoon salt

4 teaspoons lemon zest

In a heavy, nonreactive saucepan, beat the sugar and yolks until well blended. Then stir in the butter, juice, and salt and cook over medium-low heat, stirring constantly, for about a few minutes, until it thickly coats the back of a wooden spoon but is still liquid enough to pour. The mixture will change color from translucent to opaque. Whenever steam appears, remove the pan briefly from the heat, stirring constantly, to keep it from boiling. It must not be allowed to boil or the eggs will curdle.

When the curd has thickened, pour it at once through a fine-mesh strainer. Press with the back of a spoon until only coarse residue remains. Discard the residue. Stir in the lemon zest and pour it into an airtight container. The curd will continue to thicken while resting and chilling.

Store tightly covered in the refrigerator for up to 1 month.

Chocolate Ganache

MAKES 2 CUPS

G anache is the consistency of frosting. Chocolate and heavy cream combine for a chocolate that is strong in flavor and not too sweet. Use it for Eskimo Pies, Bubby's Original Peanut Butter–Chocolate Pie, Pecan-Caramel-Chocolate Tart, and your own creations.

8 ounces bittersweet chocolate, chopped	1 tablespoon cognac, rum, vanilla extract, or Cointreau (optional)
1 cup heavy cream	

Place the chocolate and the cream in a simmering double boiler. Stir the chocolate occasionally to keep it from burning or overheating. When the chocolate is completely melted and the mixture is smooth, set it aside to cool to room temperature. Stir in the optional flavoring.

Use immediately or store tightly covered in the refrigerator for up to a few weeks. To reheat the ganache use a double boiler, stirring occasionally, and allow the ganache to come to room temperature before trying to spread it. (You really need to heat it and let it cool back down to spread it.)

Caramel Sauce

Thick but pourable when warm, this flavorful caramel sauce goes well with pear, apple, and ice cream pies. It is also the flavor base for Caramel Ice Cream. You will need a candy thermometer to make it—it's more reliable than smell or color, and the caramel is far too hot to taste while it's cooking. Hot caramel can cause severe burns, so be attentive and careful while making it.

1½ cups sugar	2 tablespoons sour cream
½ cup water	1 cup (2 sticks) unsalted butter, cubed
½ cup heavy cream	

Combine the sugar and water in a heavy pot over medium heat (check the heat setting or too much water will evaporate before the sugar has had a chance to melt). Don't stir it. Clip a candy thermometer to the side so that the tip is immersed in the water but not touching the bottom of the pan.

Whisk together the heavy cream and sour cream. Set aside at room temperature.

Cook the syrup until it is a rich caramel color (340° to 380°F on the thermometer) and remove it from the heat. You can choose how dark and intense you want your caramel flavor—the lower temperatures yield a light, sweet caramel, while the higher temperatures create a darker, less sweet caramel. If the syrup gets hotter than 380°F, the caramel will be burnt and bitter, so start over.

Use caution during the next stage: The butter releases a lot of steam when it hits the caramel, so be careful not to get burned by the steam. With the caramel pot off the heat, add the butter a little at a time, stirring quickly. Add the cream and sour cream and stir well.

Cool and store the caramel sauce in an airtight container. It will keep for up to 30 days at room temperature or up to 3 months refrigerated. To reheat, warm the sauce over a double boiler, stirring occasionally.

Caramel-Orange Sauce

MAKES 2 CUPS

We use this sauce in our turtle-like Pecan-Caramel-Chocolate Tart (page 132).

2 cups fresh-squeezed orange juice	7 tablespoons unsalted butter, divided
1½ cups sugar	2 tablespoons finely minced orange zest
½ cup water	
¼ cup heavy cream	Pinch salt
2 tablespoons sour cream	

In a nonreactive pan, reduce the juice uncovered over medium heat for about 20 minutes, until it reaches a thick coating consistency and about 3 tablespoons are left. Set aside off heat.

Combine the sugar and water in a heavy pot over medium heat (check the heat setting or too much water will evaporate before the sugar has had a chance to melt). Don't stir it. Clip a candy thermometer to the side so that the tip is immersed in the water but not touching the bottom of the pan.

Whisk together the cream and sour cream. Let cool to room temperature.

Cook the syrup until it is a rich caramel color (340° to 380°F on the thermometer) and remove it from the heat. You can choose how dark and intense you want your caramel flavor—the lower temperatures yield a light, sweet caramel, while the higher temperatures create a darker, less sweet caramel. If the syrup gets hotter than 380°F, the caramel will be burnt and bitter, and you'll have to start over. Use caution now: The butter releases a lot of steam when it hits the caramel, so be careful not to get burned by the steam. With the caramel pot off the heat, add the butter a little at a time, stirring quickly. Add the cream and stir well. Add the orange reduction with zest, and a pinch of salt to taste. Stir until evenly combined. Cool until needed.

Cool and keep caramel in an airtight container. Keep up to 10 days at room temperature or for 3 months refrigerated. To reheat, warm it over a double boiler, stirring occasionally.

Hot Fudge Sauce

MAKES 2 CUPS

Chocolatey and intense, but not too sweet. Use high-quality unsweetened baker's chocolate like Valrhona or Scharffen Berger. The sweetened condensed milk helps keep this sauce liquid at room temperature. Perfect for Ice Cream Pies (page 295) and Sweetie Pies (page 298).

One 14-ounce can sweetened condensed milk

2 ounces unsweetened dark chocolate, chopped

⅛ teaspoon salt

½ cup water

½ teaspoon vanilla extract

Heat the milk, chocolate, and salt in the top of a double boiler over simmering water. Stir constantly for about 10 minutes, until the chocolate melts and mixture thickens.

Remove the sauce from the heat and stir in ½ cup water, a little at a time, until the sauce reaches the desired consistency. Cool it slightly and stir in the vanilla.

Store it covered in the refrigerator up to 3 weeks. Warm over a double boiler before serving.

Mocha Sauce

Dissolve 1 tablespoon instant espresso powder in 1 tablespoon hot water and add it to the double boiler before adding the warm water to the sauce. The espresso gives the hot fudge sauce a darker, bittersweet flavor.

RASPBERRY SAUCE

MAKES I CUP

This sauce works beautifully with any lemon pie. It's also great drizzled over a Vanilla Pudding Pie (page 240) with fresh raspberries. You can easily adapt this recipe to other berries. To use black currants, omit the lemon zest and lemon juice.

1 cup fresh raspberries (half pint)	1 lemon, juiced
½ cup sugar	1 tablespoon cassis
1 lemon, zested	(black currant liqueur)

Combine the raspberries, sugar, lemon zest, juice, and cassis in a small saucepan over medium-low heat. Do not stir, just give the pan an occasional shake until the berries release their juice and get nice and bubbly. Whisk and reduce the sauce until thickened to a coating consistency.

Strain the sauce through a fine-mesh sieve and press the berries through with a rubber spatula. Scrape the juice from the underside of the sieve and dispose of the seeds.

Refrigerate the sauce covered for up to a week.

VANILLA POURING CUSTARD

MAKES 3 CUPS

This crème anglaise sauce made with real vanilla bean is an essential addition to fruit crumbles (see page 194). It is made very much the same way as pudding but its finished consistency is thinner than pudding. We serve it warm, pooled around an individual serving of fruit crumble in a bowl.

1½ cups whole milk	8 large egg yolks
½ cup heavy cream	½ cup sugar
1 vanilla bean, split lengthwise	

In a nonreactive medium saucepan over medium heat, combine the milk, cream, and vanilla bean. When it forms small bubbles at the edge and steams slightly, turn off the heat. Remove it from the heat and scrape the seeds of the vanilla bean into the milk; dispose of the pod.

In a medium bowl, whisk together the yolks and sugar until ribbony and pale. During the next steps, stir constantly or the eggs will coagulate and you'll have scrambled eggs. Take a ladleful of hot milk and pour it in a thin stream into the eggs, whisking constantly. Continue stirring and add a few more ladlefuls of hot milk to the eggs in the same way. The tempered eggs are now ready to add back into the hot milk.

To do this, whisk the hot milk constantly and slowly and pour the tempered eggs in. When fully combined, put this mixture back on the stovetop over medium-low heat. Stir with a wooden spoon until steaming and the foam clears. Do not heat past this point or the sauce will curdle easily. It should lightly coat the back of the spoon. Remove it from the heat immediately and pour it through a fine-mesh sieve. Do not force it through, to avoid getting any congealed or curdled bits in the sauce.

Cool and refrigerate the sauce tightly covered in the refrigerator for up to 5 days.

Candied Pecans or Walnuts

MAKES 2 CUPS CANDIED NUTS

These look like glossy versions of the original nut, but they are robust with candied flavors. Serve them with Banana Cream Pie (page 246) and Pumpkin Pie (page 127) or crush them up in a Nut Crumb Crust (page 42). Leftovers are also good on salads. Use any kind of honey—clover is fine—the vanilla and whiskey dominate the flavor.

¼ cup honey

1½ tablespoons whiskey

1¾ teaspoons vanilla extract

½ teaspoon ground cinnamon

½ teaspoon salt

2 cups raw unsalted pecans or walnuts

Preheat the oven to 300°F.

In a large bowl, mix together the honey, whiskey, vanilla, cinnamon, and salt. Add the nuts and mix well.

Spread the coated nuts on a large well-greased baking sheet and bake for about 20 minutes. Stir and scrape them up every 5 minutes with a spatula and return the pan to the oven until the nuts smell good and are deep glossy brown. Be careful not to burn them.

Remove the pan from the oven and scrape the nuts up with a spatula occasionally as they are cooling or they'll stick together and to the sheet.

When the nuts are cool, dry, and set, store them in an airtight container in the refrigerator for up to 3 weeks.

Candied Hazelnuts or Almonds

MAKES 2 CUPS

Similar to candied pecans and walnuts, these are prepared with different flavors—Frangelico (for hazelnuts) or amaretto (for almonds). Use blanched (peeled raw) nuts for the best results.

¼ cup packed light brown sugar

1½ tablespoons Frangelico (for hazelnuts) or 1½ tablespoons amaretto (for almonds)

1¾ teaspoons vanilla extract

½ teaspoon ground cinnamon

½ teaspoon salt

2 cups raw, unsalted, blanched hazelnuts or almonds

Preheat the oven to 300°F.

In a medium bowl, mix together the sugar, liqueur, vanilla, cinnamon, and salt and toss the nuts in it.

Spread the coated nuts on a large well-greased baking sheet and bake for approximately 20 minutes. Stir and scrape them up every 5 minutes with a spatula and return the pan to the oven until the nuts smell rich and toasty and are deep glossy brown. Be careful not to burn them.

Remove the pan from the oven and scrape the nuts up with a spatula occasionally as they are cooling or they'll stick together and to the sheet.

When the nuts are cool, dry, and set, store them in an airtight container in the refrigerator for up to 3 weeks.

CANDIED GRAPEFRUIT PEEL

MAKES 3 CUPS

Candied grapefruit peel is divine minced and sprinkled inside a Baked Apple Dumpling in a drenching of heavy cream. It could also be added to the batter of a Apricot Gingerbuckle (page 215). The repeated boiling baths soften and remove the bitterness from the pith. This recipe is only appropriate for grapefruit peel and will not work for other citrus fruits.

3 large grapefruit	1½ cups water
Boiling water, as needed	2½ cups sugar, plus extra for coating

Peel the grapefruit by quartering it—get all the peel off and save it, pith and all. Cut long strips of thick peel, ¼ inch wide. Place them in a large saucepan and pour boiling water over them to cover. Boil the strips for 5 minutes. Drain and repeat 3 more times using fresh water each time— 4 rounds in all. Drain the peels in colander.

Select a wide, shallow pan and add the water and sugar. Clip a candy thermometer to the side. Do not stir. Dissolve the sugar over high heat and boil until just before it reaches the soft-ball stage (230° to 234°F). Add the drained peels, stir well, and reduce the heat so the syrup boils gently.

Simmer, partially covered, for about 1 hour, stirring occasionally, until the peels are tender and have absorbed almost all of the syrup. Uncover and cook slowly, stirring gently, until all the liquid has been absorbed. Place the peels on a wire rack with foil underneath to catch the drips. When they are no longer hot but still warm, roll the peels in sugar and place them back on the racks overnight, uncovered.

Dry the peels completely before refrigerating them in an airtight jar for up to 1 year.

CANDIED CITRUS SLICES

MAKES I POUND OF CITRUS SLICES

Use this recipe for oranges, blood oranges, tangerines, lemons, limes, and Key limes. The only citrus it is not suitable for is grapefruit because the peel remains too bitter if treated this way. Citrus that is very seedy inside is less well-suited, as once the seeds are removed, it will look like most of the citrus interior is missing. Candied citrus slices are great garnishes on desserts made with citrus, like Key Lime Pie (page 254), Double Lemon Chess Pie (page 255), Raspberry-Tangerine Tart (page 139), or Lemon Meringue Pie (page 263). As a variation on this recipe, you can half-dip the finished slices in melted dark chocolate. This variation would be especially good with the Blood Orange–Chocolate Pudding Tart (page 251), or as a very sweet gift.

1½ to 2 pounds citrus	1 cup water
2 cups sugar, plus extra for coating	

Wash the whole fruits in very hot water to remove any chemicals and wax. Pat them dry with paper towels. Using a very sharp knife, slice off the stem end and discard. Proceed to slice the fruit in very thin (1/16-inch) rounds. Stop when you reach the pithy end and discard it. Remove any seeds and set all the slices aside. Even if you plan to halve or quarter the slices later, prepare them as full rounds or they'll break down during cooking.

In a heavy, nonreactive skillet, combine the sugar and 1 cup water over medium heat. Do not stir. Bring to a rolling boil, then lower the heat to a simmer. Cook for 1 minute, until the liquid is clear and bubbly. Add only enough citrus slices to form a single layer. With the syrup barely simmering, cook the slices for 20 to 40 minutes (the time depends on the thickness of the slices), until the rind is softened and looks translucent.

Gently remove the slices with a slotted spatula and cool them in single layers on parchment or wax paper. Repeat the process, using the same syrup,

Candied Citrus Slices (*continued*)

cooking the fruit in single layers until all the slices are cooked. When cool, dust the candied slices with sugar. Not only does this make them beautiful and delicious; it will help prevent them from sticking to each other.

Refrigerate the candied citrus in an airtight container between layers of parchment for up to 1 month. To serve, cut the rounds in half or in quarters and use as a garnish.

Homemade Marshmallows

MAKES ABOUT 200 SMALL ½-INCH MARSHMALLOWS

We use these in our Rocky Road Ice Cream (page 288), which makes an exceptional Eskimo Pie. The delicate flavor and soft texture of homemade marshmallows is entirely superior to store-bought, which are often stale. They are fun to make, too!

1 tablespoon vegetable oil	¾ cup corn syrup
¾ cup water	¼ teaspoon salt
3 tablespoons unflavored gelatin	2 tablespoons vanilla extract
2 cups sugar	Confectioners' sugar, for coating

Oil a ½ sheet (9 × 13-inch) pan with vegetable oil.

Place ¾ cup cold water in the bowl of an electric mixer and sprinkle the gelatin evenly over the surface and allow it to soften for 10 minutes.

In a heavy, nonreactive pot, combine the sugar, corn syrup, salt, and ¾ cup water. Clip a candy thermometer to the side. Stir constantly over medium heat to dissolve the sugar. If crystals form on the sides of the pan, use a little water and a wet pastry brush to remove them or they will crystallize the whole mixture in time. Bring the mixture to 245°F and remove it from the heat.

Using the mixer, blend the gelatin mixture on low. Add an extra tablespoon or two of water if needed to loosen up any gelatin stuck to the bowl. Turn off the mixer and add a tiny bit of hot syrup to the gelatin, then mix on medium speed to combine. Repeat, adding a little more syrup each time. Do not try to add the syrup while the mixer is running or it will spin on the sides of the bowl. Continue until all of the syrup has been added. Mix on high speed, until the mix looks shiny and resembles thick marshmallow cream. Add the vanilla and mix a little more. Pour the contents of the bowl onto the oiled sheet pan and let the marshmallow (one solid surface) set up. When it is cool, lightly oil the top surface of the marshmallow, cover it with plastic wrap, and refrigerate overnight.

Using a fine sieve, generously dust the top of the marshmallow in the pan with confectioners' sugar. Place a sheet of parchment on top and invert it onto a larger cookie sheet. Take away the pan the marshmallow was in. Dust the exposed marshmallow with powdered sugar.

Prepare a tall container of hot water and use kitchen scissors to snip off ½-inch-wide strips of marshmallow and roll them in powdered sugar. Whenever the scissors start to get sticky, dip them in the hot water to clean them, and resume. Cut the strips into small ½-inch cubes and roll them again in powdered sugar. Freeze them for at least an hour if using for Rocky Road Ice Cream.

Store in an airtight container in the refrigerator for up to a month.

EQUIPMENT AND SOURCE REFERENCE

At Bubby's and at home, we give our equipment a pretty good workout. As a result, we've come up with some well-tested opinions about some tools and particular brands. Here's what we'd recommend to our friends and neighbors.

We buy most of our equipment on the Bowery or at the Broadway Panhandler in Manhattan. Wherever you live, support your local independent cooking supply store and encourage them to stock pie-making equipment. If you can't find what you need there, try searching cooking supply stores online, such as Williams-Sonoma or Sur La Table. We've included sources for rarer items like the cherry pitter we love.

Leifheit P37200 "Cherrymat" Cherry Pitter

This "Frucht und fun" modern wonder from Germany allows you to pit approximately 26 pounds (12 kilograms) of cherries per hour in its see-through hopper. It's amazingly fast, easy to use, and easy to clean. Prices vary.

It's well worth the investment. Don't get the pitter that looks like a stapler by mistake. Search online for this—we saw it at Target for $30.
http://www.leifheit.com.

Pie Weights

We use dried kidney beans. They're inexpensive and they can be used for blind-baking over and over without burning. The commercial pie weights are an unnecessary expense.

Apple Peeler/Corer/Slicer

This gadget clamps onto a counter and will impress and delight any child (or adult) who wants to be helpful. Avoid the suction ones because they are hard to secure in place. It not only peels your apples, it cores them too! All with the ease of reeling in a fish! It's an indispensable tool for production baking because it's fast and saves a lot of wear and tear on the hands (as anyone who has peeled huge batches of apples can testify)—and a good way to get family members to fight over who gets to help first.
http://www.pamperedchef.com

Apple Wedger

An apple wedger can come in handy for cutting apples into uniform slices a whole apple at a time if you're making a lot of apple pies. They work best with uniform apples and are less useful for small or oddly shaped apples.
http://www.pamperedchef.com

Salter Microtronic Digital Scale, 5 Lb

Stainless steel. Easy to clean and use. For a home cook, it's useful for dividing dough evenly for small pastries or dumplings. We use it most for reliably multiplying amounts for baking in large quantities.

http://www.williams-sonoma.com

Pie Basket

Peterboro Basket Company makes an attractive two-pie basket we like to use.
www.peterborobasket.com

Pie Safe

A pie safe can't keep pies safe from people, but it does help keep bugs, rodents, and pets away from your pies as they cool. The added advantage of a pie safe is that it is ventilated with screen mesh or punched tin, and air is allowed to circulate freely around the pastry. Pie safes come in all sorts of different sizes, shapes, and designs. Antique or new pie safes are widely available on the internet. Some are small and portable; most resemble a large piece of furniture similar to a Hoosier or kitchen hutch, with screen or punched-tin side walls and doors.

Rolling Pins

We favor a 20-inch extra-long beechwood handleless rolling pin, rounded off at the edge but not tapered. We've found that the handles on a rolling pin inevitably break off due to wear and tear, and applying the pressure directly to the pin with your palms gives you control that is more measured. The pin should be long in order to extend beyond the edges of the crust you're rolling out. It's worth getting accustomed to using this style of pin because it makes rolling out the pie dough evenly a *lot* easier.

Some bakers prefer marble or glass pins because they can be chilled, but we prefer wood because the flour adheres to the grain of the wood and keeps the dough from sticking to it. Wood pins are also a good weight to work with—not too heavy, not too light. If you are sentimental about a family heirloom or just like the way the short old-fashioned ones with handles work for you, they're nice to have around, especially for young bakers. It's lovely to know your great-grandma made pies with the same pin!

Pie Tins

It's possible to get good results with many different types of pie plates or tins. We use 9-inch and 12-inch pans most often. Look for a pie plate with a flat lip or ruffled lip, but avoid the plates with lips that slope upwards.

A Pyrex glass pie plate shows how well the bottom crust is browning and conducts heat to it very well; it's a good choice for a juicy fruit like rhubarb that, once cut, reacts and turns bluish when it comes into contact with some metal tins. Buy the kind with a flat-edged lip—the fluted one has too steep an incline for the crust edge to rest properly.

Go for a nice, heavy, dark pie plate if you're buying metal—the crust will brown better in it. (But don't pass up those beautiful old tins you come across at a yard sale. It's nice to see words stamped in the tin underneath a cut pie.) A lot of the old pie tins have small holes in the bottom to help the crust crisp. We don't really recommend these tins, but if you're using them, be aware that you'll definitely need to put a pan or foil directly below the pie plate to catch drips of butter during baking. When you cut into a pie in one of these old pie plates, you may need something underneath to catch juices that escape through these holes.

Ceramic and stoneware pie plates are beautiful for entertaining but not so great if you're bringing a pie somewhere, because they're quite heavy both coming and going. We use them for pot pies and deep-dish pies, especially for dishes without a bottom crust. Ceramic is less conductive of heat to the bottom crust in the initial high-heat setting stage of baking, but once it gets hot, it retains even high heat well.

At Bubby's we use 9-inch disposable aluminum pie tins. The uniformity of these tins works well for restaurant use. It's quite useful to have two lightweight tins that are exactly the same size for blind-baking crusts—one to hold the crust and one to nest inside it, filled with beans or weights (see page 322). We also double up the pie plates, after the pie comes out of the oven, for strength and so that there is a clean tin covering the sticky tin the pie was baked in. Disposable tins are handy for pies that must be transported to events (they can be left behind). They can be purchased at any big grocery store.

Pastry Cutter/Blender

This curved cutting device makes fast work of cutting butter into the flour manually because it makes four cuts at a time. Because speed is one control a baker has in monitoring a cool dough temperature, the advantage is well worth it. It can be a little hard on the wrist if you are making multiple pies, so in those situations, use a food processor.

There are many flimsy pastry cutters on the market. Trust us—if you have to tighten the nut on the handle every time you roll out a crust, or bend steel wires back into place, you're wasting good time. Choose a sturdy one with a plastic or soft handgrip, a securely attached handle with no movable parts, and rigid stationary stainless steel blades. If need be, you can use two table knives or a pastry scraper to cut the butter into the flour, but it'll slow down the process, putting you at a disadvantage insofar as the fat temperature is concerned.

Pastry Scrapers

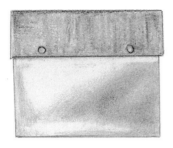

Some bakers use their scraper to cut the butter into the flour on a flat work surface. Do whatever works best for you. This is an invaluable tool for cleaning the rolling surface quickly and efficiently between rolling out crusts. It's also handy for loosening a sticky patch of dough from the work surface and the rolling pin. We recommend both the plastic and the metal—the former for cleaning counters and bowls, and the latter for cutting fats, or trimming dough edges, and scraping stubborn dough off counters. Sometimes the metal ones have a ruler on them that comes in handy for cutting dough for pastries such as Homemade Pop Tarts.

Food Processor

We use a Cuisinart® 6-quart food processor at home. We buy them from companies that offer a lifetime warranty because we give ours a decent workout. We use it quite often in the recipes in this book and highly recommend having one around.

Electric Mixer

The Kitchen-Aid stand mixers are durable and well-designed. Our favorite is the Professional 8-quart Kitchen-Aid Stand Mixer because it is flexible if you are cooking in larger quantities. Stand mixers are better than handheld because they allow you to have an extra hand free. You'll need it for custards, ice creams, and the like.

Baking Sheets

You'll want to have on hand at least two 13 x 18-inch-wide, heavy baking sheets with a lipped edge for resting pies on while they bake. They are indispensable for catching juices or melted drops of butter as they bubble over in the oven and preventing them from landing on the oven floor, where they smoke up the oven, the pie, and the house.

Metal Offset Pastry Spatula

Choose a long, thin one for spreading meringue, ganache, pudding, peanut butter mousse, and ice cream in ice cream pies, among other uses.

Baking Parchment Paper (Unwaxed)

Unwaxed baking parchment paper is useful for lining par-baked and blind-baked pastry pie shells. It is also often used for lining baking sheets under pastries—it prevents sticking and makes for easy cleanup.

Tin/Aluminum Foil

Aluminum foil comes in handy for lightly covering crusts that are browning too much, for making armatures (see Pork Pie Hats, page 185), and for covering leftovers that will be reheated in the oven.

Wide Plastic Wrap

Plastic wrap, 12 to 18 inches wide, makes it easy to cover a pie or batch of pudding as it cools.

Wire Cooling Rack

You'll want one that's large enough to fit a couple of pies.

Pastry Brush

We use a 1- or 2-inch pastry brush for painting milk or cream on pastry crusts and cobblers.

Pie Serving Spatula

A pie (triangular) spatula is indispensable for serving pie. It helps lift a wedge-shaped piece out of the tin intact.

Ravioli Cutter

We use a ravioli cutter for cutting lattice crust strips because we like the ruffled edge.

Cake Decorating Tips

It's useful to have few different sizes of metal cake decorating tips with round holes. Use either end of the tip for cutting decorative vent holes in rolled out pastry.

Cookie Cutters

Use cookie cutters for cutting decorative vent holes in rolled-out pastry. A few different small ones in metal are best.

Melon Baller

A melon baller makes quick and clean work of coring pears, apples, and quinces, especially for baked dumplings. It's also good for half-moon shaped cuts in a pastry crust.

Fine-Mesh Sieves

Fine-mesh sieves are useful for straining custards and berry sauces, dusting powdered sugar, and for washing fragile fruits. Buy a sturdy, stainless steel one about 8 inches in circumference.

Candy, Deep-Fat, Meat, Freezer, and Oven Thermometers

All four of these thermometers are extremely helpful: candy thermometers for making caramel, deep fat thermometers for frying pastries, meat thermometers for roasting meats for savory pies, freezer thermometers for making ice cream, and oven thermometers for making sure your oven is properly calibrated and up to speed. Opt for a good quality thermometer—the whole point is accuracy, and often the cheap ones are off.

Tart Pans

If you like tarts, it's good to have a number of sizes of tart pans on hand. Our recipes often call for a 10-inch tart pan, but you can always make small individual ones instead. Tart pans typically have a removable disc-shaped bottom that nests inside a fluted straight-walled edge.

Silicone Spatulas

Silicone spatulas are useful for scraping down anything you make in an electric mixer.

Pie Birds

Pie birds (or pie funnels, as they are sometimes called) are optional ornaments that serve the same purpose as a vent hole in a top crust (see page 17). They are hollow upright ceramic birds that nest in the center of a pie to vent steam out through their open mouths. There are beautiful birds (and a good deal of other species) to collect—ours is black with a yellow beak in a crowing posture. They are often available at cooking supply stores, and many unique ones, both antique and new, are available online.

Ice Cream Makers

We recommend the wooden electric motor-driven version of the old-fashioned hand-cranked machine that uses rock salt and ice, or the good old-fashioned hand-cranked machine itself. The reason why we like these best: They offer the best control over the temperature; you can keep adding ice and salt to chill down the mixture. White Mountain™ makes a 4- or a 6-quart Holmes Rival traditional electric/hand-crank ice-cream maker that is easy to find online through websites like NextTag.

WEIGHTS AND MEASURES

Standard American measures are mostly based on the volume of an ingredient, rather than its weight. There are three main categories of measuring: dry, wet, and solid. Dry measures are typically metal or plastic cups and spoons that are filled to the brim and leveled off; liquids are measured in graduated glass or plastic pitchers with extra room at the top to prevent spillage; and solids or odd-sized ingredients like nuts are measured in dry measuring cups or on a scale.

The weight within a cup measure varies dramatically from one ingredient to another. Think about the weight of a cup of dried beans versus a cup of powdered sugar. If you get into multiplying (or scaling) recipes to make bigger or smaller batches, for many ingredients it's more accurate to do so by weight. These time-saving charts should help with ingredients like fats and eggs, when the conversions are confusing or hard to break down.

There are also specialized, antiquated terms that pertain to dry, liquid, and solid measures: gills, pecks, and bushels, for example. For our recipes you'll need only the basics, but this chart might come in handy if you're adapting an old recipe.

DRY INGREDIENTS: GENERAL MEASURING CHART

Teaspoons	Tablespoons	Cups	Ounces/Pounds	Grams/Kilograms
—	—	4⅜	2 pounds, 3 ounces	1 kilogram
—	—	4	32 ounces/2 pounds	908 grams
—	32	2	16 ounces/1 pound	448 grams
—	16	1	8 ounces	224 grams
	8	½	4 ounces	112 grams
	5⅓	⅓	2⅔ ounces	74 grams
—	4	¼	2 ounces	57 grams
6	2	⅛	1 ounce	28 grams
3	1	—	½ ounce	14 grams
1½	½	—	¼ ounce	7 grams

pinch = the amount held between two fingers (less than ⅛ teaspoon)

Flour and Other Dry Ingredients	Method of Measure	Ounces per Cup	Grams per Cup
All-purpose unbleached flour	dip and sweep	4	113.4
Cornstarch	sifted	4.2	120
Cocoa	sifted	2.6	75
Granulated white sugar	dip and sweep	8	227
Light brown sugar	packed	7.6	217
Dark brown sugar	packed	8.4	239
Powdered confectioners' sugar	dip and sweep	4	115
Tapioca	dip and sweep	5.3	150.2
Gelatin	dip and sweep	5.3	150.2
Baking powder	sifted	8	227
Baking soda	sifted	8.5	240
Salt	dip and sweep	10.7	303.3

FLUID INGREDIENTS: GENERAL MEASURING CHART

Fluid ounces	Tablespoons	Cups	English System	Pints	Quarts/ Liters	Gallons
128	—	16	—	8	4	1
32	—	4	—	2	1	—
25	50	—	1 fifth	—	—	—
16	32	2	4 gills	1	½	—
8	16	1	2 gills	½	¼	—
7	14	⅞	—	—	—	—
6	12	¾	—	—	—	—
5⅓	10⅔	⅔	—	—	—	—
4	8	½	1 gill	—	—	—
2⅔	5⅓	⅓	—	—	—	—
2	4	¼	—	—	—	—
1	2	⅛	—	—	—	—
1½	3	—	1 jigger	—	—	—
½	1	—	—	—	—	—

dash = a few drops

Water and Other Fluid Ingredients	Method of Measure	Weight per Cup (Ounces)	Grams per Cup
Sour cream	liquid measure	8.5	242
Sweetened condensed milk	greased liquid measure	11	316
Honey	greased liquid measure	12	345
Molasses	greased liquid measure	11.2	322
Maple syrup	greased liquid measure	11	312
Corn syrup	greased liquid measure	11.5	328

Dry Cups		Pounds	Pecks	Bushels
128	32 quarts	64	4	1
32	8 quarts	16	1	¼
4	1 quart	2	—	—
2	1 pint	1	—	—
1	½ pint	½ (8 ounces)	—	—

Fat Measures

BUTTER

Cups	Tablespoons	Ounces	Pounds	Sticks
2	32	16	1	4
1⅓	21⅓	10.66	⅔	2⅔
1	16	8	½	2
¾	12	6	⅜	1½
⅔	10⅔	5.33	⅓	1⅓
½	8	4	¼	1
$7/16$	7	3.5	—	—
⅜	6	3	—	¾
⅓	5½	2.66	—	⅔
¼	4	2	—	½
⅙	2¾	1.33	—	⅓
⅛	2	1	—	¼

LARD

Cups	Tablespoons	Ounces
2	32	15
1⅓	21⅓	10
1	16	**7.5**
¾	12	5.625
⅔	10⅔	5
½	8	3.75
⅜	6	2.8
⅓	5⅓	2.5
¼	4	1.875
⅙	2¾	1.25
⅛	2	0.94

VEGETABLE SHORTENING

Cups	Tablespoons	Ounces
2	32	13.4
1⅓	21⅓	8.93
1	16	**6.7**
¾	12	5.025
⅔	10⅔	4.47
½	8	3.35
⅜	6	2.513
⅓	5⅓	2.23
¼	4	1.675
⅙	2¾	1.117
⅛	2	0.84

Solid Ingredients	Ounces per Cup	Grams per Cup
Bittersweet chocolate, melted	10	283.5
Peanut butter, smooth	16.6	266
Walnuts, pecans, hazelnuts, pistachios, or macadamias, coarsely chopped	4	114
Almonds, coarsely chopped	3	85
Almonds, finely ground	3.7	107
Coconut, fresh grated	2.7	79
Coconut, packaged shredded	3	85
Citrus zest	—	2 grams/teaspoon

To convert grams into ounces, multiply by 0.03527.

To convert ounces into grams, multiply by 28.35.

EGGS

	Liquid measure	Weight
5 large eggs	1 cup	253 grams
1 large egg	3 tablespoons plus ½ teaspoon	50 grams
8 large egg whites	1 cup	240 grams
1 large egg white	2 tablespoons	30 grams
13 to 14 large egg yolks	1 cup	255 grams
1 large egg yolk	3½ teaspoons	18.6 grams

OVEN TEMPERATURES

	Fahrenheit	Celsius
Slow	250 to 300°F	121°C–149°C
Slow moderate	325°F	163°C
Moderate	350°F	177°C
Quick moderate	375°F	191°C
Moderately hot	400°F	204°C
Hot	425 to 450°F	218°C–232°C
Very hot	475 to 500°F	246°C–260°C

BIBLIOGRAPHY

Abell, Mrs. L. G., *The Skillful Housewife's Book*. New York: R. T. Young, 1852.

Beard, James, *American Cookery*. Boston: Little, Brown, 1972.

Beecher, Catherine E., *Miss Beecher's Domestic Receipt-Book*. New York: Harper & Brothers, 1858.

Beranbaum, Rose Levy, *The Cake Bible*. New York: William Morrow and Company, Inc., 1988.

———, *The Pie and Pastry Bible*. New York: Scribner, 1998.

Betty Crocker's New Picture Cookbook. New York: McGraw-Hill, 1950.

Brillat-Savarin, Jean-Anthelme, *The Physiology of Taste*. Translated by M. F. K. Fisher. New York: Knopf, 1971.

Child, Mrs. Lydia Maria, *The American Frugal Housewife, Dedicated to Those Who Are Not Ashamed of Economy*. New York: S. S. & W. Wood, 1838.

Child, Julia, and Bertholle, Louisette, and Beck, Simone, *Mastering the Art of French Cooking, Volume One*. New York: Knopf, 1970.

Child, Julia, and Beck, Simone, *Mastering the Art of French Cooking, Volume Two*. New York: Knopf, 1970.

Croft, Susan, *A Lesson in Pastry Making*, No. 3 of the Series. London: Van Den Berghs & Jurgens, Ltd., pamphlet date unknown.

Cunningham, Marion, *The Fannie Farmer Baking Book*. New York: Wings Books, 1984.

Donovan, Mary; Hatrak, Amy; Mills, Frances; and Shull, Elizabeth, *The Thirteen Colonies Cookbook: A Collection of Favorite Receipts from Thirteen Exemplary Eighteenth-Century Cooks with Proper Menus for Simple Fare and Elegant Entertainments and Selected Notes of Historic Interest Being a Guide to Open-Hearth and Bee-Hive Oven Cookery Adapted for Twentieth Century Use*. Montclair, New Jersey: Montclair Historical Society, 1982.

Escoffier, A., *The Escoffier Cook Book*. New York: Crown, 1941.

Farmer, Fannie Merritt, *The Boston Cooking School Cook Book*. Boston: Little, Brown, and Company, 1896.

Farm Journal's Best Ever Pies. Garden City, N.Y.: Doubleday, 1981.

Fisher, Mrs. Abby, *What Mrs. Fisher Knows About Old Southern Cooking*. San Francisco: Women's Cooperative Printing Office, 1881.

Fisher, M.F. K., *The Art of Eating*. Hoboken, N.J.: John Wiley & Sons, 1990.

Fobel, Jim, *Jim Fobel's Old Fashioned Baking Book*. New York: Lake Isle Press, 1987.

Good, Phyllis Pellman, *The Best of Amish Cooking*. Intercourse, Pennsylvania: Good Books, 1988.

The Great Cooks' Guide to Pies and Tarts (The Great Cooks' Library). New York: Random House, 1977.

Heatter, Maida. *Maida Heatter's Book of Great Desserts*. Kansas City: Andrews McMeel Publishing, 1999.

Hibben, Sheila, *The National Cookbook*. New York: Harper Brothers, 1932.

Hibler, Janie, *The Berry Bible*. New York: HarperCollins, 2004.

Junior League of Little Rock, Inc., *Little Rock Cooks*. Little Rock: Junior League of Little Rock, Publications, 1972.

Kander, Mrs. Simon, *The Settlement Cook Book: Tested Recipes from The Milwaukee Public School Kitchens Girls Trades and Technical High School, Authoritative Dieticians and Experienced Housewives*. Milwaukee: The Settlement Cook Book Co., 1941.

The Ladies Auxillary of St. Luke's Sunday School, Buffalo, Wyoming, *Buffalo Cookery: A Collection of Choice Recipes Carefully Selected and Arranged for Western Housewives*. Hamilton, Ohio: Brown & Whitaker, 1916.

Liddell, Caroline, and Weir, Robin, *Frozen Desserts: The Definitive Guide to Making Ice Creams, Ices, Sorbets, Gelati, and Other Frozen Delights*. New York: St. Martin's Griffin, 1996.

Lutes, Della, *The Country Kitchen*. Boston: Little, Brown, and Co., 1936.

McGee, Harold, *On Food and Cooking: The Science and Lore of the Kitchen*. New York: Scribner, 2004.

Naughton, Anita, *Tea and Sympathy*. New York: G.P. Putnam's Sons, 2002.

New Favorite Honey Recipes. Madison, Wisconsin: American Honey Institute, 1947.

Robbins, Maria Polushkin, *Blue Ribbon Pies*. New York: St. Martin's Press, 1987.

Root, Waverly, *Food*. New York: Simon & Shuster, 1980.

Stamp, Catherine. *Be-Ro Flour Home Recipes*, 40th edition, pamphlet date unknown.

Stewart, Martha, *Martha Stewart's Pies and Tarts*. New York: Clarkson Potter, 1985.

Toklas, Alice B., *The Alice B. Toklas Cook Book*. Garden City, New York: Doubleday, 1960.

Walter, Carole, *Great Pies and Tarts*. New York: Clarkson Potter, 1998.

Waters, Alice, *Chez Panisse Menu Cookbook*. New York: Random House, 1982.

———, *Chez Panisse Fruit*. New York: HarperCollins, 2002.

Yockelson, Lisa, *Country Pies*. New York: Harper & Row, 1988.

Davidson, Alan, *The Oxford Companion to Food*. Oxford: Oxford University Press, 1999.

Parsons, Russ, *How to Read a French Fry: And Other Intriguing Stories of Kitchen Science*. Houghton Mifflin, 2003.

Thomas, Pamela, *Greenmarket: The Complete Guide to New York City's Farmer's Markets with 5 5 Recipes*. New York: Stewart, Tabori, and Chang, 1999.

Zanger, Mark, *The American History Cookbook*. Westport, CT: Greenwood Press, 2003.

PERPETUAL PIE CALENDAR
AND HOME RECORD

APRIL

Lamb Cobbler

Shepherd's Pie with Mashed Potato
and Cheddar Crust

Goat Cheese Pie with Pomegranate
Molasses

Leek and Onion Pie

MAY

Rhubarb Custard Pie

Raspberry-Rhubarb Pie

Strawberry-Rhubarb Pie

Rhubarb Buckle

Rhubarb Crisp

Asparagus-Cheddar Quiche

Wild Ramps and Morel Pie

Wild Ramps and Stilton Pie

Spring Vegetable Risotto Pie

JUNE

Strawberries and Cream Pie

Fresh Strawberry Pie in Chocolate
Crumb Crust

Fresh Blueberry Pie with Crème
Fraîche

Baked Blueberry Pie

Bluebarb Pie

Strawberry Ice Cream

Mint Chip Ice Cream

JULY

Blackberry Pie

Blackberry Buckle

Raspberry–Red Currant Pie

Raspberry–Black Currant Pie

Raspberry–Two Currant Pie

Gooseberry Crumble Pie

Blue Goose Pie

Sour Cherry–Almond Crumble Pie

Sour Cherry Lattice Pie

Apricot–Sour Cherry Pie

Blueberry-Nectarine Biscuit-Style
 Cobbler

Southern Batter-Style Cobbler

Boiled Plum Dumplings

Plum Buckle

Plum Crumble

Apricot Crumble

Buttermilk Pie with Fresh Berries

Buttermilk Ice Cream

AUGUST

White Peach Crumble Pie

Blueberry-Peach Pie

Peach Pastry-Style Cobbler

Fried Peach Pies

Peachy Brown Betty

Peach Ice Cream

SEPTEMBER

Concord Grape Pie with Crème
 Fraîche

Mile-High Apple Pie

Whiskey-Apple Crumble Pie

Apple-Caramel Upside-Down Pie
 (Tarte Tatin)

Apple Pie with Blackberry Glaze

Ginger–Honey Apple Pie

Autumn Apple Crisp

Fried Apple-Whiskey Pies

Fried Sweet Potato Pies

Molasses-Apple Pandowdy

Baked Apple Dumplings

Tomato-Parmesan Custard Pie

Fig and Prosciutto Pie

Apple-Roquefort-Bacon Pie

Duck Confit Pie with Glazed Figs and
 Blackberry Glaze

OCTOBER

Pear-Ginger Crisp

Pear Pie with Caramel Sauce and
 Crème Fraîche

Open-Faced Pear Pie with Red
 Currant Glaze

Lemony Pear Pie

Ginger Ice Cream

NOVEMBER

Quince-Pear Pie

Quince Turnovers

Viola's Sweet Potato Pie

Cranberry-Pear Crumble Pie

Pumpkin Pie with Caramel Sauce and
 Candied Pecans

Pecan Pie

Mocha-Pecan Pie

Pecan-Caramel-Chocolate Tart

Maple Syrup Ice Cream

Caramel Ice Cream

DECEMBER

Bubby's All-Fruit Mincemeat

Mince Pocket Pies with Clotted Cream

Nesselrode Pie

Blood Orange–Chocolate Pudding Tart

Raspberry-Tangerine Tart

Candied Grapefruit Peel

Candied Citrus Slices

ANYTIME

Homemade Pop-Tarts™

Apricot Gingerbuckle

Vanilla Cream Pie

Put-Up Peaches and Cream Pie

Banana Cream Pie with Candied
    Pecans

Banana-Mocha Pudding Pie

Chocolate Pudding Pie

Bubby's Original Peanut
    Butter–Chocolate Pie

Key Lime Pie

Double Lemon Chess Pie

Mile-High Lemon Meringue Pie

Lofty Coconut Cloud Pie

Coconut Custard Pie

Sour Cream–Raisin Pie

Chicken Pot Pie

Brandon's Steak and Guinness Pie

Todd's Beef Chuck Chili Pie

Salmon Tweed Kettle Pie

Paella Pie

Lobster Empanadas

Steak Pasties

Pork Pie Hats

Potato Knishes

Vanilla Ice Cream

Espresso Ice Cream

Chocolate Ice Cream

Rocky Road Ice Cream

Banana-Chocolate Chip Ice Cream

Ice Cream Pie

Eskimo Pie

Banana–Chocolate Eskimo Pie

Grasshopper Eskimo Pie

Sweetie Pie

Cappuccino Meringue Pie

PIE AND CRUST
COMPATIBILITY CHARTS

SINGLE CRUSTS

	All Butter	Sour Cream	Butter Shortening	Nut	Cookie	Lard
Apple Pie with Blackberry Glaze	X	X	X	X		
Apple-Caramel Upside-Down Pie (Tarte Tatin)	X	X	X			
Asparagus–Cheddar Quiche	X	X	X			
Banana-Chocolate Eskimo Pie					X	
Banana Cream Pie with Candied Pecans	X	X	X	X	X	
Banana-Mocha Pudding Pie	X	X	X	X	X	

	All Butter	Sour Cream	Butter Shortening	Nut	Cookie	Lard
Blood Orange–Chocolate Pudding Tart	X	X	X	X	X	
Bubby's Original Peanut Butter–Chocolate Pie					X	
Buttermilk Pie with Fresh Berries	X	X	X	X	X	
Cappuccino Meringue Pie					X	
Chocolate Pudding Pie	X	X	X	X	X	
Coconut Custard Pie	X	X	X			
Coconut Sweet Potato Pie	X	X	X	X	X	
Cranberry-Pear Crumble Pie	X	X	X	X		
Double Lemon Chess Pie	X	X	X		X	
Duck Confit Pie with Glazed Figs and Blackberry Glaze	X		X			X
Eskimo Pie					X	
Fig and Prosciutto Pie	X		X	X		X
Fresh Blueberry Pie with Crème Fraîche	X	X	X		X	
Fresh Raspberry and Sugared Currant Pie	X	X	X	X	X	

	All Butter	Sour Cream	Butter Shortening	Nut	Cookie	Lard
Fresh Strawberry Pie in Chocolate Crumb Crust					X	
Goat Cheese Pie with Pomegranate Molasses	X			X		
Gooseberry Crumble Pie	X	X	X			
Grasshopper Eskimo Pie					X	
Ice Cream Pie					X	
Key Lime Pie					X	
Leek and Onion Pie	X		X			
Lofty Coconut Cloud Pie	X	X	X		X	
Mile-High Lemon Meringue Pie	X	X	X		X	
Mocha-Pecan Pie	X	X	X	X		
Nesselrode Pie	X	X	X	X	X	
Open-Faced Pear Pie with Red Currant Glaze	X	X	X	X		
Pecan Pie	X	X	X	X		
Pecan-Caramel-Chocolate Tart	X	X	X	X		
Pumpkin Pie with Caramel Sauce and Candied Pecans	X	X	X	X	X	
Put-Up Peaches and Vanilla Cream Pie	X	X	X	X	X	

	All Butter	Sour Cream	Butter Shortening	Nut	Cookie	Lard
Raspberry-Tangerine Tart	X	X	X		X	
Rhubarb Custard Pie	X	X	X			
Small Mince Pocket Pies with Clotted Cream	X					
Sour Cherry–Almond Crumble Pie	X	X	X	X		
Sour Cream–Raisin Pie	X	X	X	X	X	
Strawberries and Cream Pie	X	X	X	X	X	
Sweetie Pie					X	
Tomato-Parmesan Custard Pie	X	X	X			
Vanilla Pudding Pie	X	X	X	X	X	
Viola's Sweet Potato Pie	X	X	X	X	X	
Whiskey-Apple Crumble Pie	X	X	X			
White Peach Crumble Pie	X	X	X			
Wild Ramps and Morel Pie	X	X	X			
Wild Ramps and Stilton Pie	X	X	X			

	All Butter	Butter Shortening	Lard	Herbed	Garlic
Apple-Roquefort-Bacon Pie	X	X	X	X	
Apricot–Sour Cherry Pie	X	X			
Baked Blueberry Pie	X	X			
Blackberry Pie	X	X			
Blue Goose Pie	X	X			
Bluebarb Pie	X	X			
Blueberry-Peach Pie	X	X			
Brandon's Steak and Guinness Pie	X		X	X	
Chicken Pot Pie	X	X	X	X	X
Concord Grape Pie with Crème Fraîche	X	X			
Ginger–Honey Apple Pie	X	X			
Lemony Pear Pie	X	X			
Mile-High Apple Pie	X	X	X		
Peach–Vanilla Bean Pie	X	X			
Pear Pie with Caramel Sauce and Crème Fraîche	X	X			
Quince-Pear Pie	X	X			
Raspberry–Black Currant Pie	X	X			

	All Butter	Butter Shortening	Lard	Herbed	Garlic
Raspberry–Red Currant Pie	X	X			
Raspberry-Rhubarb Pie	X	X			
Sour Cherry Lattice Pie	X	X			
Strawberry-Rhubarb Pie	X	X			

INDEX

Banana
-Chocolate Chip Ice Cream,
291–292
-Chocolate Eskimo Pie, 297
Cream Pie with Candied Pecans,
246
-Mocha Pudding Pie, 247
Béchamel Sauce, 156–157
Beef
Chili Pie, 149–151
Steak Pasties, 183–184
Steak and Guinness Pie, Brandon's,
147–148
Biscuit-style cobblers
Blueberry-Nectarine, 206–207
information about, 204–205
Blackberry(ies)
Buckle, 214
Glaze, 112–113, 158–160
information about, 74
Pie, 75
Black currants
information about, 78
Raspberry and Sugared Currant
Pie, Fresh, 80–81
-Raspberry Pie, 79
Blind-baking
information about, 15–16
nut crusts, 31
short crusts, 33
Blond Roux, 146
Blood oranges
Candied Citrus Slices, 317–318
-Chocolate Pudding Tart, 251
Blueberry(ies)
Bluebarb, 73–74
Blue Goose, 84
information about, 70
-Nectarine Biscuit-Style Cobbler,
206–207
-Peach Pie, 98

Pie, Baked, 72
Pie with Créme Fraîche, Fresh,
71
Boiled Plum Dumplings, 225–226
Bread Crumb Crust, 43
Brown betty(s)
information about, 218
Peach, 219
Brown sugar, in fruit pies, 53
Bubby's All-Butter Pastry Pie
Dough, 23–26
Bubby's Original Peanut Butter-
Chocolate Pie, 252–253
Buckle(s)
Apricot, 215–216
Apricot Gingerbuckle, 215–216
Blackberry, 214
Buttermilk, 211
Chocolate, 211
Ginger, 211
information about, 210–211
Plum, 213
Rhubarb, 212
Butter
dripping off crust, 58
in fruit pies, 54
making pastry crust, 3–5
Pastry Pie Dough, Bubby's All-,
23–26
pie/crust compatibility chart,
344–348
and Shortening Pastry Pie Dough,
Basic, 27
weights and measures, 334
Buttermilk
Buckle, 211
Ice Cream, 274–275
Pie with Fresh Berries, 255–256

C

Candied fruit
  Citrus Slices, 317–318
  Grapefruit Peel, 316
Candied nuts
  Hazelnuts/Almonds, 315
  Pecans/Walnuts, 314
Cappuccino Meringue Ice Cream
    Pie, 299–300
Caramel
  -Apple Upside-Down Pie (Tarte
      Tatin), 110–111
  basic recipe, 110
  Ice Cream, 282–283
  -Orange Sauce, 310
  -Pecan-Chocolate Tart, 132
  Sauce, 309
  Sauce, Pear Pie with Créme
      Fraîche and, 119–120
  Sauce, Pumpkin Pie with Candied
      Pecans and, 127–128
Cheddar cheese
  -Asparagus Quiche, 170
  Pastry Crust, Sharp, 44
  Savory Cheese Scones, 153–154
Cheese. See Cheddar cheese; Cheese
    pies; Cheese-based crusts; Goat
    cheese; Manchego cheese;
    Parmesan cheese; Roquefort
    cheese; Stilton cheese
Cheese-based crusts
  Bread Crumb, 43
  Cheddar Cheese Pastry, Sharp, 44
Cheese pies
  Apple-Roquefort-Bacon, 161–162
  Fig and Prosciutto, 169
  Goat Cheese with Pomegranate
      Molasses, 167–168
  Tomato-Parmesan Custard, 174
  Wild Ramps and Stilton, 173

See also Quiche
Cherry(ies)
  cherry pitter, 321–322
  information about, 85
  Pies, Fried, 228–229
  See also Sour cherry(ies)
Chestnut(s), Nesselrode Pie, 259–260
Chicken
  Paella Pie, 165
  Shepherd's Pie with Mashed
      Potato and Cheddar Crust,
      154–155
  Stock, basic recipe, 143–144
Chiffon pies
  Buttermilk with Fresh Berries,
      257–258
  Coconut Cloud, Lofty, 265–266
  information about, 239
Chili pie, Beef Chuck, 149–151
Chocolate
  -Banana Eskimo Pie, 297
  -Blood Orange Pudding Tart, 251
  Buckle, 211
  Chip-Banana Ice Cream,
      291–292
  Cookie(s), Homemade, 40
  Crumb Crust, 41
  Ganache, 132, 252–253, 308
  Hot Fudge Sauce, 311
  Ice Cream, 286–287
  Mint Chip Ice Cream, 289–290
  -Peanut Butter Pie, Bubby's
      Original, 252–253
  -Pecan-Caramel Tart, 132
  -Peppermint Crumb Crust, 41
  pudding, half-batch ratios, 248
  Pudding Pie, 248–250
  Sweetie Pie, 298
Chorizo sausage, Paella Pie, 165
Cinnamon and Sugar Scrap Buddies,
    22

Citrus
    in fruit pies, 54
    Slices, Candied, 317–318
Clams, Paella Pie, 165
Clotted cream, 304
Cobbler(s)
    Blueberry-Nectarine Biscuit-
        Style, 206–207
    information about, 204–205
    Peach Pastry-Style, 208
    Southern Batter-Style, 205, 209
Coconut
    Cloud Pie, Lofty, 265–266
    Custard Pie, 267
    Sweet Potato Pie, 135
Coffee. *See* Espresso
Concord grapes
    information about, 100
    Pie with Créme Fraîche,
        101–102
Cookie crusts
    pie/crust compatibility chart,
        344–346
    See also Sweet crumb crusts
Cookie cutters, 328
Cookies
    Chocolate, 40
    Cinnamon and Sugar Scrap
        Buddies, 22
    Gingersnaps, 39
Cornbread Crust, 149, 151
Cornstarch, as thickening agent,
    51–52
Cranberry, -Pear Crumble Pie,
    121–122
Cream
    brush top crust with, 20
    clotted, 304
    Whipped, 302
Créme anglaise, Vanilla Pouring
    Custard, 313

Créme fraîche
    basic recipe, 303
    Blueberry Pie with, Fresh, 71
    Concord Grape Pie with, 101–102
    Pear Pie with Caramel Sauce and,
        119–120
    Quick, 304
    Vanilla Pie, 242
Crimping crust
    double-crust, 16–17
    single crust, 14–15
Crisp(s)
    Autumn Apple, 202
    Pear-Ginger, 201
    Rhubarb, 200
    Topping, 199
Crumb crusts
    Bread Crumb, 43
    See also Sweet crumb crusts
Crumble(s)
    Almond Topping, 196
    Apricot, 198
    information about, 194
    Plum, 197
    Topping, 195
    with Vanilla Pouring Custard, 313
Crumble-topped pies
    Cranberry-Pear, 121–122
    Gooseberry, 82–83
    Sour Cherry-Almond, 86–87
    Whiskey-Apple, 108–109
    White Peach, 96–97
Crust(s). *See* Pastry pie dough; Pie
    crusts
Curd
    Lemon, 317–318
    Tangerine, 139–140
Currants
    information about, 76
    See also Black currants; Red
        currants

Custard pies
  Coconut, 267
  information about, 239
  Key Lime, 254
  Nesselrode, 259–260
  Rhubarb, 65
  Sour Cream-Raisin, 261–262

D

Decorating tips, cake, 328
Double-crust pies
  finishing touches, 19–20
  fruit pies, storing, 61
  pie/crust compatibility chart,
    347–348
  trimming/crimping, 16–17
Dry ingredients, weights and
    measures, 332
Duck Confit Pie with Glazed Figs
    and Blackberry Glaze, 158–160
Dumpling(s)
  Baked Apple, 222–223
  Boiled Plum, 225–226
  information about, 221, 224

E

Egg(s), weights and measures, 336
Egg wash, 20
Electric mixers, recommended type,
    326
Empanadas
  dough, 177, 181–182
  Lobster, 176–182
Eskimo Pie, 296–297
Espresso
  Cappuccino Meringue Ice Cream
    Pie, 299–300

Ice Cream, 284–285
Meringue, 306
Mocha Sauce, 311

F

Fats
  pastry dough options, 5–7
  weights and measures, 334–335
Fennel, Spring Vegetable Risotto Pie,
    163–164
Fig(s)
  and Prosciutto Pie, 169
  Glazed, 158–159
Fine-mesh sieves, 328
Flaky pastry crusts
  Basic Butter and Shortening Pastry
    Pie Dough, 27
  Bubby's All-Butter Pastry Pie
    Dough, 23–26
  Lard Pastry Pie Dough, 28
  Nut Pastry Pie Dough, 30–31
  Short Dough for Tarts, 32–33
  Sour Cream Pastry Pie Dough, 29
Flour
  for pastry crust, 4–5
  as thickening agent, 51
Fluid ingredients, weights and meas-
    ures, 333
Food processors
  mixing dough, 8–9, 24
  recommended type, 326
Freezing dough, 21
Fried pastries
  frying guidelines, 181–182, 227
  Lobster Empanadas, 176–182
Fried pies
  Apple-Whiskey, 231–232
  Cherry, 228–229
  information about, 227

Fried pies (*continued*)
    Peach, 230
    Sweet Potato, 233–234
Fruit pie(s)
    assembling, steps in, 55–59
    bubble-and-brown method, 58
    cooling, 59
    dry, causes of, 52
    flavor heighteners, 54–55
    juicy-to-dry fruits (chart), 51
    local/in-season fruit, 48–49
    reheating, 61
    Rhubarb, 63–68
    roast ripening fruit, 93, 120
    runny, causes of, 53, 109
    serving sizes, 59–60
    soggy bottom, causes of, 95
    storing, 60–61
    sweeteners, 53–54
    thickening agents, 50–53
    transporting, 60
    See also recipes under specific fruits
Fruit, poached, Pears in Port, 117

G

Ganache, 132, 252, 308
Garlic Pastry Crust
    pie/crust compatibility chart,
        347–348
    recipe, 45
Ginger
    Apricot Gingerbuckle, 215–216
    Buckle, 211
    -Honey Apple Pie, 114–115
    Ice Cream, 278–279
    -Pear Crisp, 201
Gingersnap(s)
    Crumb Crust, 39
    Homemade, 37–38

Glaze
    Blackberry, 112–113, 158–160
    Red Currant, 118
    Tangerine, 139–140
Goat cheese
    Fig and Prosciutto Pie, 169
    Pie with Pomegranate Molasses,
        167–168
Gooseberry(ies)
    Blue Goose, 84
    Crumble Pie, 82–83
    information about, 81
Graham cracker(s)
    Crust, 36
    Homemade, 34–35
Grape(s)
    Concord, Pie with Créme Fraîche,
        101–102
    skinning, 101
Grapefruit peel, Candied, 316
Grasshopper Eskimo Pie, 297
Grunts, information about, 220
Guinness stout, and Steak Pie,
    Brandon's, 147–148

H

Hazelnuts, Candied, 315
Herbed Pastry Crust
    pie/crust compatibility chart,
        347–348
    recipe, 43
Homemade Marshmallows,
    319–320
Homemade Pop-Tarts™, 235–236
Honey
    drizzle top crust with, 20
    in fruit pies, 53
    -Ginger Apple Pie, 114–115
Hot Fudge Sauce, 311

Hot Water Pastry Crust, 45, 185, 187–188

I

Ice cream
    Banana-Chocolate Chip, 291–292
    Buttermilk, 274–275
    Caramel, 282–283
    Chocolate, 286–287
    Espresso, 284–285
    Ginger, 278–279
    Maple Syrup, 293–294
    Mint Chip, 289–290
    Peach, 276–277
    Rocky Road, 288
    Strawberry, 280–281
    Vanilla, 272–273
Ice cream makers, 271
    recommended type, 330
Ice cream pies
    Banana-Chocolate Eskimo, 297
    Cappuccino Meringue, 299–300
    crust for, 270, 295
    Eskimo, 296–297
    Grasshopper Eskimo, 297
    information about, 295
    Sweetie Pie, 298
Italian Meringue, 305–306

K

Key lime(s)
    Candied Citrus Slices, 317–318
    Pie, 254
Knishes, Potato, Joy's, 189–192

L

Lamb
    Cobbler, 152–153
    Shepherd's Pie with Mashed
        Potato and Cheddar Crust,
        154–155
Lard
    Hot Water Pastry Crust, 45, 185,
        187–188
    in pastry crust, 6
    Pastry Pie Dough, 28
    pie/crust compatibility chart,
        344–348
    rendering, 28
    weights and measures, 335
Lattice crusts, making, 18–19
Leek(s), and Onion Pie, 175
Lemon(s)
    Candied Citrus Slices, 317–318
    Chess Pie, Double, 255–256
    Lemon Curd, 307
    Lemony Pear Pie, 123
    Meringue Pie, Mile-High, 263–264
Liqueurs, in fruit pies, 54–55
Lobster Empanadas, 176–182

M

Manchego cheese, Paella Pie,
    163–164
Maple syrup
    in fruit pies, 53–54
    Ice Cream, 293–294
Marshmallows
    Homemade, 319–320
    Rocky Road Ice Cream, 288
Meat cobblers, Lamb, 152–153
Meat fats
    rendered, in pastry crust, 6–7